Recipe for Writing and Spelling

An Integrated Program

THIRD EDITION

Frances Bloom
Deborah Bloom Coates

pro·ed
An International Publisher

8700 Shoal Creek Boulevard
Austin, Texas 78757-6897
800/897-3202   Fax 800/397-7633
www.proedinc.com

An International Publisher

© 2007, 2000, 1984 by Frances Bloom and Deborah Bloom Coates
8700 Shoal Creek Boulevard
Austin, Texas 78757-6897
800/897-3202   Fax 800/397-7633
www.proedinc.com

ISBN 1-4164-0069-9

Printed in the United States of America

1 2 3 4 5 6 7 8 9 10   11 10 09 08 07

This book is dedicated to Kenny, a bright fifth grader with a seemingly intractable spelling problem. His need challenged us to develop a better method for stimulating and encouraging all students to learn to spell.

Contents

Contents

Write and Spell on Your Own   201

Contents

More Sounds   343

/oi/ as in *boil, boy*

/oo/ as in *boot, grew, group, brute, through*

/yu/ as in *cube, cue, few*

/sh/ as in *ship, precious, nation, mansion, conscious, chef, sure*

/f/ as in *photo*

/ough/ as in *tough*

/n/ as in *knit, gnash*

/r/ as in *wrap*

/g/ as in *ghost*

Acknowledgments

We express our appreciation for help with this third edition to Kim Carnes, creative writing instructor, School for the Creative and Performing Arts, Lexington, Kentucky; Tamara Flanagan, consulting teacher for special education, Loudon County Public Schools, Loudon County, Virginia; and Sandra Gillespie, head of lower school, Duke School, Durham, North Carolina, for their comments on and suggestions for the added writing skills exercises.

We would like to thank the following teachers from Lexington, Kentucky, who tested materials for the second edition: Virginia Adkins, Veterans Park Elementary School; Chris Zachritz Hoover, Providence Montessori School; Sandra Gillespie, The Lexington School; Pat Miller, primary resource teacher, Veterans Park Elementary School. We also thank Dr. Patricia Young Smith, poet and retired professor of English, for her contributions, and Anne Bloom Graff for her artwork.

We would like to express our appreciation to Midge Myers for her support in the early years of this project. We also wish to acknowledge the contributions of the following teachers in Westchester County, New York, who helped in the development of the materials in the first edition: Joanne Bundy, Myrna Cable, Irene Judd, Patricia Manuel, Beatrice Matzkin, Jane McKinley, Mary Morrissy, Joan O'Rourke, Phyllis Ossen, Rochelle Pollens, Marcia Price, Donne Sauer, Barbara Schroeder, Eileen Schwartz, Elaine Sherrier, and Balbina Usefoff. We also thank Dr. Patrick Stone of the Tucker Maxon Oral School of Portland, Oregon, for making us aware of the vital role that cognition plays in all areas of education.

We appreciate the continuous support and encouragement we have received from Bill Bloom, Fred Coates, and Anne and Wayne Graff, as well as the critical review and useful comments of Jane Bloom Grise and the computer support from Bill Grise. Our special thanks to Jennifer Coates for the initial copyediting of this edition. Finally, we enjoy watching our family, Jennifer, Michelle, Kaitlin, Justin, and Joshua, lead their generation of spellers into the 21st century.

Introduction

Recipe for Writing and Spelling is designed to enrich all contemporary language arts classes or to stand alone as a basic program of instruction. It contains essential ingredients for developing skills in spelling, writing, and reasoning for students in grades kindergarten through 6. It also may be effectively used for remedial instruction with students in middle school or high school. It is a multisensory program that uses phonics, language patterns, and language experience. *Recipe for Writing and Spelling* is a sequential, structured, and logical approach for teaching spelling through word study, word analysis, and word use. Students are first introduced to words that follow spelling rules and patterns, so that they can quickly and easily master a substantial spelling vocabulary. Students are also prepared to handle less predictable words by using them in a variety of written work.

The multisensory approach enables students to enjoy the process of learning to communicate in writing. It also instills in them a growing feeling of competence as they grasp the fundamentals of good spelling. This teaching method, which has been confirmed by extensive research, complements current developments in the teaching of reading and, as testing has shown, significantly improves spelling skills.

Recipe for Writing and Spelling, Third Edition provides many new writing activities while retaining most of the spelling lessons found in *Recipe for Spelling, Second Edition*. The writing activities incorporate the target spelling skills from each unit. Students will strengthen both their writing and spelling skills while they complete enjoyable assignments using creative, informative, or personal narrative writing styles.

The worksheets in the Write and Spell on Your Own section and the Graded Word Lists in Appendix A may be reproduced for classroom or personal use. The CD-ROM included with *Recipe for Writing and Spelling, Third Edition* contains these materials as PDF files. Many teachers will find it convenient to use their computer printer to print these reproducible pages for their students. Those who prefer may reproduce the Write and Spell on Your Own pages and Graded Word Lists using a copy machine.

Writing Activities

Each unit suggests writing activities that

- use a building block approach by starting with words and phrases and gradually moving to more complex paragraphs;
- focus on specific writing skills, such as idioms, rhymes, analogies, synonyms, and dictionary skills;
- use the words presented in each spelling unit to develop writing skills; and
- emphasize the use of written expression as the end product of spelling.

These activities target the following writing styles:

- creative: writing that comes from the imagination of the writer, such as poems, short stories, dialogues

- informative: writing produced for an authentic audience and having a purpose in the real world, such as posters, letters, newspaper articles
- personal narrative: writing that focuses on an event in the life of the writer or on an idea supported by incidents in the writer's life, such as journals

Spelling Activities

The spelling activities in each unit

- present the phonic structure and regularities in our language as a base to help the student discover consistencies in the spelling patterns of words;
- use the building block approach by starting with simple CVC (consonant-vowel-consonant) words and gradually evolving to more complex word structures;
- group related spelling rules in logical clusters so that the student "discovers" them while working on the exercises and activities;
- enrich and expand the student's vocabulary while promoting thinking skills; and
- require the student, through activities and exercises, to think of appropriate words and spell them correctly, rather than copy them from a list.

Learning Activities

The learning activities

- stress the development of general reasoning skills such as analyzing, categorizing, classifying, hypothesizing, and sequencing;
- aid in the development of a sight vocabulary to facilitate spelling and writing the most frequently used words;
- emphasize the development of spelling skills in the context of writing; and
- develop the skills needed to use a dictionary to find and verify the spelling of words.

The book is organized into four parts: Spelling Sounds, Spelling Choices, Spelling Rules, and Complementary Skills. Each part focuses on a major set of concepts. The Scope and Sequence chart following the introduction lists the topic and focus of all the units in Parts 1 to 3, to assist in lesson selection and planning.

Part 1: Spelling Sounds

The 14 units in Part 1 deal with the majority of words in the English language that are phonetically consistent for particular letter patterns. These lessons teach the phonic structure and regularities in our language and introduce dictionary skills. The first six units cover the spelling of short vowel sounds. Unit 7 covers the digraphs *sh, ch, th,* and *wh.* The next three units deal with blends, and the remaining units focus on patterned sounds, the spellings of which are regular and predictable. Acquiring these skills enables students to discover consistencies in the patterns of words. Once students master these basic spelling patterns, they are ready to study irregular words.

Part 2: Spelling Choices

The purpose of the 11 units in this section is to teach students the alternate spellings for each of the major long vowels and variant consonant sounds of the language. Students are not expected to memorize the spellings for each sound; however, they receive extensive practice in choosing the correct spelling of a word from among the options available for the particular sound. Students are exposed to the various options, which are reinforced through

- logical classification and presentation of each sound, and
- emphasis on homophones, homonyms, and word meaning.

The units in Part 2 cover the spellings of the principal long vowel sounds and the alternate spellings of additional sounds; for example, /k/, /ch/, /j/, /f/, /r/, and /n/.

Part 3: Spelling Rules

Spelling generalizations and rules are presented in the six units of Part 3. Because spelling rules are easier to remember if taught in groups and inductively, we have carefully clustered the rules to help students become aware of the patterns in the rules rather than having to memorize them. By understanding and using these generalizations, students expand their spelling vocabulary.

Part 4: Complementary Skills

The four units in this section may be used in conjunction with any of the earlier units in the book. The introduction of prefixes and suffixes will substantially enlarge students' writing vocabulary. Because a large proportion of commonly used words contain prefixes and suffixes, it is beneficial to add them frequently to daily spelling instruction at all levels.

Part 4 also presents spelling rules for plurals and the use of the apostrophe in contractions and possessives. It is helpful frequently to present the rules in these units—as well as those in the unit on prefixes and suffixes—in the context of daily spelling instruction. The final unit in Part 4 introduces common abbreviations.

Organization of the Teaching Units

Each of the 30 teaching units contains the following elements: Focus, Word Lists, Pretest, Posttest, Spell Together, and Write and Spell on Your Own (grouped separately on pages 201–394).

Focus

Targeted skills for spelling and writing are stated at the beginning of each unit to assist in preparing lesson plans and formulating goals. The spelling section sets forth the particular sound or principle being presented. The writing section is divided into two parts, writing development and writing style. Writing development identifies specific writing skills presented in the unit, such as analogies, dictionary skills, or poetry forms. Writing style specifies which of the three styles of writing (creative, informative, and personal narrative) appear in the unit. The Scope and Sequence chart following the introduction summarizes these target skills for the units in Parts 1 to 3.

Word Lists

Each unit contains a comprehensive word list so that the teacher may

- select words to reinforce the concept taught;
- choose words in a particular category that are suitable for the grade level and ability of each student;
- add new and unfamiliar words to daily instruction in order to expand students' reading, writing, and speaking vocabulary; and
- develop additional spelling and language arts activities as needed.

In order to develop a balanced spelling program, you may include irregular words in each unit, selecting words from the following sources:

- the graded word lists in Appendix A;
- content-area words (i.e., words used in other subjects, such as science, math, or social studies);
- words a student selects (i.e., words the student wants to learn or needs for writing).

Suggested sight words are included in each unit in Part 1.

Pretest

The purpose of a pretest is to determine how much emphasis and time students will require to achieve mastery of a particular unit. It is also a learning experience for the students, because misspelled words are immediately identified and corrected. You may also use the pretest to individualize the spelling program for each student. If a student knows all of the words in a particular unit, you may decide to advance the student to the next unit.

Pretest Procedure
1. Select sight words to present in addition to the list of pretest words.
2. Briefly discuss the concept or focus presented in the unit. (For example, "Listen for a blend—the two consonants at the beginning of a word—and then spell the word.")
3. Dictate each word, use it in a phrase, and then repeat the word. (For example, "Spin. Spin the top. Spell spin.")
4. When students have completed the test, write each test word on the board so that they may correct their own papers or pair off and correct a partner's paper.

Posttest

The purpose of the posttest is to determine students' mastery of the words, concepts, and suggested sight words of that unit, and to identify areas where they may need additional reinforcement. With the exception of the sight words, different words are presented in the pretest and posttest so that students' mastery of the concept introduced in the unit is tested, rather than their ability to memorize the pretest words. Sentences and phrases for dictation, incorporating words from the unit and review words from previous units, are also included in the posttest.

Posttest Procedure

1. Include in the posttest the same sight words presented in the pretest.
2. Dictate words using the following procedure:
    a. Say each word.
    b. Use the word in a sentence or phrase.
    c. Say the word again.

Note. When dictating homophones, be sure the sentence clarifies which word the students are to spell.

3. Dictate phrases or sentences using the following procedure:
    a. Read the sentence or phrase.
    b. Read each word in the phrase slowly.
    c. Read the phrase again at a normal rate.

Note. The suggested phrases for dictation in Parts 1 and 2 serve as a review because they include words from previous units.

4. Encourage students to proofread their own papers in the posttest (as in any writing activity).
5. Write dictated words on the board after the test so that students may correct their own tests or pair off and correct each other's tests.

Spell Together

Spell Together consists of suggested activities and presentations to help students focus on concepts being taught and develop the necessary cognitive skills for spelling, writing, reading, language arts, and other content areas. These activities are designed to do the following:

- reinforce concepts introduced in each unit;
- give students ample opportunities to see and hear each word;
- stimulate interest in the structure of words;
- stress encoding (spelling) and, at the same time, aid in the process of decoding (reading);
- provide material to teach spelling in the context of writing;

- allow for flexibility of presentation (for example, pairs of students, small groups, or the entire class can play the suggested games);
- encourage every student to participate;
- familiarize students with new and different approaches before assigning the material in worksheets; and
- develop positive attitudes toward spelling and writing.

In Part 1, the Spell Together section includes a dictionary strand. In the early lessons, students learn to alphabetize words. They then learn to use a dictionary to look up spellings and word meanings. They are also encouraged to cultivate the habit of using a dictionary to proofread their written work and enlarge their vocabularies. In Units 6 through 14, students create their own alphabetized dictionaries. The teacher dictates designated groups of words in a specific order, and the students write these words in their dictionaries.

One of the features of Part 2 is to provide an answer for students who ask, "How can I find a word in the dictionary if I can't spell it?" The answer is, "By knowing the various ways each sound can be spelled, students can make an educated guess." They can try one spelling for the sound. If that fails, they try another.

Write and Spell on Your Own

The Write and Spell on Your Own section of this book consists of reproducible worksheets to provide students with a further opportunity for spelling and writing mastery. The same worksheets are contained on the CD-ROM for printing by computer. The exercises are designed to require the student to think of a specific word and spell it, rather than to copy words from a list or word bank. Exercises range from the simple to those that will challenge bright students or high achievers. The exercises encompass educational objectives that apply to other subject areas. You may reproduce any of the Write and Spell on Your Own pages for use in your classroom.

The exercises develop spelling and writing skills by stressing the following:

- development of writing skills (sentence or paragraph completion and writing original sentences, paragraphs, rhymes, and haiku);
- visual images of words;
- devices for expanding vocabulary;
- development of skills used in critical thinking (categorizing, classifying, hypothesizing, and drawing analogies);
- dictionary techniques; and
- fun with words through the use of puzzles.

You may adapt many of the activities and exercises suggested in Write and Spell Together and Write and Spell on Your Own and use them in other units by substituting appropriate words from a unit's word list. You may also adapt them for paired activities. Answers for Write and Spell on Your Own exercises appear in Appendix B. For the Write and Spell on Your Own exercises, or any other activities in the book, if students provide different answers that they can justify, accept those answers as correct.

Notation System

Sentences in quotation marks in the Spell Together sections suggest language you may use for instruction. The words that follow in parentheses indicate the desired student response. For example,

"What do the words have in common?" (They end in *y*.)

The boxes headed "On the Board" contain material you should write on the chalkboard or whiteboard. For example,

ON THE BOARD

1. Pound the stake in firmly.

2. I got my dog at the pound.

3. Sixteen ounces equal one pound.

Sounds are presented between slanted lines. For example,

/a/ as in *apple*
/ow/ as in *cow* or *ouch*

The spelling for a sound is in italics. For example,

/ar/ is usually spelled *ar*.

Conclusion

Learning to spell can be an enjoyable process. It need not be difficult, dull, or complicated. *Recipe for Writing and Spelling* has been designed to provide a positive experience for both teacher and student. It gives the teacher the ingredients and instructions needed to challenge students to explore and use their language creatively. It gives students the ability to communicate their ideas and thoughts effectively in writing. The result is a positive and rewarding experience for all.

Scope and Sequence

Unit	Sounds	Focus		
		Spelling	**Writing Development**	**Writing Style**
Part 1: Spelling Sounds				
1	/a/ as in *bag*	To hear and spell words with the short *a* (/a/) sound	Idioms, categorization, synonyms, dictionary skills	Informative
2	/i/ as in *big*	To hear and spell words with the short *i* (/i/) sound	Idioms, phrases, riddles, dictionary skills	Informative, creative
3	/o/ as in *bog*	To hear and spell words with the short *o* (/o/) sound To introduce simple plurals	Idioms, classification, simple plurals, dictionary skills	Informative
4	/u/ as in *bug*	To hear and spell words with the short *u* (/u/) sound	Idioms, analogies, rhymes	Creative
5	/e/ as in *beg*	To hear and spell words with the short *e* (/e/) sound	Idioms, homonyms, dictionary skills	Creative
6	Short vowel review	To review all short vowels	Synonyms, antonyms, dictionary skills	Creative
7	/sh/ /ch/ /th/ /wh/ as in *ship, chip, path, that, when*	To hear and spell consonant digraphs /sh/ /ch/ /th/ /wh/	Idioms, question words, dictionary skills	Creative, personal narrative
8	Beginning *l* and *r* blends as in *flap, drip*	To hear and spell words with beginning *l* and *r* blends	Hypothesizing, dictionary skills	Personal narrative
9	More beginning blends as in *spin*, ending blends as in *fact*	To hear and spell words with beginning blends other than *l* or *r* and words with ending blends	Similes, dictionary skills	Creative
10	Dual blends as in *brand*	To hear and spell words with both beginning and ending blends	Rhymes, dictionary skills	Creative

Scope and Sequence

Unit	Sounds	Focus		
		Spelling	Writing Development	Writing Style
11	Compounds as in *hatbox*	To hear and spell compound words	Dialogue, dictionary skills	Creative
12	/ar/ as in *hard*	To hear and spell words with the /ar/ sound	Syllables, dictionary skills	Creative, personal narrative
13	*–ng , –nk* as in *sing, sang, song, sung, wink, hank, honk, hunk*	To hear and spell words that end in *–ing, –ang, –ong, –ung,* and *–ink, –ank, –onk, –unk*	Rhymes, haiku, hypothesizing, fact and opinion, dictionary skills	Creative, informative
14	*–ed* as in *blasted, blushed, charmed*	To hear and spell *–ed* endings that are pronounced /ed/, /d/, /t/	Past tense, syllables, dictionary skills	Personal narrative
Part 2: Spelling Choices				
15	/ī/ as in *pine, fly, high, bind, pie, eye, style, child*	To recognize the different spellings of words with the long *i* (/ī/) sound	Homophones, homonyms, nouns, verbs, adjectives	Creative, personal narrative
16	/ā/ as in *cake, play, sail, great, eight, reign, vein* /ār/ as in *dare, fair, bear*	To recognize the different spellings of words with the long *a* (/ā/) sound and the /ār/ sound	Mnemonics, homophones	Creative
17	/ō/ as in *vote, boat, snow, doe, bold, though, roll*	To recognize and use the different spellings of the long *o* (/ō/) sound	Homophones, headlines, anagrams	Creative, informative
18	/ē/ as in *deep, beach, chief, theme, neither, key, baby, we* /ēr/ as in *cheer, clear, here, pier*	To recognize and use the different spellings of words with the long *e* (/ē/) sound and the /ēr/ sound	Homophones, adjectives	Creative, informative
19	/ow/ as in *cow, out*	To recognize and use the different spellings of words with the /ow/ sound	Homophones, homonyms, analogies	Creative
20	/aw/ as in *saw, fault, ball, talk, caught, bought*	To recognize and use the different spellings of words with the /aw/ sound	Mnemonics, homophones, homonyms, classification	Creative

Unit	Sounds	Focus		
		Spelling	**Writing Development**	**Writing Style**
21	/k/ as in *luck, ask, cake, cat, keep, chorus, quiz, box*	To recognize and use the different spellings of words with the /k/ sound	Homonyms	Creative
22	/ch/ as in *inch, itch* and /j/ as in *page, edge*	To recognize and use the different spellings of words with the /ch/ and /j/ sounds	Definitions, newspaper writing	Personal narrative, informative
23	/or/ as in *born, more, four, roar, door*	To recognize and use the different spellings of words with the /or/ sound	Homophones	Creative, personal narrative
24	/er/ as in *winter, stern, bird, burn, word, learn*	To recognize and use the different spellings of words with the /er/ sound	Letter writing, proverbs	Informative, creative, personal narrative
	More sounds /oi/ as in *boil, boy* /oo/ as in *boot, grew, group, brute, through* /yu/ as in *cube, cue, few* /sh/ as in *ship, precious, nation, mansion, conscious, chef, sure* /f/ as in *photo* /ough/ as in *tough* /n/ as in *knit, gnash* /r/ as in *wrap* /g/ as in *ghost*	— —	Homophones, analogies, headlines	Creative, informative, personal narrative
Part 3: Spelling Rules				
25	Double *f, l, s, z* endings as in *staff, frill, lass, buzz*	To understand and apply the doubling rule: If a one-syllable word with one short vowel ends in *f, l, s,* or *z,* the final consonant is usually doubled	Word pictures, feeling poems	Creative

Scope and Sequence

Unit	Sounds	Focus		
		Spelling	**Writing Development**	**Writing Style**
26	Doubling rule as in *bottle, ladle,* and other similar words ending in *–ble, –fle, –gle, –kle, –ple, –zle*	To understand and apply the doubling rule when adding an ending that begins with a vowel or adding an ending to an accented syllable	Syllables, diamonte	Creative
27	*–le* rule as in *apple, candle,* and other similar words	To understand and apply the doubling rule in words that end in *–le*	Classification, cinquain	Creative
28	Doubling rule for *–y* as in *baby, funny,* and other similar words ending in *–ly, –vy, –dy, –ty, –fy, –py, –sy, –ky, –ry*	To understand and apply the doubling rule for words ending in *–y*	Adjectives	Creative
29	More endings for words ending in silent *e* as in *aging, careful*	To understand and apply the doubling rule for words ending in silent *e*	Suffixes, free verse	Creative
30	*y* to *i* as in *carried, carrying* *i* before *e* as in *belief, ceiling, eight*	To understand and apply (1) the rule about changing *y* to *i* in words that end in *y* preceded by a consonant and (2) the *i* before *e* rule	Mnemonics	Creative

Write and Spell Together

PART 1

Spelling Sounds

And gladly wolde he lerne, and gladly teche.
(And gladly would he learn, and gladly teach.)

—Geoffrey Chaucer

general prologue to *The Canterbury Tales,* 14th century

UNIT 1 | /a/

Focus

Spelling: To hear and spell words with the short *a* (/a/) sound
Writing development: idioms, categorization, synonyms, dictionary skills
Writing style: informative

Word List

ad	cab	gab	lab	nag	rat	van
am	can	gag	lad	nap	sad	vat
an	cap	gap	lag	pad	sag	wag
at	cat	had	lap	pal	sap	wax
ax	dab	hag	lax	pan	sat	yak
bad	dad	ham	mad	pat	tab	yam
bag	dam	hat	man	rag	tag	yap
bam	fad	jab	map	ram	tan	zap
ban	fan	jag	mat	ran	tap	
bat	fat	jam	nab	rap	tax	

Suggested Sight Words*

is	as	his	has	was

Pretest

bat	fan	ham	man	rat
cap	gag	lad	pal	tax

Posttest

bag	dad	jab	ran	am
cab	fat	lap	ax	van

Sentences for Dictation

His cap was tan.
Dan can use the ax.
Sam is mad at Nan.

---

*All sight words in the following units are suggestions. You may select your own sight words from the graded word lists in Appendix A. Appendix A also contains methods for presenting these words.

Spell Together

■ **To get started:** Introduce the short vowels using a series of words that have the same beginning and ending consonants. Point out that only the vowel changes.

ON THE BOARD

bag   big   bog   bug   beg

■ **Listening for short *a* (/a/):** Use an apple or a picture of an apple to firmly establish the short *a* sound. Use the word *bag* to demonstrate that if students can hear the sounds in a word and identify the letters that make those sounds, they can spell the word.

Teacher says	Student says	Student writes
"bag"		
"What is the first sound you hear?"	/b/	b
"What is the second sound you hear?"	/a/	a
"What is the last sound you hear?"	/g/	g
"Spell *bag*."	b-a-g	bag

Continue with other words from the list.

■ **Complete the idiom:*** Discuss what an idiom is: "An idiom is an expression we often hear. It is a phrase that can have meaning other than its literal one. Complete each idiom with a word that has the sound of short *a*."

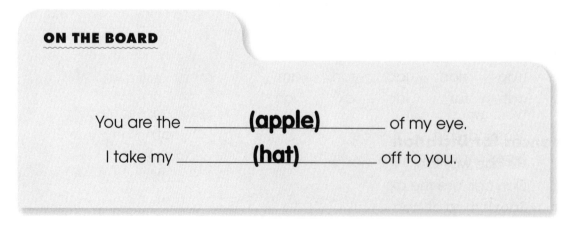

ON THE BOARD

You are the _____ **(apple)** _____ of my eye.

I take my _____ **(hat)** _____ off to you.

———————————————

*This is an exercise for older or more advanced students.

© 2007, 2000, 1984 by Frances Bloom and Deborah Bloom Coates

SPELLING SOUNDS

■ **ZAP**

1. Write the word *ZAP* in the center square of a nine-square bingo sheet (see sample). Copy and provide a sheet for each student.
2. Dictate eight short *a* words from the word list.
3. Have students write each word in the square of their choice on the bingo board (one word per square).
4. Call out the words again in a different order.
5. Have students cross off each word on their sheets as you call it out.
6. The first student to cross off a full row, as in bingo, calls out "ZAP." If all of the words on the sheet are correctly spelled, the student wins.

		ZAP

■ **Categorizing:** Introduce categorization by using groupings such as colors, foods, or animals. In this activity, the words need not contain short *a.* This feature is introduced in the next activity.

"I will say three words. Try to think of another word that is in the same category, or group."

Use the following groups:

Names:

Mary, Susan, Jane, __**(any girl's name)**__

Parts of the head:

ear, nose, mouth, __**(any part of head)**__

Colors:

red, green, orange, __**(any color)**__

Drinks:

water, juice, soda, __**(any drink)**__

■ **Thinking of short *a* words:** "I will say three words. Try to think of a short *a* word that is in the same category, or group, and then say and spell the word."

Word group	Possible answer
Clothing: shirt, coat, shoe	(hat)
Types of people: girl, boy, woman	(man)
Animals: dog, horse, cow	(cat)
Baseball equipment: glove, mitt, ball	(bat)

Encourage students to think of their own categories.

It might be helpful to use pictures to represent categories for younger students.

■ **Posters for a garage sale:** Discuss writing to inform. "Letters, brochures, how-to manuals, and advertisements are used to share your ideas, give instructions, and to sell things. Imagine you have some items that you want to sell. What are some of the ways you might let friends or classmates know what you are trying to sell?" Answers will vary. "We are going to make posters to sell some of the following items. You must use at least one of these words in your poster. You can use pictures to attract attention to it."

ON THE BOARD

FOR SALE

bag	bat	can	cap	cat	fan
ham	hat	mat	rag	tag	van

■ **Different words—same meanings:** "Words that mean the same thing are called *synonyms*. *Happy* and *glad* are synonyms." Write the following list of words on the board or on a sheet of paper for each student:

ON THE BOARD

father _____

cap _____

plump _____

friend _____

Dictate each of the following words, one at a time. If the word is a synonym of one of the words on the preceding list, students should write it next to its synonym:

pal   nap   hat
sad   fat   dad

■ **Tick-Tack-Tuck:** Direct students' attention to the tic-tac-toe grids on the board (see illustration). "Tuck a letter into the empty corners to complete the words in the squares. Each letter you add must make a word across and down." Do the first square with the class. Students can fill in the other squares at the board or on individual sheets of paper.

ON THE BOARD

(omit letters in parentheses)

(b)	a	g		(h)	a	m		r	a	(t)		(l)	a	d
a	TICK TACK TUCK	a		a	TICK TACK TUCK	a		a	TICK TACK TUCK	a		a	TICK TACK TUCK	a
t	a	(p)		t	a	(n)		n	a	(p)		(p)	a	(d)

■ **Getting ready to use the dictionary:** Use the following procedure to begin reinforcing alphabetical order:

1. Write the alphabet in lowercase letters on the board or on strips of poster board.
2. Name a letter and ask students, in turn, to recite the letters that follow it in the alphabet.
3. Cover or remove the alphabet and repeat the procedure.

Write and Spell on Your Own

Independent practice exercises for the objectives targeted in this unit are located in the corresponding Write and Spell on Your Own section of this book (see pp. 205–210).

UNIT 2 /i/

Focus

Spelling: To hear and spell words with the short *i* (/i/) sound
Writing development: idioms, phrases, riddles, dictionary skills
Writing style: informative, creative

Word List

bib	dim	gig	it	pig	rim	wig
bid	din	hid	jig	pin	rip	win
big	dip	him	lid	pip	sin	wit
bin	fib	hip	lip	pit	sip	yip
bit	fin	hit	lit	rib	six	zip
did	fit	if	nib	rid	tin	
dig	fix	in	nip	rig	tip	

Suggested Sight Words

do	you	of
does	your	off

Pretest

fix	lid	rib	jig	big
dip	hit	pin	zip	sip

Posttest

bit	lip	him	win	bid
rig	did	fib	rip	wig

Sentences for Dictation

Tim has a can of wax.
Does your cat nip you?
Min can do a jig.

Spell Together

■ **Listening for short *i* (/i/):** Use a picture or drawing of an igloo to firmly establish the short *i* /i/ sound. Use the word *big* to demonstrate that if the students can hear the sounds in a word and identify the letters that make those sounds, they can spell the word.

Teacher says	Student says	Student writes
"big"		
"What is the first sound you hear?"	/b/	b
"What is the second sound you hear?"	/i/	i
"What is the last sound you hear?"	/g/	g
"Spell big."	b-i-g	big

Continue with other words from the word list.

■ **Auditory discrimination:** Use this procedure to distinguish /i/ from /a/.

1. On the board or individual sheets of paper, have students make two columns, one labeled /i/, the other /a/.
2. Dictate the short *a* and short *i* words listed below.
3. Have the students write each word in the proper column under /i/ or /a/.

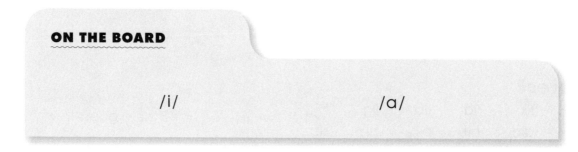

ON THE BOARD

/i/	/a/

Suggested words

pit	sat	zip	lid	win	van	lip
cat	had	map	rag	pad	rig	hid
tip	big	wig	fix	jam	can	rib

■ **Complete the idiom:** "Complete the idiom with a word that has the sound of short *i*."

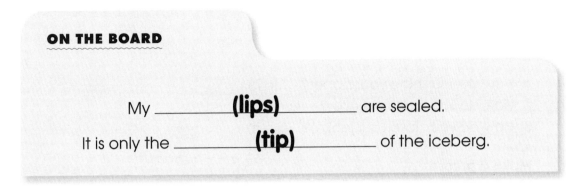

ON THE BOARD

My _____ **(lips)** _____ are sealed.

It is only the _____ **(tip)** _____ of the iceberg.

■ **Thinking of short *i* words:** Read the following clues to students:

"Try to guess the correct short *i* word after you hear all the clues."

1. I'm part of your face.
   You talk with me.
   You use me to kiss.

   I am a _____ **(lip)** _____ .

2. I am one-half dozen.
   I rhyme with *fix*.
   I am four more than two.

   I am _____ **(six)** _____ .

3. I live on a farm.
   I like the mud.
   My tail is curly.

   I am a _____ **(pig)** _____ .

4. I can help you sew.
   I hold cloth together.
   I am sharp.

   I am a _____ **(pin)** _____ .

The first student to guess the correct answer writes it on the board. Encourage students to make up and write their own riddles. Have them guess the answers to each other's riddles.

■ **How do you?** Discuss phrases. Phrases are two or more words that form a unit but are not a complete sentence.

bit of jam   at the rim   in the bag

Pick a phrase

Have students pick one of the following phrases to answer the question "How do you ...?"

dig a pit   hit a big hit   pin on a bib

How do you ...?

1. How do you make a pig happy?
2. How do you get a home run?
3. How do you keep a baby clean?

Use a phrase

Have students use a phrase to answer the following questions. If necessary, list the following words on the board.

rip   him   dig   hit   lit
pin   zip   big   tip   it

1. How do you share your paper?   (rip it)
2. How do you thank a waiter?   (tip him)
3. How do you close your jacket?   (zip it)

Make a phrase

Have students make up their own "How do you …" questions to share with a partner.

■ Dictionary skills: Alphabetizing or ABC order

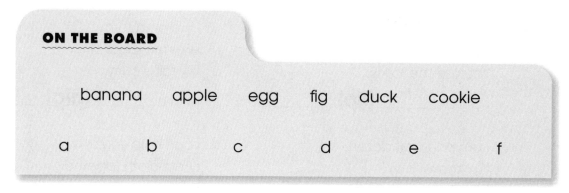

ON THE BOARD

banana   apple   egg   fig   duck   cookie

a   b   c   d   e   f

1. Have students take turns writing each word under the letter that matches the first letter of the word.
2. Discuss with students: "Alphabetical, or ABC, order means putting words in order according to the first letter in each word." (Second- and third-letter alphabetizing will follow.)
3. Repeat the procedure with the rest of the alphabet in two more groups, *g* to *p* and *q* to *z*.

If desired, present additional words from the word lists in Units 1 and 2.

Write and Spell on Your Own

Independent practice exercises for the objectives targeted in this unit are located in the corresponding Write and Spell on Your Own section of this book (see pp. 211–216).

UNIT 3 | /o/

Focus

Spelling: To hear and spell words with the short *o* (/o/) sound
To introduce simple plurals
Writing development: idioms, classification, simple plurals, dictionary skills
Writing style: informative

Word List

bob	cop	hog	log	on	rot	yon
bog	cot	hop	lot	ox	sob	
box	dog	hot	mob	pod	sod	
cob	dot	job	mom	pop	sop	
cod	fog	jog	mop	pot	sox	
cog	fox	jot	nod	rob	top	
con	got	lob	not	rod	tot	

Suggested Sight Words

toy	boy	girl	all	tall	ball

Pretest

cop	dot	job	lot	on
box	fog	hot	nod	rod

Posttest

cot	bog	rob	fox	pod
jog	hop	log	not	mob

Sentences for Dictation

The toy was in a big bag.
The girl hid your ball in a van.
The tall boy got on top of the box.

Spell Together

■ **Listening for short o (/o/):** Use a picture of an octopus to firmly establish the short o (/o/) sound. Use the word *bog* to demonstrate that if the students can hear the sounds in a word and identify the letters that make those sounds, they can spell the word.

Teacher says	Student says	Student writes
"bog"		
"What is the first sound you hear?"	/b/	b
"What is the second sound you hear?"	/o/	o
"What is the last sound you hear?"	/g/	g
"Spell *bog*."	b-o-g	bog

Continue with other words from the word list.

■ **Auditory discrimination:** "Listen to the following words. Make an O with your hands (demonstrate for the students) each time you hear the sound of short *o*." (Optional: Have students write all short *o* words on a sheet of paper.)

jam	box	gag	big	rid
zip	at	pig	mop	pal
got	in	nap	cop	him
rap	on	tax	hid	not
jog	rip	cat	hot	van
lit	lot	rod	fix	fog

Use additional words from the word lists if students need more practice.

■ **Complete the idiom:** "Complete the idiom with a word that has the sound of short *o*."

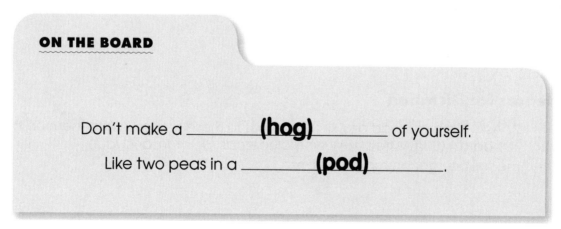

ON THE BOARD

Don't make a _____ **(hog)** _____ of yourself.

Like two peas in a _____ **(pod)** _____.

■ **Classification:** To introduce classification, use one or both of the following approaches.

Procedure A

1. Mix six red circles with six blue circles on a table. The circles should all be the same size.
2. Say, "Put together the circles that are alike." The student should sort red circles into one group and blue circles into another group.
3. Point to each group of circles. Ask, "How are the circles in each group alike?" The student should state that all the circles in one group are red and all the circles in the other group are blue.
4. Point to both groups of circles. Ask, "How are these two groups different?" The student should note that the circles in each group are a different color.

Procedure B

1. Write boys' and girls' names on the board in random order.
2. Say, "How could you divide these names into two groups? How would you classify them?" The desired classification could be as simple as, "This is a group of boys and this is a group of girls."

Note: If a student uses another classification and can justify it (such as "Those students are tall and those are short"), state that this is a correct classification and encourage the class to suggest additional classifications until the expected one is reached. Give examples until students understand the concept.

■ **Thinking about short *o* words:** Write the following words on the board:

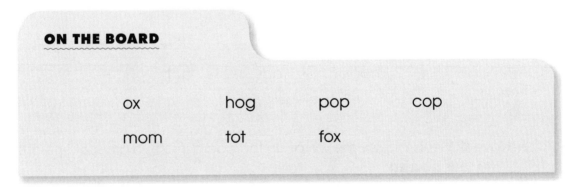

ON THE BOARD

ox	hog	pop	cop
mom	tot	fox	

1. If necessary, discuss the meanings of these words. Then say, "How would you classify these words?" (people and animals)
2. Ask, "Can you add any short *a* words to these groups? Write them on the board." (Suggested answers include *cat, rat, man,* and *lad.*)

■ **Poster for an animal clinic:** "What if we had a new animal clinic in town? What kind of poster do you think the vet might make to let people know that he or she would be treating many kinds of animals? Use at least some of the words on the board. You can make a silly poster with pictures if you think it might attract more attention."

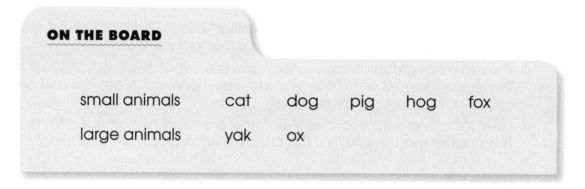

> **ON THE BOARD**
>
> small animals   cat   dog   pig   hog   fox
>
> large animals   yak   ox

More words to use

sad   mad   fat   hot   wag   lip   bit   hip   big

■ **Regular plurals***

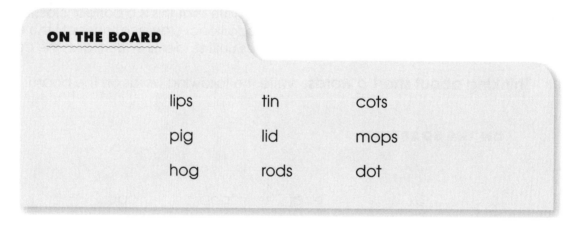

> **ON THE BOARD**
>
> lips   tin   cots
>
> pig   lid   mops
>
> hog   rods   dot

1. Have students classify the words on the board into two groups: *one* and *more than one.*

2. Using the words *singular* and *plural,* explain that, for words that describe a thing, not an action, *s* makes the word mean more than one.

■ **More than one (simple plural concentration)**

1. Cut out 20 cards from poster board, or use unlined index cards.

2. Draw a picture of each of the following objects or animals on two cards:

cat   log   pig   bat   pot

mop   hat   bag   cot   dot

---

*For discussion of irregular plurals, refer to Part 4, Unit CS2.

3. Mix the cards randomly. Turn all cards face-down on a table.

4. The student must turn up a matching pair of cards and spell the plural form correctly to get a point. The student then keeps that pair. The student with the most points wins.

■ **Dictionary skills:** Before, after, and in between

1. Write the alphabet in lowercase letters on the board or on strips of poster board to be hung on the wall.

2. Ask students the following:

   "Which letter comes before *d*, before *g*, before *l*?" Continue with other letters.

   "Which letter comes after *k*, after *u*, after *s*?" Continue with other letters.

   "Between which two letters would you find words that begin with *d*, with *p*,

   with *s*?" Continue with other letters.

Write and Spell on Your Own

Independent practice exercises for the objectives targeted in this unit are located in the corresponding Write and Spell on Your Own section of this book (see pp. 217–222).

UNIT 4 | /u/

Focus

Spelling: To hear and spell words with the short *u* (/u/) sound
To introduce analogies
Writing development: idioms, analogies, rhymes
Writing style: creative

Word List

bud	cup	hub	mug	run
bug	cut	hug	nun	rut
bum	dub	hum	nut	sum
bun	dud	hut	pug	sun
bus	fun	jug	pun	tub
but	gum	jut	pup	tug
cub	gun	lug	rub	up
cud	gut	mud	rug	us

Suggested Sight Words

one   two   three   to   or   for

Discuss the meanings of *to* and *two* using an example such as the following:
Two boys can go *to* the hut.

Pretest

bug	cup	gum	hug	mud
nut	rub	sun	up	tub

Posttest

bud	cut	gun	hut	mug
run	pun	us	tug	hum

Sentences for Dictation

You had one lid for the pot.
The boy is as tall as Dad.
It is fun to sit in the sun.

Spell Together

■ **Listening for short _u_ (/u/):** Use a picture of an umbrella to firmly establish the short _u_ sound. Use the word _bug_ to demonstrate that if the students can hear the sounds in a word and identify the letters that make those sounds, they can spell the word.

Teacher says	Student says	Student writes
"bug"		
"What is the first sound you hear?"	/b/	b
"What is the second sound you hear?"	/u/	u
"What is the last sound you hear?"	/g/	g
"Spell _bug_."	b-u-g	bug

Continue with other words from the word list.

■ **Auditory discrimination:** "Stand up if you hear a short _u_ in the word. Sit down (or stay sitting down) for all other words." Dictate the following words:

hip	hop	fat	pin	pan	bug	mob	bit
bat	cup	lid	nut	rub	six	bus	dot
not	big	pop	had	fog	run	sat	tub
wag	us	mud	hit	pup	up	ham	zip

■ **Complete the idiom:** "Complete each idiom with a word that has the sound of short _u_."

ON THE BOARD

You are my _____ **(cup)** _____ of tea.

Tom is in a _____ **(rut)** _____.

■ **Analogies:** Introduce analogies by using these diagrams.

ON THE BOARD

boy	girl		toothbrush	teeth
man	(woman)		comb	(hair)

Talk through these examples: "Analogies are relationships in meaning between words. A boy is to a girl as a man is to what?" (If necessary, give some answers for students to choose from: "cat, house, woman?") "Toothbrush is to teeth as comb is to what?"

Have students take turns completing the following analogies with short *u* (/u/) words.

ON THE BOARD

night	moon	out	in	slow	walk
day	**(sun)**	down	**(up)**	fast	**(run)**
milk	glass	ax	chop	table	tablecloth
coffee	**(cup)**	knife	**(cut)**	floor	**(rug)**

Have students make up their own analogies and try them on each other.

■ **Listening for short *u* (/u/) rhymes:** Use the following words on the board to illustrate the task. First, students select the two words that rhyme from a group of three (text above the line). Then, they make up a sentence containing the two rhyming words (text below the line).

ON THE BOARD

fun   fin   run

fun—run
_____
It is fun to run.

"As I read each group of words, write the words that rhyme." Dictate the following groups of words. Have students identify and write the two words that rhyme:

1. rat	jug	mug	4. dot	lap	cot	7. sun	fox	fun
2. cup	hog	fog	5. got	dig	pig	8. cat	fat	run
3. rip	nap	zip	6. pit	rug	hug	9. us	sad	bus

Divide the class into small groups and have each group make up as many rhyming sentences as they can from their list of rhyming words. Read the rhymes and post them around the room.

Write and Spell on Your Own

Independent practice exercises for the objectives targeted in this unit are located in the corresponding Write and Spell on Your Own section of this book (see pp. 223–228).

UNIT 5 | /e/

Focus

Spelling: To hear and spell words with the short *e* (/e/) sound
Writing development: idioms, homonyms, dictionary skills
Writing style: creative

Word List

bed	hem	men	red	web
beg	hen	met	set	wed
bet	jet	net	sex	wet
den	led	pen	ten	yen
fed	leg	pep	vet	yes
get	let	pet	vex	yet

Suggested Sight Words

under   over   ever   very   easy

(Note the –*er* ending.)

Pretest

bed	fed	leg	men	bet
vet	web	yes	red	pen

Posttest

beg	den	jet	led	met
wet	yet	hem	vex	pep

Sentences for Dictation

It is very easy to do a jig.
His pet bug is under the rug.
Ben can hop over the net.

Spell Together

■ **Listening for short e (/e/):** Use an egg or a picture of an egg to firmly establish the short *e* sound. Use the word *beg* to demonstrate that if the students can hear the sounds in a word and identify the letters that make those sounds, they can spell the word.

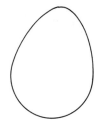

Teacher says	Student says	Student writes
"beg"		
"What is the first sound you hear?"	/b/	b
"What is the second sound you hear?"	/e/	e
"What is the last sound you hear?"	/g/	g
"Spell *beg*."	b-e-g	beg

Continue with other words from the word list.

■ **Auditory discrimination:** Use the following procedure to distinguish the five short vowel sounds introduced thus far.

1. Divide the class into five groups.
2. Assign a short vowel sound to each group (/a/ /e/ /i/ /o/ /u/) and have each student in the group write the assigned vowel on a piece of paper or a card. Say, "Raise your card (or paper) if you hear your vowel sound in the words I will say."

Suggested words

men	bib	mop	pop	pen	man	lot	pun
fan	hit	six	log	nut	pug	tip	sag
mom	leg	pet	hut	job	kid	sad	ham
den	hum	red	rot	win	hen	hot	ten

■ **Complete the idiom:** "Complete each idiom with a word that has the sound of short *e*."

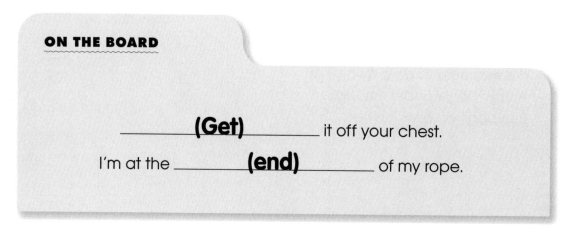

ON THE BOARD

_____ **(Get)** _____ it off your chest.

I'm at the _____ **(end)** _____ of my rope.

Egg hunt

1. Cut out egg-shaped cards from poster board or index stock.
2. Print each of the following pairs of letters on three or four cards.

   be   fe   he   je   le   me   ne
   pe   re   se   te   ve   we   ye

3. Print each of the following ending letters on three or four cards.

   b   d   g   t   m   p   s   x   n

4. Shuffle all the cards and hide them around the room.
5. Students hunt for the egg cards and try to put together two eggs to make a word.

Homonyms

ON THE BOARD

Bob dropped his new <u>pen</u> into the pig's <u>pen</u>.

He grabbed his <u>bat</u> to hit the <u>bat</u> flying in the attic.

1. Underline the homonyms *pen, pen* and *bat, bat* in the example sentences on the board.
2. "Draw a picture of each of the underlined words."
3. "In each sentence, did you draw different pictures for the two words that are spelled the same? Why?"
4. Discuss the fact that these words are spelled the same but have different meanings. "These words are called homonyms. They are spelled the same but have more than one meaning. Can you think of any other homonyms?"
5. As an ongoing activity, set aside a space on a bulletin board or blackboard/ whiteboard where students can list additional homonyms as they discover them in their reading and writing.

A round-robin story: Have students write a story about "Ben Who Is Ten." You can present this as a round-robin story for a class project. Students pass around an exercise book. Each student reads the story thus far and then contributes a set amount of text to continue it. Or each student can write an individual story on a sheet of paper. You may wish to display a list of short *e* words that might suggest story ideas, such as these:

beg   fed   hen   leg   pet   web   vet   jet   led

■ **Building short *e* words:** In each of two separate areas of the board, write two columns of different letters, as shown.

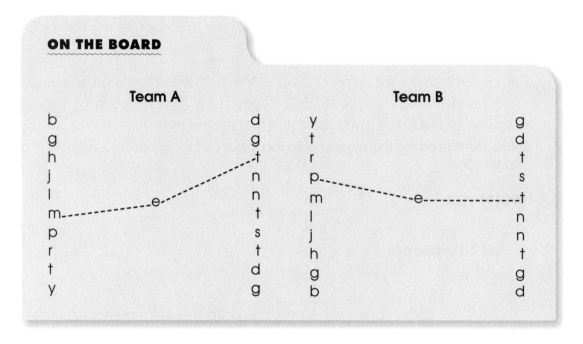

1. Divide the class into two teams.
2. Have a student from each team come to the board and make a short *e* word by connecting any of the listed beginning and ending consonants with an *e* in the middle.
3. Whichever team spells the most words correctly using the designated letters wins.

■ **Dictionary skills:** Make a column on the board for each letter of the alphabet, as shown.

Dictate the following words. Students either take turns coming to the board and writing the word under its beginning letter, or all students do this on individual sheets of paper.

bag	cap	mix	get	cut	wet	hop
jab	nap	on	den	tin	yip	fun
pad	leg	hen	in	rod	zag	
am	fat	six	up	vim	us	

Write and Spell on Your Own

Independent practice exercises for the objectives targeted in this unit are located in the corresponding Write and Spell on Your Own section of this book (see pp. 229–233).

UNIT 6 | **Short Vowel Review**

Focus

Spelling: To review all short vowels
Writing development: synonyms, antonyms, dictionary skills
Writing style: creative

Word List

Use any of the words listed for Units 1–5, plus other words that fit the patterns targeted in those units, if desired.

Optional Extension

Introduce the following compound words using the approach described in Unit 11.

bedbug	cobweb	humbug	sunlit	tiptop
bobcat	hatbox	lapdog	sunset	upset
catnap	hotbed	pigpen	suntan	zigzag
catnip	hubcap	ragbag	sunup	

Pretest

log	fig	top	sat	lit
dot	red	bug	jam	nip
hid	pen	tub	had	pet
box	cut	yet	led	rug

Posttest

lag	bad	six	rot	tan
fin	pup	nap	fun	tin
got	bun	let	ten	mop
sob	net	leg	jug	wit

Sentences for Dictation

She is on a big mat.
Not all of the men had met Sam.
Ben can go to the den.
We can use two or three pots.

Spell Together

■ **Acting out the short vowels:** Display the series of pictures used to cue the short vowels. Have the students perform an action that relates to each picture. Examples: eating an *apple,* cracking an *egg,* being cold near an *igloo,* waving arms like an *octopus,* holding an *umbrella.*

ON THE BOARD

Say to students, "Act out the vowel you hear in the words I will say." Read the following words:

Suggested words

rap	wet	run	hid	pot	yes
wet	fix	bat	fad	pod	hug
rub	vet	pop	mud	fun	lip
on	beg	hit	top	rod	dad
sad	bed	gum	six	gag	rob

■ **Same and different**

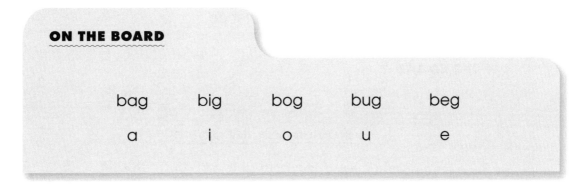

ON THE BOARD

bag	big	bog	bug	beg
a	i	o	u	e

Teacher says

"Bag, big, bog, bug, beg—
   how are these words alike?"

"How are they different?"

"How are these vowels the same?"

Student says

The /b/ and /g/ sounds are the same.

The vowel in the middle is different.

All of the vowels are short.

Dictate words from the list of suggested words and have students, in turn, write each word on the board under the corresponding short vowel sound.

■ **Synonyms and antonyms**

ON THE BOARD

good—bad	big—little	dad—father
cry—sob	wet—dry	up—down
rob—steal	lid—top	hot—cold

1. Read each pair of words with the class.
2. Say, "These word pairs can be classified into two groups. How would you group these word pairs?" Guide students to the desired classifications: words that have the same meaning versus words that have opposite meanings. If necessary, discuss the relationship of the words in each pair.
3. Explain, "Words that have the same meaning are called *synonyms,* and words that have the opposite meaning are called *antonyms.*"

■ **Contrasting sentences:** "We can use antonyms to compare and contrast things in our writing." Point out that each underlined word in the first sentence on the board has an antonym in the second sentence.

ON THE BOARD

1. <u>Women</u> can <u>stand</u> <u>here</u>.

2. <u>Men</u> can <u>sit</u> <u>there</u>.

Present two more pairs of sentences on the board. Have the students fill in the blanks in the second sentence with an antonym of the underlined words in the first sentence.

ON THE BOARD

The <u>moon</u> is going <u>down</u>.

The _____ is coming _____.

The <u>bottom</u> of the lake is <u>cold</u>.

The _____ of the lake is _____.

Have students write contrasting sentences for each of the following sentences.

1. It is a <u>cold</u>, <u>dry</u> day. (It is a hot, wet day.)
2. <u>Women</u> can go <u>out</u>. (Men can go in.)
3. <u>Mom</u> is <u>happy</u> when she is <u>dry</u>. (Dad is sad when he is wet.)

■ **Tap that word (a game of synonyms and antonyms)**

1. Divide the class into two teams.
2. Stand behind your desk. Have a student from each team come up to your desk.
3. Ask the student to name a short vowel word that is the synonym or antonym of the word you read. Example: "Think of a short vowel word that is the antonym of *small*."
4. The first student to tap your desk can try to answer the question. If the answer is correct, the student writes the word on the board. If the answer is incorrect, the student from the opposing team has an opportunity to answer.

5. Continue the game. The team that accumulates the most correctly spelled words within a prescribed time wins.

Suggested synonyms

cot—bed	jump—hop	hog—pig	cap—hat	work—job
baby—tot	run—jog	police officer—cop	crowd—mob	

Suggested antonyms

cold—hot	off—on	dry—wet	no—yes	out—in
women—men	bottom—top	happy—sad	lose—win	thin—fat

■ **Students' own dictionaries:** Students will create their own dictionaries by writing in words you dictate from the Words for Students' Own Dictionaries activities in Units 6 through 14. Dictate the words in the order listed so that the words on each page of the students' dictionaries will be in alphabetical order. (*Example:* Word #5 in Unit 6 is *mad,* and word #4 in Unit 7 is *mat.* Thus, in Unit 6, students write *mad* on the *m* page; in Unit 7, they will add *mat* beneath it. The dictionary words have been introduced in previous units and serve as a review.

Procedure for making individual dictionaries

1. Have each student either staple together 13 sheets of lined paper and insert these sheets into a folder, or use a copy book with at least 26 pages.
2. Students write one letter of the alphabet, in sequence, at the top of each page.
3. Dictate the words listed in Units 6 through 14 in alphabetical order.

■ **Students' own dictionaries:** an optional approach

1. Students may divide each page of their dictionary into two columns. They list the dictated words in the first column and write any new words they want to learn to spell in the second column.
2. After students have written the dictated dictionary words, they can define each word or use it in a sentence. If desired, have students write these in column 2.
3. Have students add guide words to each page after they complete their dictionaries.

■ **Words for students' own dictionaries:** Dictate the following words in order. Afterward, have students check each word against a model or trade off and check each other's work.

1. bag	3. dad	5. mad	7. rag	9. web
2. cap	4. fed	6. on	8. up	10. yam

Write and Spell on Your Own

Independent practice exercises for the objectives targeted in this unit are located in the corresponding Write and Spell on Your Own section of this book (see pp. 235–240).

UNIT 7 | /sh/, /ch/, /th/, /wh/

Focus

Spelling: To hear and spell consonant digraphs /sh/, /ch/, /th/, /wh/
Writing development: idioms, question words, dictionary skills
Writing style: creative, personal narrative

Word List

sh

shag	shin	shop	shun	shut
shed	ship	shot	shush	

ash	dash	gash	hash	lash	mush	sash
bash	dish	gosh	hush	mash	rash	wish
cash	fish	gush	josh	mesh	rush	

ch

chap	chat	chin	chip	chop	chug	chum

th

bath	path	that	then	this	thug	with
math	than	them	thin	thud	thus	

wh

when	which	whim	whip	whiz

Suggested Sight Words

who	what	why	where	here	there

Pretest

chap	when	shop	thin	shag
chum	this	ash	rash	cash

Posttest

chug	thud	math	whiz	then
bash	shot	gosh	dash	sash

Sentences for Dictation

It was easy to jog on the path to the shed.
Why did every girl get one toy?
Who let the man hop over the net?

Spell Together

■ **Listening for consonant digraphs (/sh/, /ch/, /th/, /wh/):** Introduce and identify each digraph separately (two letters that make one sound) to distinguish and emphasize it.

ON THE BOARD

Sharon will rush to shop for fish.

Say, "What sound do you hear repeated?" (the /sh/ sound) "How many sounds do you hear in /sh/?" (one) "/Sh/ is a consonant digraph. It is spelled *sh*. Two letters, *s* and *h*, work together to make one new sound: /sh/."

Use the word *ship* to demonstrate that if the students can hear the sounds in a word and identify the letters that make those sounds, they can spell the word.

Teacher says	Student says	Student writes
"ship"		
"What is the first sound you hear?"	/sh/	sh
"What is the second sound you hear?"	/i/	i
"What is the last sound you hear?"	/p/	p
"Spell *ship*."	sh-i-p	ship

Continue with other /sh/ words from the word list. Then proceed in the same manner with /ch/, /th/, and /wh/. First have the students identify the sound that is repeated in each of the following sentences. Then have them listen for the sounds and write the word that is listed after the sentence.

Sound	Sentence	Written word
/ch/	A chap will chat with his chum.	chip
/th/	The thin man led them to the path.	
	(Note the hard and soft /th/ sound.)	bath
/wh/	Who can tell me when he lost the whip?	when

■ **Complete the idiom:** "Complete each idiom with a word that has the sound of /ch/ or /sh/."

ON THE BOARD

He had a _____ **(chip)** _____ on his shoulder.

I'll be happy when my _____ **(ship)** _____ comes in.

■ **Auditory discrimination:** Have the students write each digraph, /sh/, /ch/, /th/, /wh/, on a separate card. Read aloud each of the following suggested words slowly. Have the students hold up the correct card to indicate the digraph the word contains. Use additional words from the word list if desired.

Suggested words

ship	wish	them	when	whip	chum
thud	hush	whiz	shot	bath	chat
fish	chug	then	ship	why	where

■ **Question words:** If possible, post a large picture that can elicit a story. Using the words on the board, start a round-robin story by having the first student describe "who," the second student add "did what," and so on. You may wish to audiotape the story and play it back to the class.

ON THE BOARD

?   who   did what   when   why   where   how   ?

Change the order of the words on the board and have the students retell the story.

■ **What do you wish for?** Suggest topics to start a "What do you wish for?" journal. Some samples follow:

I wish I had a dish of _____ because _____.

I wish I had a pal who _____.

I wish I had a path that went to _____.

I wish I could get a job in a shop that was _____.

■ **Dictionary skills:** Alphabetizing

ON THE BOARD

cash   fish   bath   dish

Have students do the following, in turn:
1. Underline the first letter in each word.
   c̲ash   f̲ish   b̲ath   d̲ish
2. Write the underlined letters in alphabetical order:
   b   c   d   f
3. Write the words in alphabetical order:
   bath   cash   dish   fish
4. Repeat with additional groups of words from the word list.

■ **Words for students' own dictionaries:** Have students add the following words, in the order given, to their dictionaries.*

1. ham	3. lad	5. net	7. ten	9. vet
2. nap	4. mat	6. sad	8. us	10. yap

Write and Spell on Your Own

Independent practice exercises for the objectives targeted in this unit are located in the corresponding Write and Spell on Your Own section of this book (see pp. 241–246).

*See Unit 6 for instructions for making the dictionaries.

UNIT 8 | Beginning *l* and *r* Blends

Focus

Spelling: To hear and spell words with beginning *l* and *r* blends
Writing development: hypothesizing, dictionary skills
Writing style: personal narrative

Word List*

L blends

blab	clap	flap	flit	glum	slab	slip
bled	clash	flash	flog	plan	slam	slit
blip	clip	flat	flop	plod	slap	slop
blob	clod	flax	flush	plop	slash	slosh
blot	clog	fled	glad	plot	slat	slot
blush	clot	flesh	glen	plug	sled	slug
clam	club	flex	glib	plum	slid	slum
clan	flag	flip	glob	plush	slim	slush

R blends

brag	crab	drop	grab	pram	thrash	trip
bran	crash	drug	grid	prim	thresh	trot
brash	crib	drum	grim	prod	throb	
brat	crop	fresh	grin	prop	thrush	
brim	crush	fret	grip	shred	trap	
broth	drag	frog	grit	shrub	trash	
brush	drip	from	grub	shrug	trim	

Suggested Sight Words

other   another   mother   brother   father   sister

Pretest

blot	clash	slap	plop	clip
brim	trip	from	trash	shrub

---

*Where necessary, introduce the *l* blend first, and then proceed to the *r* blend.

Posttest

slot	plush	flap	plug	flash
crush	brag	shrug	prod	trim

Sentences for Dictation

The girl was glad to get the big sled.

Did Fred grab your drum?

I will be glad to get another brush.

Where does your mother get fish?

Spell Together

■ **Review consonant digraphs**

> **ON THE BOARD**
>
> _____ hip   _____ hop
>
> _____ hip   _____ hop

"What letters can you put before *hip* and *hop* to make new words?"

s: ship, shop   c: chip, chop

"We changed the consonant *h* to a consonant digraph. A consonant digraph is two letters used together for one sound."

■ **Introduce beginning blends:** Introduce *l* and *r* blends separately, following the same procedure for each.

L blends

> **ON THE BOARD**
>
> _____ lap   _____ led
>
> _____ lap   _____ led

"What letters can you put before *lap* and *led* to make new words?"
f, c: flap, clap   f, s: fled, sled

"Say each word. You can hear two sounds at the beginning of the new words. These are consonant blends."

Dictate the following groups of words, stressing each beginning blend:

bl	cl	fl	gl	pl	sl
blab	clap	flat	glad	plan	slap
blot	clam	flip	glen	plum	slid
blob	clot	flop	glib	plop	slum
blush	clash	flesh	glum	plush	slush

R blends

ON THE BOARD

_____ rip   _____ rag

_____ rip   _____ rag

"What letters can you put before *rip* and *rag* to make new words?"
t, g: trip, grip   b, d: brag, drag

Dictate the following groups of words, stressing each beginning blend:

br	cr	dr	gr	pr	tr
bran	crib	drop	grin	prop	trot
brag	crab	drum	grip	prod	trap
brim	crop	drug	grab	pram	trip
brush	crush	drag	grub	prim	trash

Tell students that some consonant digraphs can combine with another letter to make a consonant blend (*shr: shred, shrub, shrug; thr: thrash, throb, thrush*).

■ **Blending:** This is a card game for two to eight players.
1. Print three sets of cards with one of the following words on each card. These are word cards.

lash	let	lad	rag	rim	rash	rip	rot
rush	lid	lot	lip	led	lap	rat	lug

2. Print six sets of cards with one of the following consonants on each card: *f, b, g, t, c, d, s,* and *p*. These are draw cards.

3. Deal six word cards to each player. Place the draw cards in a pile in the center of the table.

4. Each player, in turn, takes a draw card and tries to make a new word using the draw card and one of the word cards in his or her hand. (*Example:* word card *lash* and draw card *c* spells *clash.*)

5. If the player is not able to make a word, he or she discards the draw card and puts it at the bottom of the pile. A player who makes a word keeps both cards.

6. The first player to make six correctly spelled words wins.

What if? This activity introduces hypothesizing. "A hypothesis is something you might assume to be true. To hypothesize is to try to think of what might happen in a given situation. For example, what might happen if there were no gravity?" Have students write an *l* or *r* blend word that might answer the following questions.

What could happen if:

1. "A car goes too fast?" (crash)
2. "You get the best report card in the school?" (brag)
3. "You are embarrassed?" (blush)
4. "You pick up four books, six cups, and one chair?" (drop)
5. "You finish watching a great play?" (clap)
6. "You close the door when you are angry?" (slam)
7. "Your shoelace is untied?" (trip)
8. "You lose a lot of weight?" (slim)
9. "You drop your book on a flower?" (crush)
10. "There is a nail in your tire?" (flat)

Have the student make up a story based on one of the hypothetical questions.

Words for students' own dictionaries: Have students add the following words, in the order given, to their dictionaries.*

1. cash	3. chat	5. shed	7. when	9. which
2. fish	4. chop	6. that	8. math	10. thin

Write and Spell on Your Own

Independent practice exercises for the objectives targeted in this unit are located in the corresponding Write and Spell on Your Own section of this book (see pp. 247–250).

*See Unit 6 for instructions for making the dictionaries.

UNIT 9 | More Beginning Blends, Ending Blends

Focus

Writing and spelling: To hear and spell words with beginning blends other than *l* or *r*
To hear and spell words with ending blends
Writing development: similes, dictionary skills
Writing style: creative

Word List

Beginning blends

scab	shrug	snag	snub	spin	stag	stop	swig	twin
scan	smash	snap	snug	spit	stash	stub	swim	
scat	smog	snip	span	spot	stem	stud	swish	
scum	smug	snob	spat	stab	step	swam	twig	

scram	scrap	scrub	splash	split	sprig	strap	strip

Ending blends

act	bump	dust	gift	jilt	mast	pulp	self	tusk
and	bunch	elf	golf	jump	melt	pump	send	vast
ant	bust	elm	gulf	just	mend	punch	sent	vent
apt	camp	end	gulp	lamp	mint	punt	shaft	vest
ask	cast	fact	gust	land	mist	raft	shelf	weld
band	champ	fast	hand	last	munch	ramp	shift	went
bask	chant	felt	held	left	musk	rapt	sift	wept
belt	chest	fifth	helm	lift	must	rasp	soft	whisk
bench	chomp	film	help	lint	nest	rend	task	wilt
bend	damp	fist	hint	lisp	next	rent	tempt	wisp
bent	dent	flask	hump	list	pact	rest	tent	zest
best	depth	fond	hunt	loft	pant	risk	tenth	
bond	desk	frisk	husk	lump	pest	romp	theft	
brisk	disk	fund	imp	lunch	pinch	rust	tilt	
bulb	dusk	gasp	inch	mask	pond	sand	tint	

Tell students that the /k/ sound at the end of a word is usually spelled –*k* when it appears in a consonant blend.

Suggested Sight Words

some   come   cause   because   any   many

Pretest

spin	snag	twin	pump	best
strip	pant	inch	land	champ

Posttest

snug	swam	snub	end	weld
swish	pinch	ramp	bulb	chest

Sentences for Dictation

We thought the bench was split.

Mother got some fresh fish for father.

Many men come to our club for lunch.

Spell Together

■   **Review *l* and *r* blends:** "We have been spelling words that begin with consonant blends: the *l* blend, as in *blot,* and the *r* blend, as in *brag.* Listen for the beginning blends and write these words." Dictate the following words:

blob	clap	flip	plop	slug	brim	crop
from	grin	drug	trip	prod	shred	thrush

■   **More beginning blends**

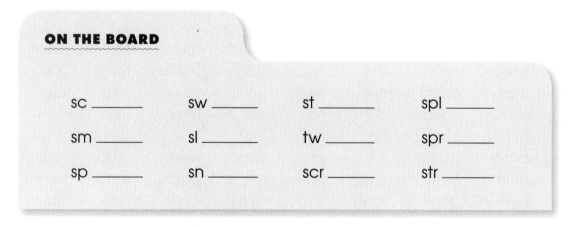

ON THE BOARD

sc _____	sw _____	st _____	spl _____
sm _____	sl _____	tw _____	spr _____
sp _____	sn _____	scr _____	str _____

"Look at these other beginning consonant blends on the board. Listen carefully and spell these words with the blends." Dictate these words:

scat   smog   spin   swim   slip   snag   stop   twin

"Listen for three beginning consonants in these words." Dictate these words:
scrub   split   sprig   strap

Continue with additional words from the word list.

▪ Ending blends

ON THE BOARD

fact	raft	gulf	melt	camp	bend
dent	wept	task	gasp	vest	pinch

"Each word on the board has a consonant blend at the end. Can you think of any other words with these ending consonant blends?" List the words students suggest.

Dictate the following additional words with ending blends:

and	cast	inch	raft	tempt	weld
band	felt	jump	self	fact	went
bump	gulp	lisp	shaft	vast	risk

▪ Bingo blend: Make up two bingo boards on separate areas of the board so two teams can work simultaneously, as shown.

ON THE BOARD

Team A				Team B			
a	e	i	o	a	e	i	u
___mp	___nd	___lt	___mp	___sp	___st	___fth	___mp
___st	___lt	___nt	___nd	___ft	___lt	___ft	___st
___sp	___lf	___sp	___lf	___nd	___lf	___nt	___nd
___ft	___st	___ft	___nd	___mp	___ft	___lt	___nch

1. Write each of the following words on a card and shuffle the cards.

chomp	last	punch	dust	melt
shift	fond	raft	hand	wilt
theft	end	champ	romp	lisp
lint	jump	pest	golf	self
gasp	pond	fifth	fund	

2. Divide the class into two teams. Assign a bingo blend board to each team.

3. Have one student from each team go up to the board. Draw a card and read the word on it. The student writes the word in the correct vowel column and the correct blend space. (Note that not all the words will fit on both boards.) Any student who spells a word incorrectly must erase it and loses a turn.

4. The first team to complete a row of words going across, down, or diagonally wins. For additional rounds, have the teams trade boards.

■ **Simile charades:** "A simile is a figure of speech in which two dissimilar things are compared by the use of the words *like* or *as.* An example is the phrase 'limp as a dishrag.'"

1. Write these similes on individual cards.

   flat as a pancake   thin as a rail

   fast as a rabbit   snug as a bug in a rug

2. Select a student to take a card and act out the simile.

3. The other students try to guess the first word of the simile and spell it correctly. If they need help, write the simile on the board, leaving off the first word.

4. Have students expand each phrase into a complete sentence.

■ **Dictionary skills:** Second-letter alphabetizing

ON THE BOARD

swim   spin   snap   shrug

1. Underline the first letter of each word. Say, "Because the first letter in these words is the same, how would you alphabetize the words?" (You use the second letter.)

2. Have students copy the words from the board. "Underline the second letter in each word."

   swim   spin   snap   shrug

3. "Write the second letters in alphabetical order."

   h   n   p   w

   "When the first letter of a group of words is the same, we put the words in alphabetical order by using the second letters."

4. "Write the words in alphabetical order."

   shrug   snap   spin   swim

5. "When the first and second letters are the same, we put words in alphabetical order by using the third letter."

6. Make up sheets with the following words in columns, or have students copy these words. Make sure each student has a card or second sheet of paper to cover the columns.

hint	lint	bend	pump	bent
help	last	belt	punch	bench
hunt	lump	best	pulp	bend

7. "Look at one column of words at a time (that is, going down). Cover the column so that only the first letter shows. If the first letter in each word is the same, uncover at the second letter. If the second letter is the same, cover the first two letters and look at the third letter. Write the words in alphabetical order."

■ **Words for students' own dictionaries:** Have students add the following words, in the order given, to their dictionaries.*

1. club   3. sled   5. drag   7. fresh   9. drum
2. flag   4. flash   6. crab   8. drop   10. frog

Write and Spell on Your Own

Independent practice exercises for the objectives targeted in this unit are located in the corresponding Write and Spell on Your Own section of this book (see pp. 251–254).

*See Unit 6 for instructions for making the dictionaries.

UNIT 10 | Dual-Blend Words

Focus

Spelling: To hear and spell words with both beginning and ending blends
Writing development: rhymes, dictionary skills
Writing style: creative

Word List

blanch	clamp	crust	grunt	shrimp	stilt	tract
bland	clasp	draft	plant	slant	stint	tramp
blast	cleft	drift	plump	slept	stomp	trend
blend	clinch	flask	primp	slump	strand	trump
blimp	clump	flinch	print	spend	strict	trust
blitz	craft	flint	prompt	spent	stump	twist
blond	cramp	gland	scalp	splint	stunt	
blunt	crept	glint	scamp	sprint	swift	
brand	crest	grand	scant	squint	thrift	
brash	crisp	grant	scrimp	stamp	thrust	
brunt	crunch	grasp	script	stand	thump	

Suggested Sight Words

should	would	could	though	thought	brought

Pretest

clasp	slant	thump	print	blast
grunt	splint	blimp	crisp	plump

Posttest

crunch	slump	cramp	stint	blunt
scalp	sprint	drift	blend	slept

Sentences for Dictation

We could twist the clamp for you.
We should help him get off the raft.
I thought she had not brought a twig.

Spell Together

■ **Hear the blend, beginning and end**

ON THE BOARD

bran	and	clam	lamp
brand		clamp	

Teacher says	Student spells
"Listen for the beginning blend: *bran*. Spell it."	b-r
"Listen for the ending blend: *and*. Spell it."	n-d
"Put the two words together. Spell *brand*."	b-r-a-n-d

Continue with the following words:

clam—lamp = clamp   plum—lump = plump
cram—ramp = cramp   scan—ant = scant

■ **Blended rhymes**

ON THE BOARD

draft—raft   You might get a draft
               as you climb on the raft.

trust—rust   How can you trust
               a car that can rust?

1. "Listen for the rhyming words within these words. Write both words."

thump	craft	draft	bland	tramp	slump	brash
trend	brunt	plump	blend	gland	sprint	flint
blast	cramp	blimp	crust	grunt	thrust	scamp

2. "Make up rhymes with some of the words you wrote."

■ Words within words

1. Divide the class into two teams with five players on each team.

2. Ask the class to think of a word that can be made by combining a letter with the definition of a different word. (*Example: s + a group of tents = scamp.*)

3. Present the following suggested combinations and have each team try to identify the target word. Set a time limit and call on each team alternately until you get the correct answer. (Do the first one with the class.)

Suggested combinations	Target word
1. *t* + a reddish coating that forms on metal exposed to air	trust
2. *b* + walk lamely	blimp
3. *g* + solid part of the Earth	gland
4. *c* + something that provides light	clamp
5. *b* + to allow temporary use of something	blend
6. *b* + after all the others	blast
7. *s* + a way to write your name in first grade	sprint
8. *b* + a very small animal	brunt
9. *c* + a floating platform	craft

■ Boxes for words:
This is a game for two players. You will need two boxes (shoebox or similar size) and two sets of cards. In the first box, put one set of cards with one of the following *beginning* blends on each card: *bl–, br–, cl–, cr–, dr–, fl–, gl–, gr–, p–, pr–, sc–, scr–, sl–, sp–, st–, tr–.* In the second box, put one set of cards with one of the following *ending* blends on each card: *–nd, –st, –nt, –mp, –sp, –ft, –pt, –lt, –ct, –nch.*

1. Each player, in turn, takes five cards from each box and makes as many words as possible by combining a beginning and an ending blend with any intervening vowel. Each beginning and ending blend may be used only once per turn. Any cards that do not make a word are returned to the box.

2. Each player says and writes each word made.

3. Each correctly spelled word earns the player one point. The first player to score 20 points wins.

■ Words for students' own dictionaries:
Have students add the following words, in the order listed, to their dictionaries.*

1. end	3. ant	5. pest	7. jump	9. snap
2. inch	4. bench	6. rest	8. slug	10. gasp

Write and Spell on Your Own

Independent practice exercises for the objectives targeted in this unit are located in the corresponding Write and Spell on Your Own section of this book (see pp. 255–260).

*See Unit 6 for instructions for making the dictionaries.

UNIT 11 | Compounds

Focus

Spelling: To hear and spell compound words
Writing development: dialogue, dictionary skills
Writing style: creative

Word List

Single consonants

bedbug	cobweb	humbug	sunlit	tiptop
bobcat	hatbox	lapdog	sunset	upset
catnap	hotbed	pigpen	suntan	zigzag
catnip	hubcap	ragbag	sunup	

Consonant digraphs

bathtub	chitchat	dishrag	hotshot	upshot
catfish	dishpan	fishnet	sunfish	whiplash

Consonant blends

bobsled	gumdrop	manhunt	snapshot	withheld
dogtrot	handbag	sandbag	sunlamp	withstand
draftsman	handclasp	sandblast	sunspot	
dustpan	handcraft	sandbox	tenpins	
filmstrip	hangman	sandman	tinsmith	
flagman	himself	slipshod	uplift	

The following compound words combine short-vowel words and sight words from previous lessons:

anyone	offhand	overlap	therefore	whereas
anywhere	overall	overrun	thereupon	whereupon
everyone	overcast	overstep	undergo	wherever
everywhere	overcome	overwhelm	underhand	whoever
forbid	overdo	popover	understand	
forget	overhand	someone	underwent	
herewith	overland	somewhere	whatever	

Pretest

handbag	catnip	sandbox	cobweb	uplift
dishrag	gumdrop	dustpan	sunset	lapdog

Posttest

hatbox	catnap	pigpen	upset	bathtub
hubcap	dishpan	snapshot	tiptop	himself

Sentences for Dictation

Someone could stand here or there.

His brother can stamp whatever you send.

Everyone left the trash in a trashcan.

Spell Together

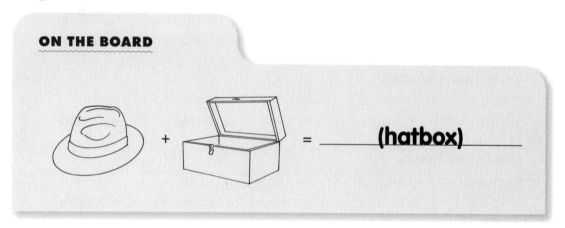

ON THE BOARD

+ = _____ **(hatbox)** _____

- **Two to make one:** Explain that compound words consist of two or more simple words combined to make a new word. "In some compound words, the meaning of both words together gives the meaning of the whole word. Other compound words have a different meaning than the simple words that make them up. For example: a *hatbox* is a box for a hat, but is *humbug* a bug that can sing?"

  "Listen for the two words you know. Spell each word. Put them together to make a new word."

Teacher says	Student writes
"Spell *hat.*"	hat
"Spell *box.*"	box
"Put them together and spell *hatbox.*"	hatbox

Continue with other words from the word list.

Composing compounds

1. Divide the class into two teams.
2. With a student from one team at the board, dictate a simple word that is part of a compound word on the suggested word list.
3. If the student can make a compound word using that simple word and write it on the board correctly, his or her team receives a point. (Give a point for each correct compound, even if it is not on the word list.)
4. If the student's answer is incorrect, a student from the other team tries to complete the compound word for a point. Alternate which team gets first shot to spell a word.
5. The team that completes the most compounds wins.

Suggested words

bath	hum	sun	hand	cob	gun	sand
cat	pig	up	snap	shot	dish	whip

As a review of sight words introduced in previous units, have students compose compounds using the following words:

some	any	one	who	under	where	there
every	over	ever	come	for	what	

Compound concentration

1. Make 20 to 24 cards.
2. Write each half of 10 to 12 compound words on a card. Use words from the list that follows.
3. Place all the cards face-down on a table.
4. The first player turns up one card and then a second card. If both cards match (in either order) to make a compound word, the player keeps the cards. If not, the player turns the cards face-down on the table again and tries to remember the words on them.
5. The second player concentrates on where specific word cards are located and continues in the same manner.
6. The player who collects the most compound words wins.

Suggested words

bath	tub	bed	bug	cat	nap	dish	rag
hand	bag	him	self	man	hunt	sun	set
tip	top	snap	shot	sand	box	cob	web
some	one	who	ever	under	stand	over	come

Compound lineup

1. Write on a card a compound word from the word list, leaving a space between the two simple words that compose it. Make a card for every two students.
2. Cut the cards in half between the two simple words and mix up the halves.

3. Give each student half a card.

4. Tell the students to find a partner whose card completes their compound word and to line up in pairs.

■ **Dialogues**

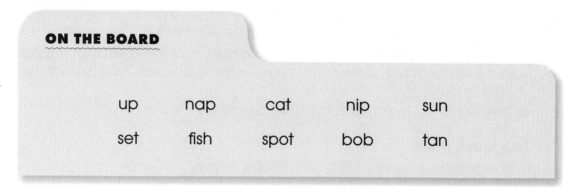

ON THE BOARD

up	nap	cat	nip	sun
set	fish	spot	bob	tan

Have the students (a) see how many compound words they can make from these words, and (b) use the compound words to complete the following dialogue. Students can work in teams or in pairs. Students might also enjoy acting out their dialogues.

The Cat and the Sun

Cat: What a tiptop catnap I had!

Sun: My, my cat, did you nap at sunup?

Cat: _____

Sun: _____

Cat: _____

Sun: _____

Scoring

4 points for every line of dialogue

3 points for every compound that has *cat* or *sun* in it

1 point for any other compound word

Possible compounds

sunfish	catnip	sunset
bobcat	suntan	catfish
sunup	catnap	sunspot

■ **Words for students' own dictionaries:** Have students add the following words, in the order listed, to their dictionaries.*

1. spend   3. stamp   5. grand   7. crunch   9. grunt

2. cramp   4. crept   6. blast   8. blend   10. thrift

Write and Spell on Your Own

Independent practice exercises for the objectives targeted in this unit are located in the corresponding Write and Spell on Your Own section of this book (see pp. 261–263).

*See Unit 6 for instructions for making the dictionaries.

UNIT 12 /ar/

Focus

Spelling: To hear and spell words with the /ar/ sound
Writing development: syllables, dictionary skills
Writing style: creative, personal narrative

Word List

arch	car	farm	mar	scarf	stark
ark	card	hard	march	shark	start
arm	cart	hark	mark	sharp	tar
art	charm	harm	marsh	smart	tart
bar	chart	harp	par	snarl	yard
barb	dark	harsh	parch	spar	yarn
bard	darn	jar	park	spark	
bark	dart	lard	part	star	
barn	far	lark	scar	starch	

armrest	boxcar	farmhand	flatcar	hardship	shipyard
barnyard	dogcart	farmyard	handcar	sandbar	starfish

artist	garnish	parsnip	varnish
bombard	marlin	tarnish	

Suggested Sight Words

earn	learn	earth	early	heard	heart

Pretest

hard	march	tar	dart	harsh
star	arm	part	art	sharp

Posttest

arch	charm	smart	darn	marsh
harp	car	start	bar	lard

Sentences for Dictation

The artist left his car in the barn.

I heard you would come to the sandbox early.

Her sister is upset because she did not learn to swim.

Spell Together

■ /ar/ is not hard

ON THE BOARD

Who left the jar

of black tar

in our _____?

I'm so smart

I can hit the chart

with a _____.

Rhyme

"Can you complete the rhyme?"

"List the rhyming words in each rhyme. How are they alike?"

Help the students discover that the words all have the /ar/ sound (and the letters *ar*).

jar—tar—car   smart—chart—dart

"Listen for the /ar/ sound. It is usually spelled *ar.*"

Dictation

Dictate the following words. Have students, in turn, write them on the board. If necessary, add more words from the word list:

arm	barn	chart	dart	hard	marsh	part
charm	mar	star	yarn	tart	tar	harp

■ **What is a syllable?** Discuss the term *syllable:* "A syllable is a word or part of a word that consists of an uninterrupted expression of sound. It consists of one or more letters, including at least one vowel. Each syllable has one beat. *Farm* has one beat. How many beats do you hear in *farmyard?* Clap out the beats for each syllable you hear in these words."

whatever	overstep	another	underhand	brought	sandbar
somewhere	father	scar	sharp	barnyard	artist

SPELLING SOUNDS

■ **Spell words of more than one syllable:** "To spell words of more than one syllable, say the first syllable, spell the syllable, then say and spell the second syllable, and continue in the same way for the remaining syllables."

Dictate the following words. Have the students say and spell each syllable.

armrest	barnyard	farmhand	tarnish	tinsmith
boxcar	farmyard	shipyard	artist	himself
bombard	varnish	parsnip	hobgoblin	chitchat

■ **Starboard:** a syllable game for two players

1. Make a board by gluing or drawing 24 stars along a pathway.
2. Write each of the following suggested words on a card. Place the cards face-down on a table.
3. Give each student a game piece. A player takes a card and counts the syllables in the word, then moves the marker along the star pathway, one star for each syllable in the word.
4. Encourage the students to monitor each other. A player who incorrectly counts the number of syllables cannot move.

Suggested words

barnyard	farm	goblet	snapshot	hard
understand	instrument	bandit	splendid	
arithmetic	artist	hobgoblin	spark	

■ **Where does it start?** Initiate a discussion about how things start. You might mention that everything starts somewhere. Ask where the following things start.

a bark (a dog)

an arm (a shoulder)

the dark (at sunset)

a march (the first step forward)

a spark (from a fire)

a yard (at a fence)

When we write we start with an idea. Suggest the following topics. Have students answer each question with a sentence or short paragraph.

1. What might you do when you feel smart?
2. How do you feel when you are in the dark?
3. What would you do if you were face-to-face with a shark?

■ **Dictionary skills:** "A dictionary helps you spell a word. A dictionary is also arranged to help you find the words you are looking for." (Give each student a dictionary, if available, or demonstrate with a class dictionary.) "Think of a dictionary as divided into three parts: the beginning, with words from *a* to *f;* the middle, with words from *g* to *p;* and the end, with words from *q* to *z.*"

ON THE BOARD

Beginning	Middle	End
a to f	g to p	q to z

Have students copy the three headings from the board on individual sheets of paper. Dictate the following words in the order listed. Have students write each one under the correct heading. (Each word list will then be properly alphabetized.)

1. hard	4. smart	7. lamp	10. charm	13. march
2. raft	5. arch	8. cart	11. farm	14. yard
3. jar	6. barn	9. tar	12. tart	15. part

■ **Words for students' own dictionaries:** Have students add the following words, in the order listed, to their dictionaries.*

1. handbag	3. pigpen	5. gumdrop	7. dustpan	9. tiptop
2. hatbox	4. tinsmith	6. bobsled	8. zigzag	10. humbug

Write and Spell on Your Own

Independent practice exercises for the objectives targeted in this unit are located in the corresponding Write and Spell on Your Own section of this book (see pp. 265–270).

---

*See Unit 6 for instructions for making the dictionaries.

UNIT 13 | –ng, –nk

Focus

Spelling: To hear and spell words that end in –*ing*, –*ang*, –*ong*, –*ung*, and –*ink*, –*ank*, –*onk*, –*unk*

Writing development: rhymes, haiku, hypothesizing, fact and opinion, dictionary skills

Writing style: creative, informative

Word List

Final –*ng*

bring	king	sing	sting	thing	
cling	ping	sling	string	wing	
fling	ring	spring	swing	zing	

bang	fang	hang	rang	slang	twang
clang	gang	pang	sang	sprang	

bong	long	song	thong
gong	prong	strong	throng

clung	lung	sprung	stung
hung	rung	strung	sung

handspring   slingshot   strongbox

Final –*nk*

blink	drink	link	rink	slink	wink
brink	ink	mink	shrink	stink	
clink	kink	pink	sink	think	

bank	dank	lank	sank	tank
blank	drank	plank	shank	thank
clank	flank	prank	spank	yank
crank	frank	rank	swank	

conk	honk

Final *–nk* (*Continued*)

bunk	drunk	hunk	shrunk	spunk
chunk	dunk	junk	skunk	sunk
clunk	flunk	plunk	slunk	trunk

bunkbed   gangplank   inkblot

Suggested Sight Words

knot   knew   know   wring   wrap   wrong

Pretest

gong	strung	ring	slang	sung
tank	sunk	honk	drank	inkblot

Posttest

cling	gang	long	strung	thing
blank	mink	spunk	shrunk	gangplank

Sentences for Dictation

We think we can hang a ring in the fishtank.
We know the earth on the farm is hard.
Everyone knew the wrong car was in the yard.

Spell Together

■ **Listen to my rhyme**

ON THE BOARD

I love to sing	I think
as I cling	that a mink
to my swing.	can wink!

"Listen to the rhyming words in each rhyme. How are they alike?" Lead students to realize that they end in *–ing* and *–ink*, respectively. Point out that /ing/ is spelled *–ing;* /ink/ is spelled *–ink.*

■ **Listen for the changing vowel sounds:** The following series of words vary only in the vowel sound. Present the words in a group but slowly enough for students to write as you speak.

"Spell *sing*. Listen for the different vowel sounds in the following words. Spell *sang*, spell *song*, spell *sung*."

"Spell *wink*. Listen for the different vowel sounds in the following words. Spell *hank*, spell *honk*, spell *hunk*."

Dictate the following words and have students spell them:

yank	bring	conk	hang	spring	twang
lung	spunk	gong	pink	trunk	blank

If necessary, add words from the word list.

■ **Haiku:** "Haiku is Japanese poetry that deals with thoughts and feelings. The form consists of three lines, each with a specific number of syllables. Count the syllables in the first two lines of the haiku on the board. Try to write a five-syllable last line." It may be helpful to suggest a line (such as, "No one bothers me!").

> **ON THE BOARD**
>
> **Haiku**   **Bunkbed**
>
> First line: 5 syllables   I love the top bunk.
>
> Second line: 7 syllables   My space away from the world.
>
> Third line: 5 syllables   _____

If you feel that students are ready, have them try to write their own haikus. Suggest the following words to generate ideas:

ring	clunk	sing	spank	clank	spring
fling	strong	trunk	wing	stung	
drink	skunk	swing	junk	blink	

■ **Password—what if? (hypothesizing)**

1. Make two cards for each of the following words:

sting	shrink	tank	sink	dunk	ring
spank	hang	thank	flunk	wink	bank
drink	string	blink	trunk	sing	junk

2. Divide the class into two teams, Team A and Team B. Give one student from each team a card with the same word on it.

3. The player from Team A makes up a hypothetical situation to enable the members of his or her team to guess and spell the word on the card. (*Example:* For the word *sink,* the student might ask, "What would happen if you had a hole in the bottom of your boat?" Someone would answer, "sink—*s-i-n-k.*")

4. If no one on Team A can guess and spell the word on the card, the student from Team B repeats the procedure with the same word.

5. Continue with pairs of students from each team. Alternate which team gets to guess first. The team with the most correct responses wins.

■ **Commercials:** fact or opinion?

1. Discuss the difference between a fact and an opinion: A *fact* is a statement that can be proven true or false. An *opinion* is a judgment about a person, thing, idea, or animal.

2. Divide the class into two imaginary companies that produce commercials. Company A's advertisements are based on facts. (*Example:* Our drink contains only grape juice and water.) Company B's advertisements are based on opinion. (*Example:* Our grape drink is the best in town.)

3. Dictate a word (a suggested list follows). The company representative spells the word and uses it in a one-sentence "commercial" that stresses either fact or opinion.

4. The team scores a point if the representative spells the word correctly and uses it in that team's type of commercial (fact or opinion).

Suggested words

bank	drink	ink	mink	pink	shrink	sink
trunk	swing	string	bunkbed	tank	slingshot	

■ **What's missing?**

1. Read the story that follows.

2. Stop after each sentence and have students write an *–ng* or *–nk* word that could fill each blank.

3. After reading the story, have students say and spell the words they picked to fill the blanks. All reasonable responses are acceptable.

Fred and Mike were hiking in the woods. They decided to stop to

_____ some water. Mike saw something strange near the

_____ of a tree. Fred kicked some dead leaves out of the way.

They saw a small box tied with _____. Someone had written

numbers on it in red _____. They carefully opened

the box. There was a giant diamond _____ in the box.

4. Have the students continue this story or write another story, using the words they selected. To help them complete the story, ask, "What do you think Fred and Mike will do with what they found in the box? What would you do with it? Where do you think it came from?"

■ **Dictionary skills:** guide words

1. Have students open a standard dictionary to any page. Say, "Look at the top of the page. You will see a word on the left and right. Look at the first and last entries on the page. They are the same as the words at the top of the page. How do these words help you look up a word?"

2. Elicit from the students that the words on the top of the page tell you what are alphabetically the first and last words on the page so that you can quickly find the page with the word you want. Say, "These words are called guide words."

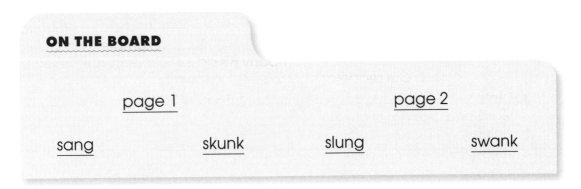

ON THE BOARD

page 1		page 2	
sang	skunk	slung	swank

3. Have students, in turn, write the words you dictate under the correct guide word. Dictate the following words in order:

1. sang	3. spring	5. shank	7. stung	9. swank
2. slung	4. sank	6. sing	8. sung	10. skunk

■ **Words for students' own dictionaries:** Have students add the following words, in the order listed, to their dictionaries.*

1. yard	3. starch	5. yarn	7. arch	9. arm
2. star	4. starfish	6. start	8. lard	10. art

Write and Spell on Your Own

Independent practice exercises for the objectives targeted in this unit are located in the corresponding Write and Spell on Your Own section of this book (see pp. 271–273).

*See Unit 6 for instructions for making the dictionaries.

UNIT 14 | -ed

Focus

Spelling: To hear and spell *–ed* endings that are pronounced /ed/, /d/, or /t/*
Writing development: past tense, syllables, dictionary skills
Writing style: personal narrative

Word List

/ed/

blasted	darted	hinted	mended	sanded	trusted
blended	dented	hunted	parted	shifted	twisted
branded	drafted	landed	planted	slanted	welded
chanted	dusted	listed	printed	started	
charted	handed	melted	rested	tinted	

/t/

barked	camped	flushed	marched	punched	stamped
blinked	clamped	grasped	marked	rushed	thanked
blushed	clanked	helped	mashed	smashed	thumped
brushed	crashed	jumped	munched	spanked	winked
bumped	crunched	linked	pinched	splashed	yanked

/d/

armed	charmed	darned	farmed	harmed	snarled

Suggested Sight Words

quit   quiet   quite   quart   quarter   queen

Point out to students that *q* is always followed by *u*.

Pretest

blasted	hinted	landed	started	helped
blushed	farmed	grasped	crunched	linked

---

*In this unit, *–ed* is added only to verbs ending in two consonants. See Unit 26 for the consonant-doubling rule when *–ed* is added to a word ending in a single consonant.

Posttest

chanted	camped	dusted	thanked	munched
harmed	shifted	brushed	welded	blinked

Sentences for Dictation

The car was not harmed or dented when we bumped.

The quiet queen could cause the men to march.

What did you wrap with the other bit of string?

Spell Together

■ **Using *-ed* endings /ed/, /t/, /d/**

> **ON THE BOARD**
>
> I plant trees.
>
> I planted trees yesterday.

"How does *-ed* change the meaning of the word *plant?*" Elicit that *-ed* tells us that *planted* happened in the past. Have students make up two sentences for each of the following words. The first sentence should be in the present or future tense and the second in the past tense. (*Example:* "Hear the dog bark"/"The dog will bark" and "The dog barked all day.")

bark	hunt	punch	trust	darn	march	wink

■ **Listen for the sounds of *-ed*:** Have students, in turn, read the words on the board out loud. "Listen to the sound at the end of each word. What are the different sounds you hear for *-ed* in these words?" (/ed/, /d/, /t/)

> **ON THE BOARD**
>
> | | | | | |
> |---|---|---|---|---|
> | rushed | stamped | harmed | shifted | thanked |
> | farmed | chanted | blended | marched | snarled |

"You may hear /t/, as in *rushed,* /d/, as in *harmed,* or /ed/, as in *shifted.* The ending is still spelled *–ed."* Have students list the words on the board under the proper headings.

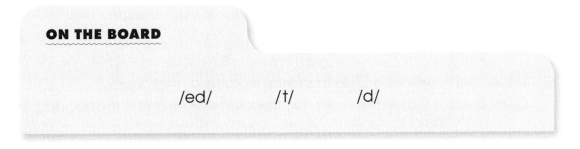

ON THE BOARD

/ed/   /t/   /d/

■ **Listen for the extra syllable**

ON THE BOARD

rushed	blended
harmed	shifted
marched	chanted

"Read the words in the first column. How many syllables do you hear in each word? (one) Now read the words in the second column; how many syllables do you hear? (two) The letters *–ed* add an extra syllable to a word when you hear the sound /ed/."

■ **Relay the sounds of *-ed:*** Set up three columns for Team A and Team B on separate areas of the board, as shown.

ON THE BOARD

Team A			Team B		
/ed/	/t/	/d/	/ed/	/t/	/d/

1. Divide the class into two teams, Team A and Team B. Assign a caller for each team.

2. Give each caller one of the following lists of words. Add more words from the word list if necessary.

	Caller A			**Caller B**	
blushed	parted	darned	blasted	snarled	started
charmed	munched	drafted	harmed	clamped	bumped
smashed	rested	armed	listed	farmed	blinked

3. The callers dictate a word to the first student on their team.

4. The student runs to the board and writes the word under the heading that matches the pronunciation of the *-ed* ending.

5. The game continues until one caller has dictated all his or her words. The game ends when a team finishes its list.

6. Check the words for correct spelling and placement.

■ **"How can I help you?"—compare and contrast:** Explain that we use different tenses to tell when things happen. "We use the present and past tenses to compare and contrast things that are happening now to things that happened in the past. Write about what you did with your mom, dad, grandparents, or a friend when you were little, in past tense. What do you do with them now?"

■ **Dictionary skills:** "Check all the pages in your dictionary. Can you find any that have no words on them?" Lead students to see that there are no words listed under *q* or *x*. "Can you think of any special words that begin with *q* or with *x*? See if you can find any in a dictionary and add them to *your* dictionary."

■ **Words for students' own dictionaries:** Have students add the following words, in the order listed, to their dictionaries.*

1. pink	3. ink	5. lung	7. wing	9. king
2. plank	4. junk	6. strong	8. trunk	10. prank

Write and Spell on Your Own

Independent practice exercises for the objectives targeted in this unit are located in the corresponding Write and Spell on Your Own section of this book (see pp. 275–280).

---

*See Unit 6 for instructions for making the dictionaries.

PART 2

Spelling Choices

A teacher affects eternity; he can never tell
where his influence stops.

—Henry Adams

UNIT 15 | /ī/

Focus

Spelling: To recognize the different spellings of words with the long *i* (/ī/) sound

Word patterns

i-e as in *pine*   *igh* as in *high*   *ie* as in *pie*   *y-e* as in *style*
y as in *fly*   *ind* as in *bind*   *ye* as in *eye*   *ild* as in *child*

Writing development: homophones, homonyms, nouns, verbs, adjectives
Writing style: creative, personal narrative

Word List

i-e as in *pine*

bike	fine	life	pine	site	tile	white
bite	fire	like	pipe	slide	time	wide
bribe	five	lime	pride	slime	tire	wipe
bride	glide	line	prize	smile	tribe	
crime	grime	mile	quite	spine	twine	
dime	gripe	mime	ride	sprite	vile	
dive	hide	mine	ripe	stride	vine	
drive	hire	nine	shine	stripe	while	
file	kite	pile	shrine	swipe	whine	

pipeline	sideline	sidestep	sunshine	whitecap	windpipe

y as in *fly*

by	fly	ply	sky	spy	wry
cry	fry	pry	sly	try	
dry	my	shy	spry	why	

igh as in *high*

blight	flight	light	plight	sight
bright	fright	might	right	slight
fight	high	night	sigh	tight

sunlight

ind as in *bind*

bind	blind	find	grind	kind	mind	rind	wind

hindsight   mankind

ie as in *pie*

die	lie	pie	tie

ye as in *eye*

dye	eye	lye	rye

y-e as in *style*

style	type	tyke

ild as in *child*

child	mild	wild
wildcat	wildlife	

Sight Words

Add 10 sight words of your or the students' choice (see Appendix A for possibilities).

Pretest

bite	dime	stripe	try	fright
type	shy	wild	light	pie

Posttest

twine	cry	vine	blight	glide
spy	slight	pride	shine	sunlight

a fine lunch   sing at night

a star in the sky   helped the child

Add words or phrases that include selected sight words.

© 2007, 2000, 1984 by Frances Bloom and Deborah Bloom Coates

Spell Together

■ **Spelling the long *i* (/ī/) sound:** Discuss symbols. "A symbol is something chosen to stand for something else. What symbols do we see every day?" Discuss traffic signs and arithmetic symbols (−, +, =, %) and any others the students suggest. "Letters are the symbols for the sounds we spell and read."

> **ON THE BOARD**
>
> If I tie the right type of string to my kite, it will fly high in the sky.

1. Read the sentence on the board.
2. Ask students, "What vowel sound do you hear repeated?" (the long *i* sound)
3. Have students identify and read the long *i* words. Contrast them with short *i* words as in *lip, sit,* and *win* (point out the short /i/ in *in, it,* and *will*).
4. Have students, in turn, underline the letters in each word that make the /ī/ sound.
5. Keeping the original sentence on the board, write the following columns. "These are different ways to spell the long *i* sound."

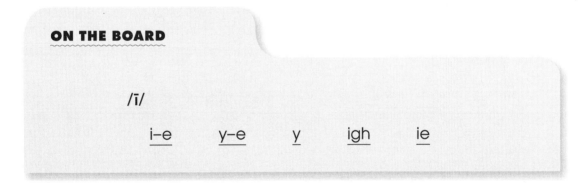

> **ON THE BOARD**
>
> /ī/
>
> i–e   y–e   y   igh   ie

6. Have students, in turn, copy the words from the sentence under the appropriate columns.
7. Ask students to suggest additional words with the long *i* sound and write them in the appropriate columns on the board.

SPELLING CHOICES

■ **Sound bank:** Say to the students, "You will be making your own booklet to list the letter symbols for each sound you learn. We will call it a Sound Bank."

1. Have each student staple together 12 sheets of paper (or continue using the copy book used for the Student's Own Dictionary in Part 1).

2. Have the students copy the following chart headings on page 1 of their Sound Bank.

ON THE BOARD

/ī/

i–e	y–e	y	igh	ie	ye	ild	ind
kite	type	sky	high	tie	eye	child	find

3. "Find as many words as you can for each letter group and write them in the proper column of your chart. Look in magazines, books, a dictionary, and on the Internet."

■ **Homophones**

ON THE BOARD

1. by _____   3. right _____

   bye _____   write _____

   buy _____   4. hire _____

2. dye _____   higher _____

   die _____

1. "How is each pair of words the same?" (They sound the same.)

2. "How is each pair different?" (They have different spellings.)

3. "Find the meanings of each pair of words in the dictionary. How else are they different?" (They have different meanings.)

4. Ask for volunteers to write a sentence for each homophone.

5. "Words that sound alike but are different in meaning and spelling are called *homophones.*" Write *homophone* on the board.

6. "Some words that sound alike and have different meanings are spelled alike. They are called *homonyms.*" Discuss the different meanings of words such as *right, die,* and *tire.*

7. "List the homophones on the board at the bottom of page 1 in your Sound Bank. Try to find more homophones that are spelled with the long *i* sound." (Suggestions: *lye—lie, rye—wry, sight—site, might—mite, stile—style*)

■ **Patterns and hints:** silent *e*

> **ON THE BOARD**
>
> a bit of a <u>bite</u>   a <u>strip</u> makes a <u>stripe</u>
>
> <u>grip</u> it and <u>gripe</u>   <u>slid</u> down the <u>slide</u>

1. Have students, in unison, read each phrase on the board.

2. "What happens to the short *i* sound when an *e* is added to the word?" (It changes to the long *i* sound.)

3. "An *e* at the end of a word makes the vowel say its name. It becomes a long vowel."

4. Have students think of additional short vowel words that are changed to the long *i* sound when *e* is added. Here are possibilities:

kit—kite	slim—slime	twin—twine	fin—fine	dim—dime
hid—hide	shin—shine	spin—spine	din—dine	quit—quite
sit—site	tin—tine	grim—grime	rip—ripe	snip—snipe

■ **Hints**

/ī/ before *nd* and *ld* is usually spelled *ind, ild,* as in *find* and *child.*

/ī/ before *t* is usually spelled *ight,* as in *light.* (Remember the most frequently used exceptions: *bite, kite, white.*)

/ī/ at the end of an open syllable is usually spelled *i,* as in *trial, dial, vial.*

■ **Ad lib:** Use ad libs to encourage descriptive writing.

1. Discuss nouns, verbs, and adjectives. Describe a noun as a person, place, or thing; a verb as an action word; and an adjective as a word that describes something.

ON THE BOARD

Verb	Noun	Adjective
drive	bike	white
hide	dime	fine
ride	kite	five
find	prize	nine
shine	light	tight
like	tie	wild

2. Call out the following parts of speech and ask the students to pick a word from the appropriate column on the board, or any other long *i* word. List the words in order on the board for reference.

   a. verb _____   f. verb _____

   b. noun _____   g. verb _____

   c. number _____   h. adjective _____

   d. number _____   i. noun _____

   e. name _____   j. verb _____

3. Use the words in the listed order to fill in the blanks to the story. Read the story to the class with the added words.

   I want to learn how to _____ **a** _____ a _____ **b** _____. I will practice

   from _____ **c** _____ in the morning until _____ **d** _____ at night.

   _____ **e** _____ wanted to _____ **f** _____ but he had to _____ **g** _____

   an _____ **h** _____ _____ **i** _____ for his mom after school. Do you think

   you will ever learn to _____ **j** _____? I sure hope so.

4. Repeat the process to get a different story.

© 2007, 2000, 1984 by Frances Bloom and Deborah Bloom Coates

■ Memory

Can you remember?

1. Collect pictures of the following /ī/ items and place them in a box or envelope.

bike	kite	lime	smile	tire
sky	tile	dime	fly	bride

2. Remove the items one at a time, name them, and arrange them face-up on a table.

3. Allow the students to look at the group of pictures for at least one minute.

4. Place the pictures back in the box or envelope and have the students write down as many items as they can remember.

Can you forget?

Have each student take two words from the list and use them in a story about "What would you do if all of your teachers forgot to come to school?"

Write and Spell on Your Own

Independent practice exercises for the objectives targeted in this unit are located in the corresponding Write and Spell on Your Own section of this book (see pp. 283–290).

SPELLING CHOICES

UNIT 16 /ā/ /ār/

Focus

Spelling: To recognize the different spellings of words with the long *a* (/ā/) sound and the /ār/ sound

Word patterns

a-e as in *cake*   *ai* as in *sail*   *eigh* as in *eight*   *ei* as in *vein*

ay as in *play*   *ea* as in *great*   *eign* as in *reign*

are as in *dare*   *air* as in *fair*   *ear* as in *bear*

Writing development: mnemonics, homophones
Writing style: creative

Word Lists

Some dictionaries present long *a* before *r* as a separate sound from long *a* alone. We list all /ār/ words separately below, but combine them with long *a* words in the Spell Together and Write and Spell on Your Own activities.

Long *a* /ā/

a-e as in *cake*

ate	cape	frame	lame	paste	scale	tape
bale	case	gale	lane	pave	scrape	taste
base	cave	game	late	plane	shade	trade
baste	crate	gape	made	plate	shape	wade
blade	crave	gaze	make	rate	slate	waste
blaze	date	glade	male	rave	slave	whale
brake	fade	glaze	mane	safe	stake	
brave	fame	grade	mate	sake	stale	
cake	fate	grape	name	sale	state	
came	flake	grate	pale	sane	tale	
cane	flame	haste	pane	save	tame	

makeshift   trademark

ay as in *play*

bay	fray	lay	play	slay	stray
bray	gay	may	pray	spay	sway
clay	gray	nay	ray	spray	tray
day	hay	pay	say	stay	way

archway	highway	parkway	playmate	playpen	subway

ai as in *sail*

aid	chain	hail	nail	raid	stain
ail	drain	jail	paid	rail	strain
aim	fail	laid	pail	rain	tail
bait	faint	maid	pain	sail	trail
braid	faith	mail	paint	saint	train
brain	frail	main	plain	snail	wait

mainland	pigtail	raindrop	sailfish	waistline

ea as in *great*

break	great	steak

eigh as in *eight*

eight	freight	neigh	sleigh	weigh	weight
eighth					

eign as in *reign*

feign	reign

ei as in *vein*

feint	rein	skein	veil	vein

Long ar /ār/

are as in *dare*

bare	dare	hare	rare	stare
blare	fare	mare	scare	
care	glare	pare	share	

bareback	hardware	nightmare

© 2007, 2000, 1984 by Frances Bloom and Deborah Bloom Coates

air as in *fair*

air   fair   hair   lair   pair   stair

ear as in *bear*

bear   pear   tear   wear

Sight Words

Add 10 sight words of your or the students' choice (see Appendix A for possibilities).

Pretest

clay	bait	stay	brain	subway
vein	fair	safe	break	freight

Posttest

paint	stray	great	eighth	scare
tray	drain	brave	archway	raindrop

made a fine steak   play on the sleigh

in the right pail   haste makes waste

Add words or phrases that include selected sight words.

Spell Together

■ **Spelling the long *a* (/ā/) sound**

> **ON THE BOARD**
>
> The weight of the pail could break the clay plate.

1. Read the sentence on the board.
2. Ask, "What vowel sound do you hear repeated?" (the long *a* sound)
3. Have a student read the sentence on the board one word at a time and underline the letters that say /ā/.
4. Explain, "These are different ways to spell the long *a* sound." Write all the word patterns as column headings on the board under the *a* sentence.

ON THE BOARD

/ā/

    a–e   ai   ay   ea   eigh   ei

5. Have students, in turn, copy the long *a* words from the sentence under the appropriate column headings.
6. Ask students to think of additional words with the long *a* sound and add them to the lists on the board.
7. "Copy the chart from the board onto page 2 of your Sound Bank. Find more words for each spelling of the long *a* sound and add them to your long *a* lists."

■ **Listen! Middle or end? (auditory discrimination):** Dictate the following words slowly, one at a time. For each word, instruct students, "Raise your hand if you hear the long *a* sound in the *middle* of the word. Put your hand on your head if you hear the long *a* sound at the *end* of the word." (Model raising your hand and putting it on your head at the appropriate junctures in the instructions.)

lay	chain	day	jail	trail	rain	play	tray
nail	aid	hay	stray	slay	fail	stair	say

■ **Patterns and hints:** /ā/ spelled *ay* or *ai*?

ON THE BOARD

You can stay and play with the paint in the pail.

1. "What vowel sound do you hear repeated?" (/ā/)
2. Have a student underline each long *a* sound in the sentence.
3. "Put the words together that are spelled alike." (*stay—play; paint—pail*)
4. "How is each pair of words alike?" (The long *a* sound is at the end of the word in *stay* and *play* and in the middle of the word in *paint* and *pail*.)
5. Discuss these patterns: /ā/ at the end of a word is usually spelled *a-y*, as in *clay* and *tray*; /ā/ in the middle of a word is usually spelled *a-i*, as in *tail* and *nail*.

SPELLING CHOICES

■ **Mnemonic memory aid:** "A mnemonic is any trick or device you can think of to help you remember something. It is spelled with an *m* (for *memory*) before the *n*. In pronunciation, the *m* in *mnemonic* is silent."

ON THE BOARD

Mnemonic

eigh—<u>Eight</u> horses that <u>weigh</u> a lot will <u>neigh</u> and pull

the <u>weight</u> of the <u>freight</u> on the <u>sleigh</u>.

ea—Let's take a <u>break</u> and enjoy a <u>great</u> <u>steak</u>.

1. "The underlined words on the board contain long *a* words spelled *e-i-g-h* and *e-a*. Try to remember the two sentences to help you remember the spelling of these words. There are no other long *a* words spelled *e-a*; additional words spelled *e-i-g-h* include *eighteen, eighteenth, eighty, eightieth,* and *eighth*."
2. Have the students make up their own mnemonic sentences to remember the spelling of the long /ā/ sound spelled *eigh* and *ea*.

■ **Homophones with long *a*:** Have the students list the following homophones at the bottom of the long *a* page in their Sound Banks.

ail—ale	great—grate	pain—pane	stair—stare
ate—eight	maid—made	pair—pare—pear	steak—stake
bail—bale	mail—male	plain—plane	tail—tale
break—brake	main—mane	rain—rein—reign	vain—vane—vein
fair—fare	nay—neigh	sail—sale	wait—weight
faint—feint	pail—pale	slay—sleigh	way—weigh

Have students try to make up short phrases that contain pairs of homophones.

Examples

fly a plain plane   charge a fair fare
pare a pair of pears   a new way to weigh

Write and Spell on Your Own

Independent practice exercises for the objectives targeted in this unit are located in the corresponding Write and Spell on Your Own section of this book (see pp. 291–296).

Focus

Spelling: To recognize and use the different spellings of the long *o* (/ō/) sound

Word patterns

o-e as in *vote*　　***ow*** as in *snow*　　***old*** as in *bold*　　***oll*** as in *roll*

oa as in *boat*　　***oe*** as in *doe*　　***ough*** as in *though*

Writing development: homophones, headlines, anagrams
Writing style: creative, informative

Word List

o-e as in *vote*

bone	doze	hope	mope	quote	sole	tone
choke	drone	joke	note	robe	spoke	tote
code	drove	lobe	ode	rode	stole	vote
cone	globe	lode	poke	role	stone	whole
cope	grope	lone	pole	rope	stove	yoke
cove	hole	lope	probe	shone	stroke	zone
dome	home	mole	prone	slope	throne	

homeland	homespun	milestone	wholesale
homemade	manhole	sunstroke	wishbone

oa as in *boat*

boast	croak	goal	loam	oath	shoal	toast
boat	float	goat	loan	poach	soak	
coal	foam	groan	moan	road	soap	
coast	gloat	load	oak	roam	throat	
coat	goad	loaf	oat	roast	toad	

boatman	coastline	roadbed	roadway	soapsuds

ow as in *snow*

blow	crow	grow	mow	shown	stow
blown	flow	grown	own	slow	throw
bow	flown	growth	row	snow	thrown
bowl	glow	low	show	sow	tow

blowgun	showboat	snowcap	snowman
overflow	showcase	snowdrift	undergrowth
scarecrow	slowpoke	snowflake	undertow

oe as in *doe*

doe	foe	hoe	roe	toe	woe

tiptoe

old as in *bold*

bold	fold	hold	old	told
cold	gold	mold	sold	

ough as in *though*

although	dough	doughnut	though

oll as in *roll*

boll	poll	loll	toll
droll	roll	stroll	troll

Sight Words

Add 10 sight words of your or the students' choice (see Appendix A for possibilities).

Pretest

bone	coat	soap	cold	tiptoe
goat	flow	stove	hoe	snowman

Posttest

coast	blow	though	globe	wishbone
vote	told	grope	toast	snowflake

a high pole	the ball was thrown
stub his toe	load the boat

Add words or phrases that include selected sight words.

© 2007, 2000, 1984 by Frances Bloom and Deborah Bloom Coates

Spell Together

- ## Spelling the long *o* (/ō/) sound

ON THE BOARD

He said he would row the boat even though

we told him that it had a hole as big as his toe.

1. Read the sentence on the board.
2. Ask, "What vowel sound do you hear repeated?" (the long *o* sound)
3. Have a student read the sentence, one word at a time, and underline the letters that say /ō/.
4. Say, "These are different ways to spell the long *o* sound." Write all the word patterns as column headings on the board under the *o* sentence.

ON THE BOARD

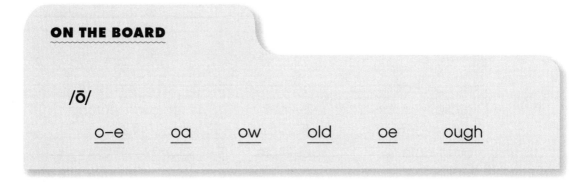

/ō/

o-e   oa   ow   old   oe   ough

5. Have students, in turn, copy the long *o* words from the sentence in the appropriate columns on the board.
6. Ask students to think of additional words with the long *o* sound and add them to the lists on the board.
7. "Copy the chart from the board onto page 3 of your Sound Bank. Find more words for each spelling of the long *o* sound and add them to your lists."

SPELLING CHOICES

■ **Patterns and hints:** /ō/ spelled *ow*

> **ON THE BOARD**
>
> | oe: | doe | foe | hoe | toe | woe |
> |-----|------|------|---------|-------|-----|
> | ough: | although | dough | doughnut | though | |

"These are most of the /ō/ words that are spelled *ough* or *oe*. At the end of most words, *o* is usually spelled *ow*, as in *snow*. Make up some silly sentences to help you remember the /ō/ words that are spelled *ough* and *oe*."

■ **Hint for *old*:** Before *–ld*, /o/ is usually spelled *o*, as in the following words:
bold   cold   fold   gold   hold   mold   sold   told

■ **Homophone swap:** List the following homophones on the board.

> **ON THE BOARD**
>
> | dough—doe | road—rode | sow—so—sew |
> |-----------|-----------|------------|
> | grown—groan | roll—role | thrown—throne |
> | loan—lone | shown—shone | tow—toe |
> | poll—pole | soul—sole | whole—hole |

1. Have students use dictionaries to look up the meanings of any homophones that are new to them.
2. Say, "Pick a pair of homophones to use in a sentence. Write them on your paper."
3. Erase the board after the students have completed their selections.
4. "Write a sentence using both of the homophones that you selected. Leave blanks where the homophones should be." *Example:* We _____ down the bumpy _____ in the new car. (rode—road)
5. Have students exchange sentences and try to guess and spell the correct homophones.

■ **Headlines (homophones for long *o*)**

> **ON THE BOARD**
>
> Boy Is _____ off Horse
>
> Sun Has Not _____ for 30 Days
>
> New Bank Offers _____ at Low Interest Rate
>
> Falling Meteorite Makes Deep _____ in Ground

1. Divide the class into groups of five people.
2. Each group selects a member to be the newscaster.
3. The groups copy the news headlines from the board and fill in each blank with a long *o* word.
4. Each group makes up a set of four new headlines using the homophones of the words in the blanks. Students may use dictionaries.
5. Each newscaster reads the new headlines to the class.

■ **Anagrams:** Anagrams are words or phrases made by transposing, or rearranging, the letters of a different word or phrase. No letters can be used twice or left out. They are fun for students and also encourage them to focus on words.

Anagram slap
1. List examples of anagrams on the board:

> **ON THE BOARD**
>
> dome—mode   lope—pole

2. List the following words on the board:

ON THE BOARD

tone	loan	poach	toast	pokes
votes	toad	roam	shone	groan
drove	poem	slope	lose	boat
veto	wolf	robe	worth	zone

---

3. Play "slap": Have pairs of students, or "pals," work together to try to make anagrams of the listed words. Only some of the words can be formed into anagrams. The "pals" shout "slap" when they think they have found all the words that can be rearranged to form new words. The team that finds the most anagrams wins.

Leftover letters

List the following sentences on the board (omitting the answers in parentheses):

ON THE BOARD

Eleven plus two = Twelve plus _____ (one)

The Morse code = Here come _____ (dots)

A decimal point = I'm a dot _____ (in place)

For each equation, have students compare the phrase to the left of the equals (=) sign with that to the right, crossing out any letters in the left-hand phrase that also appear in the right-hand phrase. They then take the letters that are not crossed out and use them to try and fill in the blank.

Write and Spell on Your Own

Independent practice exercises for the objectives targeted in this unit are located in the corresponding Write and Spell on Your Own section of this book (see pp. 297–304).

UNIT 18 /ē/ /ēr/

Focus

Spelling: To recognize and use the different spellings of words with the long *e* (/ē/) sound and the /ēr/ sound

Word patterns

ee as in *deep*	**ie** as in *chief*	**ei** as in *neither*	**y** as in *baby*
ea as in *beach*	**e-e** as in *theme*	**ey** as in *key*	**e** as in *we*
eer as in *cheer*	**ear** as in *clear*	**ere** as in *here*	**ier** as in *pier*

Writing development: homophones, adjectives
Writing style: creative, informative

Word List

Some dictionaries present long *er* as a separate sound from *e*. We list /ēr/ words separately below, but combine them with /ē/ words in Spell Together and Write and Spell on Your Own activities.

Long e /ē/

ee as in deep

bee	feed	greet	peel	seen	steep	week
beech	feel	heel	queen	seep	street	weep
beet	feet	Jeep	reed	sheep	sweep	wheel
bleed	flee	keen	reel	sheet	sweet	
breed	fleet	keep	screech	sleep	teem	
creek	free	leek	screen	sleet	three	
creep	glee	meet	see	speech	tree	
deep	greed	need	seed	speed	wee	
fee	green	peek	seem	steel	weed	

beehive	freeway	sheepskin	speedway	streetcar

ea as in *beach*

beach	dream	heat	mean	pleat	seat	teach
bean	each	lead	meat	reach	sheath	team
beat	east	leaf	neat	read	sneak	treat
cheap	eat	leak	peach	real	squeal	veal
cheat	feast	lean	peak	ream	steal	weak
clean	feat	leap	peal	scream	steam	wean
cleat	flea	leash	peat	sea	streak	wheat
deal	gleam	least	plea	seal	stream	yeast
dean	heal	meal	plead	seam	tea	zeal

leapfrog	meanwhile	seaside	streamline	teammate
meantime	seacoast	seaweed	teacup	teapot

ie as in *chief*

brief	field	priest	shriek	wield
chief	grief	shield	thief	yield

belief	infield	relief

e-e as in *theme*

mete	theme	these

ei as in *neither*

seize	sheik

either	leisure	neither	seizure

ey as in *key*

key	money	monkey	turkey

y as in *baby*

baby	lady	shady

e as in *we*

be	he	me	she	we

Long er /ēr/

eer as in *cheer*

beer	deer	leer	seer	sneer	veer
cheer	jeer	peer	sheer	steer	

ear as in *clear*

clear	ear	gear	near	sear	spear	year
dear	fear	hear	rear	shear	tear	

ere as in *here*

here   mere

ier as in *pier*

pier   tier

Sight Words

Add 10 sight words of your or the students' choice (see Appendix A for possibilities).

Pretest

free	field	clean	lady	either
she	key	cheer	heat	teacup

Posttest

neither	sheet	wheat	belief	shady
these	scream	clear	thief	speedway

pave the street   send a brief note
grind the meat   hold the baby

Add words or phrases that include selected sight words.

Spell Together

■ **Spelling the long *e* sound**

> ### ON THE BOARD
>
> The chief and the lady can see us here
>
> from either end of the pier.

1. Read the sentence on the board.
2. Ask, "What sound do you hear repeated?" (/ē/)

3. Have a student read the words in the sentence with the long *e* sound and underline the letters that say /ē/.

4. Say, "These are different ways to spell the long *e* sound." Write all the word patterns as column headings on the board under the *e* sentence.

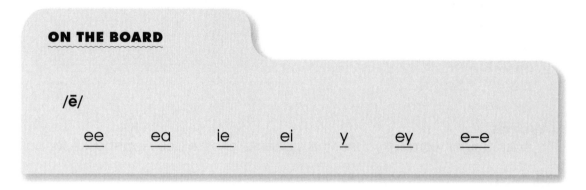

ON THE BOARD

/ē/

ee   ea   ie   ei   y   ey   e-e

5. Have a student write the long *e* words in the sentence on the board in the appropriate columns on the board.

6. Ask students to suggest additional words with the long *e* sound and add them to the lists on the board. (Accept /er/ words and simply add them in the appropriate column.)

7. "Copy the chart from the board onto page 4 of your Sound Bank. Find more words for each spelling of long *e* and add them to your lists."

■ Patterns and hints

- /ē/ at the end of words of more than one syllable is usually spelled *y:*

  baby   lady

- /ē/ is spelled *ei* in the few words listed on page 98 and after *c:*

  receive   receipt   deceit   conceit

- /ē/ is spelled *i* at the end of a few words:

  ski   broccoli   spaghetti

- /ē/ is spelled *i* in some silent *e* words:

  police   machine

- /ē/ is spelled *i* in words ending in *–que* and *–gue:*

  antique   physique   unique   intrigue
  clique   technique   fatigue

■ **Homophones:** Select 10 words from the list of homophones and write them on the board. (Select only one word from each pair.) Have students think of the homophone for each word listed and write each pair of homophones in a sentence.

bee—be	flee—flea	peek—peak	seem—seam
beech—beach	heel—heal	peer—pier	steel—steal
beet—beat	here—hear	reel—real	teem—team
deer—dear	leek—leak	reed—read	week—weak
feet—feat	meet—meat—mete	see—sea	

■ **Tell and listen**

1. Divide the class into five or six groups and have each group name a secretary.
2. Dictate a different set of words to each group (see suggestions following).
3. Have each group make up and dictate to the secretary a short story using as many of the dictated words as they can.
4. As each group, in turn, tells a story, the other groups listen for and write each long *e* word they hear.
5. The group telling the story gets one point for each long *e* word used. The groups who are listening get one point for each word they record and spell correctly.

Suggested sets for dictation

Group 1	Group 2	Group 3	Group 4	Group 5	Group 6
sheep	deer	monkey	turkey	bee	flea
shear	see	screech	squeal	cheer	wee
field	leap	lean	three	lady	queen
green	eat	dream	steal	sleep	meal
free	plead	shield	clean	sweep	street

■ **Describing things (adjectives)**

1. Divide the class into groups of five. Assign a secretary for each group.
2. Explain that adjectives are words that describe a noun or pronoun. "They help us paint a clearer word picture of something."
3. Dictate, one at a time, some or all of the following adjectives and have the group secretary list each adjective as a column heading:

free	steep	neat	lean	deep	cheap	three
clean	mean	clear	brief	wee	real	green

4. Each group must think of things that each adjective could describe. The secretary lists suggestions under the appropriate adjective. (If necessary, clarify the adjectival meaning of homonyms such as *free* or *lean*.)
5. The group that compiles the longest lists in a specified amount of time wins.

■ **How does it grow? Observations:** You will need a bean seed, a jar, paper towels, and water.

1. Line the outside of the jar with a paper towel. Place a second wadded-up paper towel inside the first to hold the outer one in place.

2. Place the bean seed between the side of the jar and the paper towel near the bottom of the jar.

3. Slowly pour water into the jar until the paper towels are completely wet.

4. Place the jar on a warm, sunny windowsill and keep the towels moist.

5. Have the students observe the bean seed every day and describe what they see in a bean seed log. Suggest that they use as many *e* words (such as those in the following list) as they can in their logs.

ON THE BOARD

see	clean	least	green	these
three	speed	speed	yield	deep
sheet	bean	leaf	sheath	be
seed	each	reach	feed	

Write and Spell on Your Own

Independent practice exercises for the objectives targeted in this unit are located in the corresponding Write and Spell on Your Own section of this book (see pp. 305–310).

UNIT 19 | /ow/

Focus

Spelling: To recognize and use the different spellings of words with the /ow/ sound

Word patterns

ow as in *cow*   **ou** as in *out*

Writing development: homophones, homonyms, analogies
Writing style: creative

Word List

ow as in cow

bow	cow	frown	jowl	prowl	vow
brow	crown	gown	now	scow	
brown	down	growl	owl	scowl	
chow	drown	how	plow	sow	
clown	fowl	howl	prow	town	

anyhow	cowhand	downtown	somehow
cowboy	downcast	downwind	sundown

ou as in out

bough	flour	house	our	round	south
bound	foul	loud	oust	scout	spout
bout	found	lout	out	shout	sprout
cloud	grouch	mound	pouch	slouch	stout
couch	ground	mount	pound	snout	trout
count	hound	mouth	pout	sound	vouch
crouch	hour	ouch	proud	sour	

outbid	outfit	outside	outwit	southbound
outcast	outlaw	outsmart	snowbound	southwest

Sight Words

Add 10 sight words of your or the students' choice (see Appendix A for possibilities).

Pretest

brown	cloud	town	growl	sour
loud	how	out	shout	downcast

Posttest

hound	frown	trout	clown	sprout
scowl	slouch	bow	mouth	downtown

mix with flour   down the right path
pound the wheat   a crown for the queen

Add words or phrases that include selected sight words.

Spell Together

■ **Spelling words with the /ow/ sound**

> **ON THE BOARD**
>
> The scout found the brown cow.

1. Read the sentence on the board.
2. Ask, "What sound do you hear repeated?" (/ow/)
3. Have a student read and underline the words in the sentence with the /ow/ sound.
4. "These are different ways of spelling the /ow/ sound."
5. Write the two patterns on the board in columns, without erasing the sentence. Have a student copy the /ow/ words from the sentence in the appropriate columns.

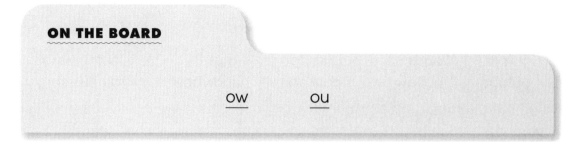

> **ON THE BOARD**
>
> ow   ou

6. Ask students to think of additional words with the /ow/ sound and add them to the lists on the board.

7. "Copy the chart from the board onto page 5 of your Sound Bank. Find more /ow/ words and add them to the appropriate lists."

Patterns and hints

ON THE BOARD

How can a clown prowl, scowl, and pout

and not shout out loud or make a sound?

1. Have a student underline each word in the sentence that contains the /ow/ sound.

2. Say, "Put the words together that are spelled alike."

how—clown—prowl—scowl   pout—shout—out—loud—sound

3. "What pattern do you notice in whether /ow/ is spelled *o-w* or *o-u*?" Discuss these generalizations:

   • /ow/ is usually spelled *o-w* at the end of a word or when followed by a final *l* or *n*, as in *town* and *owl*.

   • /ow/ is usually spelled *o-u* at the beginning or in the middle of a word, as in *ouch* and *scout*.

Hints

   • /ow/ is usually spelled *o-w* before a vowel:

bowel	coward	dowel	power	tower
bower	cower	flower	towel	vowel

   • /ow/ is spelled *o-u-g-h* only in *bough* and *plough. Plough* is the alternate spelling for *plow.*

Homophones

See Unit 15 for a suggested homophone exercise.

flour—flower   foul—fowl   bough—bow

Homonyms

See Unit 5 for a suggested homonym exercise.

bound   count   pound   sound

■ **Analogies (another approach):** Review the concept of an analogy using the diagram and sentence on the board. (See Analogies in Unit 4, page 23, for sample explanations.)

ON THE BOARD

egg	chicken	or egg is to chicken
milk		as milk is to _____ **(COW)**

List the following analogies on the board without the answers in parentheses and have students, in turn, complete them with /ow/ words:

ON THE BOARD

1. happy is to smile as sad is to _____ (frown or pout)

2. soft is to whisper as loud is to _____ (shout)

3. hear is to ear as eat is to _____ (mouth)

4. cherry is to red as chocolate is to _____ (brown)

5. honey is to sweet as lemon is to _____ (sour)

6. dog is to bark as bear is to _____ (growl)

Have the students write a short paragraph about one of the analogies on the board. *Example:* A student who chooses, *Happy is to smile as sad is to frown,* would write about what makes him or her happy and what makes him or her sad.

Write and Spell on Your Own

Independent practice exercises for the objectives targeted in this unit are located in the corresponding Write and Spell on Your Own section of this book (see pp. 311–317).

UNIT 20 | /aw/

Focus

Spelling: To recognize and use the different spellings of words with the /aw/ sound

Word patterns

aw as in *saw*   **all** as in *ball*   **augh** as in *caught*

au as in *fault*   **alk** as in *talk*   **ough** as in *bought*

Writing development: mnemonics, homophones, homonyms, classification
Writing style: creative

Word List

aw as in saw

awl	claw	drawn	jaw	raw	sprawl
bawl	crawl	fawn	law	saw	squawk
brawl	dawn	flaw	lawn	scrawl	straw
brawn	draw	gawk	paw	shawl	thaw
caw	drawl	hawk	prawn	spawn	yawn

hawklike	jawbone	jigsaw	sawdust	seesaw

au as in fault

fault	gaunt	haunt	paunch	vault
flaunt	haul	launch	taunt	
fraud	haunch	maul	taut	

all as in ball

all	call	hall	small	tall
ball	fall	mall	stall	wall

alk as in talk

balk	chalk	stalk	talk	walk

augh as in caught

caught	taught

daughter	haughty	naughty	slaughter

ough as in *bought*

bought   brought   fought   ought   sought   thought

Sight Words

Add 10 sight words of your or the students' choice (see Appendix A for possibilities).

Pretest

jaw	taught	brought	launch	tall
fault	scrawl	walk	dawn	sawdust

Posttest

fought	drawn	flaunt	naughty	prawn
paunch	flaw	chalk	small	jigsaw

fall in the hole   hide in the vault

sprawl on the couch   a bed of straw

Add words or phrases that include selected sight words.

Spell Together

■ **Spelling the /aw/ sound**

ON THE BOARD

The man brought his small daughter

to the space launch at dawn.

---

1. Read the sentence on the board.
2. Ask, "What sound do you hear repeated?" (/aw/)
3. Have a student read and underline the words in the sentence that contain the /aw/ sound.

4. "These are different spellings of the /aw/ sound." Write the various patterns on the board as column headings, without erasing the sentence.

ON THE BOARD

/aw/

aw   au   all   augh   ough

5. Have students, in turn, copy the /aw/ words from the sentence in the appropriate columns on the board.
6. Ask students to think of additional words with the /aw/ sound, and add them to the columns on the board.
7. "Copy the chart from the board onto page 6 of your Sound Bank. Find more /aw/ words and add them to the appropriate lists."

Patterns and hints: /aw/ spelled *aw* or *au*

ON THE BOARD

We saw the artist draw a gaunt man with a big paunch.

1. Have a student underline each word in the sentence that contains the /aw/ sound.
2. Say, "Put the words together that are spelled alike."

    saw—draw   gaunt—paunch

3. "What pattern do you notice in whether /aw/ is spelled *a-w* or *a-u*?" Discuss these generalizations:
    - /aw/ is usually spelled *a-w* at the end of a word or before a final *l* or *n*, as in *draw, yawn,* or *bawl.*
    - /aw/ is usually spelled *a-u* in the middle of a word, as in *fraud.* Exceptions are *haul, maul, hawk, gawk, squawk.*

■ **Mnemonics for /aw/ spelled *augh* and *ough***

ON THE BOARD

They caught the naughty daughter and

taught her not to be haughty.

1. Have a student underline the /aw/ words in the sentence.
2. "This sentence contains most of the /aw/ words that are spelled *a-u-g-h*. Remember the sentence to help you spell these words."
3. "/aw/ is spelled *o-u-g-h* only in *brought, fought, nought, ought, sought,* and *thought.* Can you think of a sentence that has all these words? Make up a silly sentence to help you remember the /aw/ words that are spelled *o-u-g-h.*"

■ **Homophones:** Have students find the meanings of *awl* and *taut,* and any other unfamiliar words, in a dictionary. Then use each pair of homophones in one sentence.

awl—all   bawl—ball   haul—hall   maul—mall   taut—taught

■ **Homonyms:** Here is a list of common homonyms. Use them with or in place of the homonyms used in the following activity.

ball   fall   fawn   saw   stall
draw   fault   hawk   stalk   vault

ON THE BOARD

flaw	wall	bought	ball
saw	fault	stall	taught
claw	caught	fall	brawl
thaw	draw	launch	vault

1. "Some of the words on the board have more than one meaning. They are homonyms." Remind students that homonyms are words that sound and are spelled the same but have different meanings.

2. Divide the class into small groups. The students in each group will use their memories or a dictionary to determine which words are homonyms, and then write sentences that use each meaning of the homonyms.

3. Set a time limit. The group with the most homonyms used correctly wins.

Which one does not belong? Dictate the following groups of words. For each group, have students identify the word that does not belong based on meaning.

- eyes, nose, claw, mouth
- small, large, big, huge
- bat, golf club, stick, ball
- saw, glue, tape, staple
- heart, lung, stomach, jaw

- man, boy, son, daughter
- friendly, naughty, cheerful, helpful
- evening, dawn, dusk, night
- cooked, boiled, raw, broiled
- walk, run, crawl, skip

Have the students, individually or in groups, write a story using one of the groups of words.

Write and Spell on Your Own

Independent practice exercises for the objectives targeted in this unit are located in the corresponding Write and Spell on Your Own section of this book (see pp. 319–321).

UNIT 21 | /k/

Focus

Spelling: To recognize and use the different spellings of words with the /k/ sound

Word patterns

ck as in *luck*   *ke* as in *cake*   *k* as in *keep*   *qu* as in *quiz*

k as in *ask*   *c* as in *cat*   *ch* as in *chorus*   *x* as in *box*

Writing development: homonyms
Writing style: creative

Word List

ck as in *luck*

back	clock	hack	nick	rock	snack	trick
beck	cluck	jack	pack	sack	sock	truck
black	crack	kick	peck	shack	speck	tuck
block	crock	lack	pick	shock	stick	wick
brick	deck	lick	pluck	shuck	stock	
buck	dock	lock	pock	sick	stuck	
check	duck	luck	puck	slack	tack	
chick	flick	mock	quack	slick	thick	
chock	flock	muck	quick	smack	tick	
chuck	frock	neck	rack	smock	track	

backfire	blacktop	homesick	nickname	sidetrack
backlog	chopstick	lipstick	nightstick	stockyard
bareback	feedback	livestock	padlock	wedlock
blacksmith	hemlock	locksmith	quicksand	yardstick

k as in *ask*

ark	bulk	flask	junk	risk	tank	yank
ask	dark	frisk	mark	shark	task	
bark	desk	hulk	mask	silk	think	
brisk	dusk	ink	park	sunk	whisk	

ke as in _cake_

bake	choke	joke	pike	smoke	strike
bike	fake	lake	poke	snake	take
brake	flake	like	rake	spike	wake
cake	hike	make	shake	spoke	yoke

clambake	makeshift	namesake	smokestack
handshake	makeup	pancake	sunstroke

c as in _cat_

cat	cave	clamp	cog	crash	crest

ch as in _chorus_

chord	chorus	chrome

qu as in _quiz_

quack	quail	quaint	quake	quench	quest	quick
quilt	quip	quit	quite	quiz	quote	

x as in _box_

box	fax	fix	fox	hex
mix	nix	tax	vex	wax

exclude	exhale	exit	exist	extreme	taxi

Sight Words

Add 10 sight words of your or the students' choice (see Appendix A for possibilities).

Pretest

duck	mark	trick	bulk	spoke
ask	thick	bake	quick	yardstick

Posttest

pack	pluck	snake	whisk	shark
brisk	hike	crack	quote	chopstick

drive the truck   make a fine shawl

a homesick daughter   a loud bark

Add words or phrases that include selected sight words.

Spell Together

ON THE BOARD

Jack and Kim can hear the chorus at the lake in the park.

1. Read the sentence on the board.
2. Ask, "What sound do you hear repeated?" (/k/)
3. Have a student read and underline the words in the sentence on the board that contain the /k/ sound.
4. "These are different spellings of the /k/ sound at the end and at the beginning of words." Write the various patterns on the board as column headings, without erasing the sentence.

ON THE BOARD

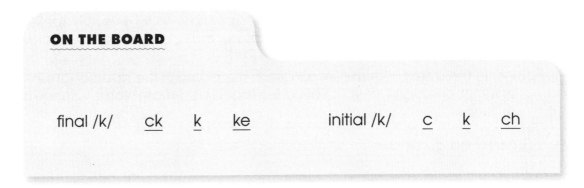

final /k/   <u>ck</u>   <u>k</u>   <u>ke</u>   initial /k/   <u>c</u>   <u>k</u>   <u>ch</u>

5. Have students, in turn, write the /k/ words from the sentence on the board in the appropriate columns on the board.
6. Ask students to think of additional words containing /k/ as a final sound and add them to the lists on the board.
7. "Copy the chart from the board onto page 7 of your Sound Bank. Find more words with various spellings of the sound /k/ and add them to your lists."

Spelling /k/ as a final sound

1. Read the sentence on the board again.
2. "What pattern do you notice for /k/ spelled *k, ck,* or *ke* at the end of words?" Also encourage students to look at the word lists in their Sound Banks to find patterns.
3. Help the students discover the rules:
   - /k/ is usually spelled *ck* after a short vowel, as in *luck.*
   - /k/ is usually spelled *k* after another consonant (such as *r, n, s, l*) and after a vowel digraph (*ee* or *ea*), as in *break* and *bark.*
   - /k/ is usually spelled *ke* (silent *e*) after a long vowel, as in *bake.*

■ **Spelling /k/ as an initial sound**

> **ON THE BOARD**
>
> The king can clap with the crowd when they see
>
> the chorus come around the curve in the coach.

1. Have a student underline each /k/ sound in the sentence, then underline the letters that follow each /k/ sound.
2. Help the students discover the rules:
   - /k/ before *i* or *e* is usually spelled *k,* as in *king, kid,* or *kite.*
   - /k/ before *a, o, u, r,* and *l* is usually spelled *c,* as in *can, clap, crowd, come, curve, coach.*
3. Discuss /k/ spelled *ch:* "/k/ is sometimes spelled *c-h.* /k/ is usually spelled this way in words related to music, art, religion, and science, such as *chorus, choral, chrome, chronic, choir, chord, Christmas.*"
4. "Write the words from the sentence on the board in the appropriate initial /k/ columns on page 7 of your Sound Bank and add more words with the initial /k/ sound."

■ **/k/ spelled *qu* and *x***

> **ON THE BOARD**
>
> Can a quail quack at a fox in a box?

1. Have a student read the sentence on the board and underline and say the words with *qu* and *x.* Point out the following to students: *qu* makes the sound /kw/; *q* is always followed by *u; x* makes the sound /ks/.
2. Dictate a group of *qu* and *x* words.

quack	quaint	queen	quest	quicksand	quit	quiz
quail	quake	quench	quick	quilt	quite	

box	fox	mix	vex
fix	hex	tax	wax

© 2007, 2000, 1984 by Frances Bloom and Deborah Bloom Coates

■ **Homonyms:** Have students find the definitions for the different meanings of *park, stick, spoke, check,* and *rock* and use each pair of homonyms in one sentence. Add any other homonyms you wish from the following suggested list.

| back | check | duck | park | quack | sack | spoke |
| block | deck | lock | pack | rock | sock | stick |

Write and Spell on Your Own

Independent practice exercises for the objectives targeted in this unit are located in the corresponding Write and Spell on Your Own section of this book (see pp. 323–329).

UNIT 22 /ch//j/

Focus

Spelling: To recognize and use the different spellings of words with the /ch/ and /j/ sounds.

Word patterns

ch as in *inch*   **ge** as in *page*

tch as in *itch*   **dge** as in *edge*

Writing development: definitions, newspaper writing
Writing style: personal narrative, informative

Word List

ch as in inch

arch	clinch	hunch	munch	punch	starch
bench	coach	inch	parch	quench	stench
branch	crunch	lunch	pinch	ranch	trench
bunch	drench	march	poach	scrunch	welch
clench	flinch	mulch	porch	squelch	

tch as in itch

batch	crutch	hatch	match	scratch	switch
botch	ditch	hitch	notch	sketch	thatch
catch	etch	itch	patch	stitch	twitch
clutch	fetch	latch	pitch	stretch	witch

hemstitch   hitchhike   hopscotch   witchcraft

ge as in page

age	change	hinge	page	sage	twinge
barge	charge	huge	plunge	singe	wage
bulge	cringe	large	rage	stage	
cage	fringe	lunge	range	strange	

dge as in edge

badge	dodge	edge	hedge	lodge	ridge	trudge
bridge	dredge	fudge	judge	nudge	sludge	wedge
budge	drudge	grudge	ledge	pledge	smudge	

Sight Words

Add 10 sight words of your or the students' choice (see Appendix A for possibilities).

Pretest

page	march	patch	coach	edge
hitch	hinge	inch	fudge	hitchhike

Posttest

cage	poach	stage	thatch	hemstitch
fetch	bulge	branch	drench	witchcraft

march to the park	scratch my back
smile at the judge	held a huge chain

Add words or phrases that include selected sight words.

Spell Together

■ /ch/—spell it *ch* or *tch*?

ON THE BOARD

We can have lunch at the ranch   /ch/

if we catch a batch of fish.   ch   tch

1. Read the sentence on the board. Say, "These are different spellings of the /ch/ sound at the end of a word."
2. Have a student write the /ch/ words in the sentence on the board in the appropriate columns on the board (*ch* or *tch*).
3. Ask students to think of additional words that have /ch/ as a final sound and add them to the lists on the board.
4. "Copy the chart on the board on page 8 of your Sound Bank. Find more words spelled *ch* or *tch*, and add them to your lists."

© 2007, 2000, 1984 by Frances Bloom and Deborah Bloom Coates

/j/—spell it *ge* or *dge*?

> **ON THE BOARD**
>
> There was a huge cage near   /j/
>
> the edge of the bridge.   ge   dge

1. Repeat the procedure used for /ch/. Say, "These are different spellings of the /j/ sound."
2. "Copy the chart on the board on page 9 of your Sound Bank. Find more /j/ words spelled *ge* or *dge* and add them to your lists."

Choosing the correct spellings for the /ch/ and /j/ sounds

1. Review the rule for /k/ spelled *k, ck,* or *ke:* "The /k/ sound is usually spelled *k* after another consonant or a vowel digraph, as in *mask* and *break; ke* after a long vowel, as in *break;* and *ck* after a short vowel, as in *duck.*
2. "The rule for the /ch/ and /j/ sounds in the middle or at the end of a word is similar. Look at your word lists in your Sound Bank. Can you figure it out?"
   - The /ch/ sound is usually spelled *ch* after a consonant or a long vowel or vowel digraph, as in *inch* and *coach;* and *tch* after a short vowel, as in *catch.*
   - The /j/ sound is usually spelled *ge* after a consonant or a long vowel, as in *large* and *stage,* and *dge* after a short vowel, as in *edge.*
3. List these exceptions to the /ch/ rule and have students add them to their Sound Banks: *rich, much, such, which,* and *sandwich.*

Word, please: Give the class the definition for a word and a word ending from the following list. Students should try to guess the word and write it correctly on the board.

Definition	Ending	Word
1. You eat it at noon.	use *ch*	(lunch)
2. Where cattle or horses live.	use *ch*	(ranch)
3. You scratch it.	use *tch*	(itch)
4. You do this to a batter.	use *tch*	(pitch)
5. It covers a hole in your pants.	use *tch*	(patch)
6. A type of chocolate candy.	use *dge*	(fudge)
7. It lets you cross over water.	use *dge*	(bridge)
8. It's around the outside of the table.	use *dge*	(edge)
9. This is a word for very angry.	use *ge*	(rage)

Definition	Ending	Word
10. This is a flat-bottomed boat.	use *ge*	(barge)
11. You reduce your thirst.	use *ch*	(quench)
12. A part of a book.	use *ge*	(page)
13. She might show up at Halloween.	use *tch*	(witch)
14. What you do in a parade.	use *ch*	(march)
15. You keep a bird in it.	use *ge*	(cage)

■ Two for one

1. Write each of the following word parts on a card.

lun_____	ca_____	pa_____	hu_____	di_____
e_____	cru_____	pun_____	ran_____	stre_____
ma_____	pi_____	ju_____	scra_____	ple_____
we_____	chan_____	lar_____	bri_____	
sta_____	ben_____	coa_____	ba_____	

2. Make five cards for each of the following endings:

   ch   tch   ge   dge

3. Shuffle each set of cards and place each set face-down on the table.

4. Each player, in turn, picks one card from each pile and tries to make one word from the two cards. *Example: lun + ch or ge makes lunch or lunge.* A player who cannot make a word returns the cards face-down to the bottom of the appropriate pile.

5. The player who makes the most words in a predetermined period of time wins.

■ Just the facts, please

1. Discuss the important features of a newpaper article. "When we write a news-paper article, we want to grab the readers' attention, keep the article short, and stick to the facts."

2. Present the following story:

   Mitch and his dog, Fudge, were eating food in the middle of the day. After they finished, Mitch played throw and catch with a stick. One time, Mitch threw the stick and it landed on a place where people sit. This was next to a large structure that went over the water. All of a sudden, a large gust of wind blew the stick into the water.

   Fudge really wanted that stick. She barked and pawed at the rail. Mitch was very worried. He did not know what to do. Mitch really wanted to run quickly after Fudge and grab her. Mitch had a feeling that that would not work and so he changed plans. Mitch did not move a muscle. Then, he slowly picked up another stick. Fudge looked at Mitch and then she looked at the water below. Fudge looked at Mitch's stick and after what seemed like a long time, Fudge ran back to Mitch.

3. Have the students rewrite the story as a newspaper article. Tell them to
   a. make up a headline or title for the story;
   b. write an introductory sentence;
   c. try to replace the highlighted words or phrases by replacing with /ch/ or /j/ words; and
   d. try to simplify the story by taking out any unnecessary words or phrases.
4. List the following words on the board and suggest that students use them to replace some of the words or phrases in the story. If necessary, rewrite the first sentence to demonstrate how it can be changed. "Mitch and his dog, Fudge, were eating lunch."

ON THE BOARD

bridge	charge	switch	bench	hunch	lunch
plunge	flinch	twitch	budge	fetch	lunge

Write and Spell on Your Own

Independent practice exercises for the objectives targeted in this unit are located in the corresponding Write and Spell on Your Own section of this book (see pp. 331–334).

UNIT 23 | /or/

Focus

Spelling: To recognize the different spellings of words with the /or/ sound

Word patterns

or as in *born*   *our* as in *four*   *oor* as in *door*

ore as in *more*   *oar* as in *roar*

Writing development: homophones
Writing style: creative, personal narrative

Word List

or as in *born*

born	dorm	fort	morn	pork	shorn	sport	torch
cord	for	forth	north	port	short	stork	torn
cork	ford	horn	or	scorch	snort	storm	worn
corn	fork	lord	porch	scorn	sort	thorn	

blowtorch	forlorn	northwest	shortcake	windstorm
corncob	forsake	pitchfork	shorthand	
cornflower	fortnight	popcorn	shortstop	
cornstarch	northbound	shopworn	snowstorm	

ore as in *more*

bore	fore	ore	shore	store	yore
chore	lore	pore	snore	tore	
core	more	score	sore	wore	

our as in *four*

four	fourth	mourn	pour	your

oar as in *roar*

boar	board	oar	roar	soar

oor as in *door*

door	floor

Sight Words

Add 10 sight words of your or the students' choice (see Appendix A for possibilities).

Pretest

more	fork	roar	door	popcorn
four	worn	tore	cork	storm

Posttest

horn	chore	pour	born	soar
store	scorch	board	stork	

sail to the northwest   a huge windstorm

husk the corn   the oar fell on the floor

Add words or phrases that include selected sight words.

Spell Together

■ **Letter symbols for /or/**

ON THE BOARD

The four men opened the door to hear
the roar of the storm near the shore.

1. Read the sentence on the board.
2. Ask, "What sound do you hear repeated?" (/or/)
3. Have a student read the words in the sentence that contain the sound /or/ and underline the letters that say /or/.
4. "These are different spellings of the /or/ sound." Write the various word patterns on the board as column headings, without erasing the sentence.

ON THE BOARD

/or/:   or   ore   our   oar   oor

© 2007, 2000, 1984 by Frances Bloom and Deborah Bloom Coates

5. Have a student copy the /or/ words from the sentence in the appropriate columns.

6. Ask students to think of additional words with /or/ and add them to the lists on the board.

7. "Copy the chart from the board onto page 9 of your Sound Bank. Find more words for each spelling of /or/ and add them to your lists."

■ **Homophone hunt**

sore—soar	for—fore—four	pore—pour	morn—mourn
bored—board	or—ore—oar	bore—boar	forth—fourth

1. Divide the class into small groups or have students work in pairs.

2. Dictate one word from each homophone group to the class.

3. Students should find homophones for each dictated word, using dictionaries when needed, and then use each word correctly in a phrase or sentence.

4. A selected member of each group or pair writes the group's sentences or phrases on the board.

■ **The leader:** You are out with a group of friends when all of a sudden, a big storm comes up. Everyone is alarmed, and no one knows what to do. Then, you have a plan. Write down your plan using as many /or/ words as you can.

ON THE BOARD

storm	morn	cork	torch	pour	wore
horn	north	short	your	shore	windstorm
ford	port	fork	more	tore	

Write and Spell on Your Own

Independent practice exercises for the objectives targeted in this unit are located in the corresponding Write and Spell on Your Own section of this book (see pp. 335–337).

SPELLING CHOICES

UNIT 24 | /er/

Focus

Spelling: To recognize the different spellings of words with the /er/ sound

Word patterns

er as in *winter* (syllabic) *ir* as in *bird* *or* as in *word*

er as in *stern* *ur* as in *burn* *ear* as in *learn*

Writing development: letter writing, proverbs
Writing style: informative, creative, personal narrative

Word List

Syllabic *er* as in *winter*

amber	bluster	flower	master	voucher
barber	ember	gather	summer	whisper
barter	farmer	limber	temper	winter
blunder	farther	lumber	timber	

er as in *stern*

berth	germ	herd	serf	term
fern	her	pert	stern	verb

ir as in *bird*

birch	dirt	flirt	quirk	squirm	third
bird	fir	gird	shirt	squirt	thirst
birth	firm	girl	sir	stir	twirl
chirp	first	irk	smirk	swirl	whirl

birthday	blackbird

ur as in *burn*

blur	church	curl	hurl	purge	spurt
blurt	churn	curt	hurt	slur	surf
burn	cur	fur	lurch	spur	urge
burst	curb	furl	lurk	spurn	urn

or as in *word*

word	world	worse	worth
work	worm	worst	

worship

ear as in *learn*

dearth	earn	heard	pearl	yearn
early	earth	learn	search	

Sight Words

Add 10 sight words of your or the students' choice (see Appendix A for possibilities).

Pretest

burn	stir	term	hurt	learn
worth	flower	firm	word	birthday

Posttest

earth	first	curl	world	worse
verb	urge	sir	temper	blackbird

patch his shirt	found a pearl
get the right worm	work in a brickyard

Add words or phrases that include selected sight words.

Spell Together

■ **Spelling the /er/ sound**

ON THE BOARD

When the stern farmer heard that a bird was nesting in the birch tree, he gave his word that he would not hurt it.

1. Read the sentence on the board.
2. Ask, "What sound do you hear repeated?" (/er/)

3. Have a student read the sentence and underline the words containing the /er/ sound.

4. "These are different spellings for the /er/ sound." Write the various word patterns on the board as column headings under the /er/ sentence.

ON THE BOARD

/er/:   <u>er</u>   <u>ir</u>   <u>ur</u>   <u>or</u>   <u>ear</u>

5. Have a student copy the /er/ words from the sentence in the appropriate columns on the board.

6. Ask students to think of additional /er/ words and add them to the lists on the board.

7. "Copy the chart from the board onto page 10 of your Sound Bank. Find more /er/ words and add them to your lists."

■ **/er/ in the middle of a word:** Present these hints to help students recognize which /er/ spelling to use in particular words:

/er/ spelled *or*

/er/ is spelled *or* after *w*, as in *word, world*, and *work*.

/er/ spelled *er, ir, ur*

"If you know the different spellings for the /er/ sound, you can easily find the correct spelling for most words by using a dictionary."

Select *er, ir,* and *ur* words that are appropriate for the age and grade of the students. Have them make up a mnemonic sentence to remember the spelling for these words. *Example: /er/ spelled ir: A bird in a birch can chirp at a girl.*

/er/ spelled *ear*

This spelling occurs in just a few words, such as *earn, early, search*.

A mnemonic sentence can help the students learn this group. *Example: Many try to search the earth to earn an early fortune.*

■ **/er/ at the end of a word:** Present these hints to help students recognize which spelling of final /er/ to use:

/er/ spelled *er*

/er/ spelled *er* occurs at the end of a word to show comparison (*smarter, darker, taller*) or to describe what a person does (*hunter*—one who hunts; *painter*—one who paints).

/er/ spelled *or*

/er/ is spelled *or* in some words that name a condition or a quality, such as *honor, odor, vapor, splendor, major,* and *minor.*

/er/ is spelled *or* in some words that tell what people do, such as *doctor, inventor, mayor, visitor, director,* and *conductor.*

■ **Hangman:** Draw a gallows on the board, review the rules of hangman with the class, if needed, and select a leader to begin the game.

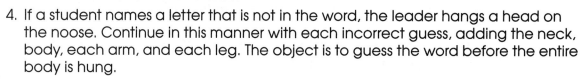

1. The designated leader thinks of an /er/ word (spelled *er, ir, ur, ear*) and puts a blank on the board under the hangman for each letter of the word.
2. Students, in turn, try to guess the letters in the word.
3. If a student names a letter in the word, the leader writes it in the correct blank or blanks.
4. If a student names a letter that is not in the word, the leader hangs a head on the noose. Continue in this manner with each incorrect guess, adding the neck, body, each arm, and each leg. The object is to guess the word before the entire body is hung.

You can adapt hangman, a classroom favorite for generations, to almost any group of words or unit. It is also effective in whole-class or small-group formats.

■ **Adding *r*'s**

1. Divide the class into two teams. The first student from each team comes to the front of the room.
2. The teacher or designated leader reads one of the suggested words from the following list.
3. The object is to place an *r* in the word to make it into an /er/ word. *Example:* cub—curb
4. As soon as a student thinks of a word, he or she raises a hand and writes the word on the board. If the word is correct, that team earns a point. If it is not correct, the player on the opposing team tries to win the point by thinking of an appropriate word.
5. If the student can use the word correctly in a sentence, his or her team earns an additional point.
6. Continue in this manner with one student at a time from each team. You may want to have a rule that each student can play only once until everyone has had a turn.
7. The team with the most points wins.

Suggested words

spun	hut	cut	head	pet	gem	chip
fist	bid	flit	bun	lean	wok	death

■ **Summer or winter?** "Your family is going to move. They want to go somewhere where it is either always summer or always winter. Write a letter to tell them which you would prefer. Include reasons and examples to try to convince them to agree with you."

ON THE BOARD

Suggested words

blunder	fur	bluster	burn	dirt
winter	early	chirp	yearn	world
fir	summer	urge	ember	first
worth	birch	search	bird	worm
farther	hurt	flower	work	shirt
fern	earth	thirst	timber	worst

■ **All about proverbs:** Discuss proverbs: "Proverbs are usually words of wisdom that have been shared around the world. They can be humorous or serious and are kept short so that they are easily remembered."

Read the following proverb: "A bird in the hand is worth two in the bush." Initiate a discussion about what this might mean.

Present another proverb, "The early bird gets the worm." Have students write about
- a time when they were the early bird and they got the worm; or
- a time when they were the early bird but they did not get the worm.

Write and Spell on Your Own

Independent practice exercises for the objectives targeted in this unit are located in the corresponding Write and Spell on Your Own section of this book (see pp. 339–342).

More Sounds

Focus

This unit presents additional sounds with their spellings and offers classroom activities that can be adapted for any of the sounds. The teacher can present the material as a separate unit or select one or more of the sounds as part of earlier units in Part 2.

Writing development: homophones, analogies, headlines
Writing style: creative, informative, personal narrative

Word Patterns and Word List

/oi/

oi as in *boil*

boil	coin	hoist	loin	point	toil
broil	foil	join	moist	soil	void
coil	foist	joint	oil	spoil	

oilburner	oilcan	oilcloth	oilskin	tinfoil

oy as in *boy*

boy	cloy	coy	joy	soy	toy

Patterns
- /oi/ at the end of a word is usually spelled *oy*.
- /oi/ in the middle or at the beginning of a word is usually spelled *oi*.

/oo/

oo as in *boot*

bloom	brood	loon	pooch	roost	stoop	woo
boom	broom	mood	pool	root	swoon	zoo
boost	droop	moon	proof	shoot	swoop	zoom
boot	gloom	moot	roof	soon	tooth	
booth	loom	noon	room	spoon	troop	

bootblack	moonbeam	noonday	roommate
broomstick	moonlight	noontime	toothbrush
loophole	moonstruck	rooftop	toothpick

SPELLING CHOICES

ew* as in *grew

brew	dew	flew	shrew	yew
chew	drew	grew	threw	

dewdrop

ou* as in *group

group	route	soup	troupe	you

u-e* as in *brute

brute	flute	rude	rule

ough* as in *through

through	throughout

Homophones

root—route	troop—troupe
threw—through	you—yew

/yu/

u-e* as in *cube

cube	cure	cute	mule	mute

ue* as in *cue

argue	continue	cue	hue

ew* as in *few

few	hew	mew	pew

/sh/

sh* as in *ship

See Unit 7 for a more extensive list of *sh* words. Selected examples appear here for comparison with other spellings of the /sh/ sound.

fishnet	rash	shed	shock
mash	shape	ship	

ci* as in *precious

precious	social	special

ti* as in *nation

fraction	nation	station

si as in *mansion*

mansion   session   tension

sci as in *conscious*

conscience   conscientious   conscious

ch as in *chef*

chauffeur   chef   chiffon   chute

su as in *sure*

sugar   sure

/f/

ph as in *photo*

graph   phase   phlox

phonic   photo   photograph   triumph

/ough/

ough as in *tough*

cough   enough   rough   tough

/n/

kn as in *knit*

knack	knee	knife	knob	know
knave	kneel	knight	knot	knuckle
knead	knew	knit	knotty	

knapsack   kneecap   knicknack   knighthood   knothole

Homophones

knead—need   knight—night   knot—not

knew—new   knit—nit   know—no

gn as in *gnash*

gnarled   gnash   gnaw   gnome   gnu

SPELLING CHOICES

/r/

wr as in wrap

wrangle	wreath	wrest	wring	writhe	wrung
wrap	wreck	wrestle	wrinkle	wrong	wry
wrath	wren	wretch	wrist	wrote	
wreak	wrench	wriggle	write	wrought	

Homophones

wrap—rap	wrest—rest	wring—ring	wrung—rung
wreak—reek	wretch—retch	write—right	wry—rye

/g/

gh as in ghost

ghetto   ghoul   ghost

Spell Together

■ **Analogies:** Have students make up and exchange analogies for the various word groups. Point out that analogies can be written in two ways:

Frown is to smile	as	sadness is to joy.
frown : smile	::	sadness : joy

Some suggested analogies for some of the word groups are:

/oi/	Frown is to smile	as	sadness is to (joy).
	cake : bake	::	spaghetti : (boil)
/oo/	hot : sandal	::	cold : (boot)
	frog : jumped	::	bird : (flew)
/u/	see : blind	::	speak : (mute)
	auditorium : chair	::	church : (pew)
/sh/	big : size	::	square : (shape)
	2 : one half	::	whole : (fraction)
/f/	instrument : musician	::	camera : (photographer)
	flu : fever	::	cold : (cough)
/n/	piecrust : roll	::	bread : (knead)
	dress : sew	::	sweater : (knit)

■ **Mood words:** Select a few words from each group and write them on the board. Ask the students to use the words in a short paragraph describing how the words make them feel.

/oi/	joy, spoil	/n/	knighthood, kneel
/oo/	mood, swoon, rude	/r/	wrath, wrong
/u/	argue, mew	/g/	ghost, ghoul
/sh/	tension, precious	/n/	gnarled, gnash
/f/	triumph, tough	/sh/	special, sugar

■ **News headlines:** Students are to pretend they are reporters for a newspaper. They gather pictures that include suggested words and use them in headlines.

Suggested words

wrench	nation	knee	fishnet	coin
mansion	wreath	shed	ghost	chef
wreck	station	knapsack	chauffer	

Write and Spell on Your Own

Independent practice exercises for the objectives targeted in this unit are located in the corresponding Write and Spell on Your Own section of this book (see pp. 343–345).

PART 3

Spelling Rules

I have learned much from my teachers,
even more from my colleagues,
but I have learned the rest from my students.

—Maimonides

Focus

Spelling: To understand and apply the following rule: If a one-syllable word with one short vowel ends in *f, l, s,* or *z*, the final consonant is usually doubled.*
Writing development: word pictures, feeling poems
Writing style: creative

Word List

Double *f*

bluff	cuff	huff	ruff	skiff	snuff	stuff
buff	fluff	muff	scoff	sluff	staff	tiff
cliff	gruff	puff	scuff	sniff	stiff	whiff

Double *l*

bell	dull	gull	mill	shrill	swell	well
bill	dwell	hill	pill	sill	swill	will
chill	fell	hull	quell	smell	tell	yell
cull	fill	ill	quill	spell	thrill	
dill	frill	kill	sell	spill	till	
drill	grill	lull	shell	still	trill	

handbill	molehill	pillbox	spellbound
hillside	numbskull	sawmill	uphill
hilltop	nutshell	shellfish	

Double *s*

bass	chess	floss	hiss	mass	muss	toss
bless	class	fuss	kiss	mess	pass	
bliss	cross	glass	lass	miss	press	
brass	dress	grass	less	moss	stress	

classmate	crosswalk	password

---

*Part 3 deals with the application of spelling rules. Most students are already familiar with the *f, l, s, z* doubling rule, making it a useful initial step before presenting the spelling rules that follow.

SPELLING RULES

Double *z*

buzz   fizz   fuzz   jazz   razz   whizz

Sight Words

Add 10 sight words of your or the students' choice (see Appendix A for possibilities).

Pretest

puff	dull	quill	less	pillbox
sniff	tell	class	buzz	shellfish

Posttest

staff	frill	chill	floss	classmate
thrill	quell	stress	jazz	hillside

a torn cuff   a game of chess
a steeper hill   cross the bridge

Add words or phrases that include selected sight words.

Spell Together

- **Review syllables:** A syllable is a word or a part of a word that consists of one or more letters, contains at least one vowel, and is pronounced as one unit. It does not always contain a consonant. *Examples:* fill–ing, e–vent, o–pen, on–ly, ev–er

- **Double letters:** Directing students' attention to the words on the board, ask the following questions:

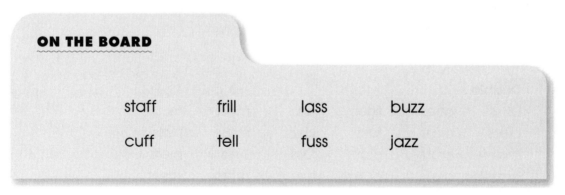

ON THE BOARD

staff	frill	lass	buzz
cuff	tell	fuss	jazz

1. "How many syllables are in each word?" (one)
2. "How many vowels are in each word?" (one)
3. "What are the final letters in each word?" (*ff, ll, ss, zz*)

SPELLING RULES

4. "Two letters that spell one sound are called *double letters.*" Help the students discover the rule for doubling the final *f, l, s,* and *z* in one-syllable words: If a one-syllable word with one vowel ends in *f, l, s,* or *z,* the final consonant is usually doubled.

5. Discuss these exceptions: *if, plus, us, gas, bus, pal, gal, this, fez, quiz, yes, thus.*

■ **Association:** Have students think of and spell any one-syllable words ending in *f, l, s,* or *z* that are associated with the following words. Encourage students to use their imaginations.

Suggested word	Possible association
sick	ill, pill
nose	sniff, smell, bill
letters	spell, drill
angry	cross, fuss, yell
girl	miss, lass
window	sill, glass
school	class, pass
beach	gull, shell
dentist	drill, fill
climb	hill, cliff, huff, puff

■ **Word circle relay**

1. Divide the class into two teams and have them line up for a relay race.

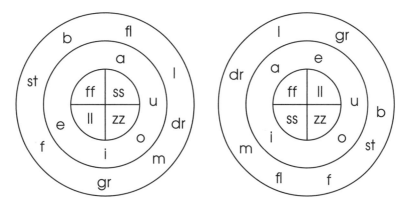

2. At a given signal, a student from each team goes to the board and makes a word from the rings of letters in the circle. The students must choose one beginning sound from the outside ring, a short vowel from the middle ring, and one ending sound from the center, and then write the word on the board.

3. The team with the most correctly spelled words wins.

■ **Word pictures**

© 2007, 2000, 1984 by Frances Bloom and Deborah Bloom Coates

ON THE BOARD

Press   c l i
        f
        f   mis's

1. "These words illustrate their meanings. They make the word look like what it says."
2. Have the students try to print the following words to match their meanings: *chill, stiff, bell, mess, toss, fell, hill, cross, frill, fuzz, smell.*
3. Post the word pictures around the room.
4. Students can also make word pictures from appropriate vocabulary presented in previous units. Here are a few of many possibilities:

slim	smile	bowl	cloud	stretch	flower
kite	chain	stream	fall	fork	
eye	cold	deep	tall	worm	

■ **Spell last first (focus on the ending sound)**

1. Divide the class into two teams.
2. Say, "Listen for the ending of each word. When I say the word, spell it *backwards.* Remember the rule for doubling words ending in *f, l, s,* or *z.*"
3. Dictate a word to each player in turn. Players who spell their word correctly remain standing. Those who do not spell the word backwards, or who spell it incorrectly, sit down. The next player on the opposing team then has an opportunity to spell the word.
4. Continue for a designated time. The team with the most students standing wins.

Suggested words

puff	yes	pal	bill	sip	tiff	hill
bed	shell	press	stiff	cliff	fit	win
fix	pot	big	bus	tell	sap	
well	mess	den	pass	this	miss	
stop	ill	brass	fan	lot	sell	

- **Feeling poems:** "Words that you read or hear can sometimes create an image in your mind. A poet might put these images into words. Some words might also make you think about your feelings."

ON THE BOARD

bluff   puff   cliff   huff

Feeling Poem

Huff puff
A cliff?
A bluff?
I will huff and puff
but still
keep going up.

Have the students use any of the following words and any additional words to write "feeling" poems.

| bell | shrill | trill | yell | thrill | bliss |
| fell | mess | razz | stiff | fluff | stress |

Write and Spell on Your Own

Independent practice exercises for the objectives targeted in this unit are located in the corresponding Write and Spell on Your Own section of this book (see pp. 349–353).

UNIT 26 | Doubling Rule

Focus

Spelling: To understand and apply the following rules:

1. When adding an ending that begins with a vowel (*–ing, –ed, –er, –est*) to a one-syllable word that ends in one consonant preceded by one vowel, double the final consonant.

2. Many words of more than one syllable double the final consonant before an added ending if the last syllable of the root word is accented.

Writing development: syllables, diamante
Writing style: creative

Word List

One-syllable words: final consonant doubles

batting	fatter	kidding	quitter	snipping
biggest	fittest	lugging	quizzing	splitting
blotter	flapped	madder	rubbed	stepped
chipped	flatter	napping	runner	stirring
chopping	grabbed	padded	scarred	thinnest
clipped	hitting	planning	shopping	wettest
dimmer	hottest	plotted	skidded	winner
dripping	jogger	prodded	slimmest	

One-syllable words: final consonant does not double

aiming	counting	handful	oiling	shipment
blasted	darkest	helpless	oldest	shortly
blindly	dented	joined	quickest	sinful
boastful	dimly	joyful	quickly	snatching
bolder	fitness	kindly	reaching	snugly
boldly	freshest	madly	rested	stranded
buzzer	freshly	marker	restful	weighing
cheapest	greatest	mindful	sadness	witless
chewing	grimly	moaning	sailing	

Multisyllable words: final consonant doubles

admitted	deterring	forgotten	preferred	repelled
beginner	equipped	occurred	propelled	submitting
committed	expelled	omitting	rebelling	transferred
compelling	forbidding	patrolled	referring	transmitted
controlled	forgetting	permitted	regretted	

Multisyllable words: final consonant does not double

affected	enjoying	hammered	orbiting	prevented
carpeting	entered	invented	ordering	profiting
concerned	exiting	limiting	pardoned	remaining
contained	galloped	objected	persisted	revealed
differing	gardener	offering	piloting	subtracted
employed	gathered	opening	presented	visiting

Sight Words

Add 10 sight words of your or the students' choice (see Appendix A for possibilities).

Pretest

batting	visiting	scarred	sailing	aiming
admitted	snipping	oldest	marker	rebelling

Posttest

sailed	flatter	forgotten	stirring	expelled
counting	oiling	chipped	orbiting	limiting

flapped its wings   submitting a plan

enjoying the game   chewing some gum

Add words or phrases that include selected sight words.

Spell Together

■ **Adding an ending can change the spelling:** "You can change the meaning or tense of a word by adding an ending. Sometimes we change the spelling of a word when we do this."

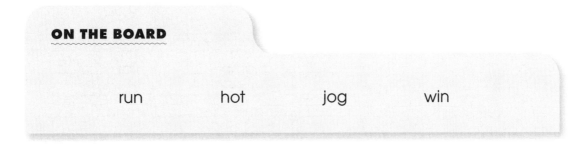

ON THE BOARD

run   hot   jog   win

Read the words on the board, asking the following questions.

- "How many syllables are in each word?" (one)
- "How many consonants are there at the end of each word?" (one)
- "How many vowels are there before the final consonant in each word?" (one)
- "There is a rule called the one-one-one rule (or doubling rule) for doubling letters when adding an ending to a word. The ending you add to the word must start with a vowel for the rule to apply."

ON THE BOARD

When adding an ending that begins with a vowel to a one-syllable word that ends in one consonant preceded by one vowel, double the final consonant.

Present the following examples and show how the one-one-one rule applies. If necessary, use more examples from the word list.

ON THE BOARD

flat + er = flatter   flat + ly = flatly

meet + ing = meeting   rest + ed = rested

SPELLING RULES

■ **Use the rule:** Have students, in turn, add *–ed, –er, –est,* or *–ing* to the words in columns A, B, and C, and *–ful, –ly, –ment,* or *–ness* to the words in column D.

ON THE BOARD

<u>A</u>	<u>B</u>	<u>C</u>	<u>D</u>
bat _____	aim _____	camp _____	flat _____
blot _____	boil _____	blast _____	ship _____
drip _____	sail _____	dust _____	mad _____
big _____	weed _____	melt _____	dim _____
dip _____	play _____	old _____	sin _____

■ **Apply the one-one-one rule to words of more than one syllable**

1. "The one-one-one rule applies to words of more than one syllable if the accent is on the final syllable of the word."

2. Define *accent:* extra force or stress pronounced on one of the syllables of a multisyllabic word. Point out the dictionary symbol for an accented syllable (' in front of the syllable). *Example: 'or • bit* means the first syllable is accented. (The placement of stress marks varies in different dictionaries.)

3. "How are Group A and Group B different?" (The consonant doubles in Group A but not Group B.)

ON THE BOARD

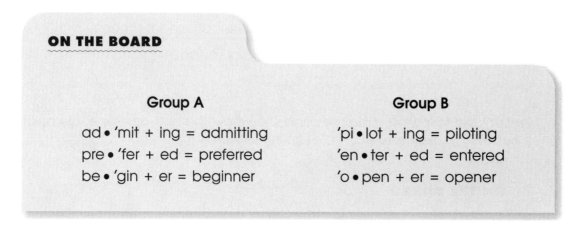

Group A	**Group B**
ad • 'mit + ing = admitting	'pi • lot + ing = piloting
pre • 'fer + ed = preferred	'en • ter + ed = entered
be • 'gin + er = beginner	'o • pen + er = opener

---

4. "Which syllable is accented in Group A? In Group B?"

5. "Notice that when the accent is on the final syllable and that syllable fits the other conditions of the one-one-one rule, the final consonant is doubled."

◼ Patterns and hints

Never double *x, y,* or *w*

The one-one-one rule does not apply to words ending in *x, y,* or *w:*

box—boxing   play—playing   snow—snowing

q + *u* = a consonant

Qu stands for the /kw/ sound. When the vowel *u* is combined with *q,* it is treated as a consonant. The vowel that follows *qu* is treated as one vowel. *Example: quit + ing = quitting*

Keep *c* hard

To retain the /k/ sound in words ending in *c,* add *k* before endings that begin with *e, i,* or *y.*

picnic–picnicking   panic–panicking–panicky
traffic–trafficking   frolic–frolicking

Exceptions:
critic—critical   cubic—cubical   logic—logical

Words ending in *–fer*

Do not double the final consonant in words ending in *–fer* before *–ence.* When *–ence* is added, the accent shifts to the first syllable.

in • 'fer   in • 'ferred   'in • fer • ence
de • 'fer   de • 'ferred   'def • er • ence
pre • 'fer   pre • 'ferred   'pref • er • ence

◼ Pick-up sticks

1. Write base words on ice-cream sticks or tongue depressors.
2. A player heaps all the sticks in a pile on the floor.
3. The object of the game is to remove one stick without moving any of the others.
4. If successful, the player adds any ending to the base word, writes the word with the ending on the board or on a sheet of paper, and keeps the stick.
5. If the player spells a word incorrectly or moves a stick, he or she places the stick back on the pile and the other player takes a turn.
6. The player with the most sticks wins.

Suggested base words

chop	rub	clip	scrub	boil	scar
plan	aim	melt	blast	stir	drain
pin	sail	dot	wag	flop	drip

SPELLING RULES

■ **Finish my word (listen for the accented syllable)**

1. Divide the class into small groups and have the students in each group sit or stand in a circle.
2. The first student says one syllable of a two-syllable word. An example is *for*.
3. The next student adds another syllable to make a word, such as *get*.
4. The group then claps for each syllable, with a louder clap for the accented syllable. *Example: for*—soft clap, *get*—loud clap
5. A third student chooses an ending to add to the two-syllable word and spells the word.
6. If the word is spelled correctly, the student starts a new word.
7. Play for a predetermined period of time. If necessary, post the following suggested words on the board:

ON THE BOARD

invent	consent	begin	rebel	control	object	limit
enjoy	exit	permit	expel	equip	admit	profit

■ **Diamante:** A diamante is a poem that forms the shape of a diamond. It follows a set pattern that can be created by counting syllables or words.

ON THE BOARD

Diamante

Line 1: 1 word (noun)   Maze
Line 2: 2 words (adjectives)   Confus_____, dizzy
Line 3: 3 words (verbs ending in –*ing*)   Begin_____, search_____, wind_____
Line 4: 4 words (nouns or a phrase)   Go_____ every which way
Line 5: 3 words (verbs ending in –*ing*)   Think_____, persist_____, exit_____
Line 6: 2 words (adjectives)   Joyful, successful
Line 7: 1 word (noun—synonym for topic)   Puzzle

_____

Answers: confusing, beginning, searching, winding, going, thinking, persisting, exiting

1. Remind the students of the doubling rule.
2. Have the students complete the diamante on the board by adding –*ing* in the blanks.
3. Have groups of students work together to create a diamante.

Write and Spell on Your Own

Independent practice exercises for the objectives targeted in this unit are located in the corresponding Write and Spell on Your Own section of this book (see pp. 355–360).

UNIT 27 | –le Rule

Focus

Spelling: To understand and apply the following rules:
1. When a consonant plus *–le* follows a short vowel, the consonant is usually doubled.
2. When a consonant follows another consonant and precedes *–le,* it is not doubled.

Writing development: classification, cinquain
Writing style: creative

Word List

Short vowel + consonant + *–le*

apple	dribble	jiggle	nuzzle	saddle	struggle
babble	drizzle	juggle	paddle	scribble	supple
baffle	fiddle	kettle	pebble	scuffle	tattle
battle	fizzle	little	peddle	scuttle	throttle
bottle	giggle	meddle	puddle	settle	topple
brittle	gobble	middle	puzzle	shuffle	tussle
bubble	grapple	muddle	quibble	shuttle	whittle
cattle	griddle	muffle	rabble	sizzle	wiggle
cripple	guzzle	muzzle	raffle	snuffle	wobble
cuddle	haggle	nettle	rattle	snuggle	
dabble	hobble	nibble	riddle	straddle	
dazzle	huddle	nozzle	ripple	straggle	

Short vowel + two consonants + *–le*

amble	crinkle	humble	nimble	speckle	trample
angle	crumble	hurdle	pickle	spindle	tremble
ankle	crumple	hurtle	pimple	sprinkle	trickle
buckle	dawdle	jingle	ramble	startle	tumble
bundle	dwindle	jumble	rumble	strangle	twinkle
bungle	fickle	jungle	sample	stumble	uncle
cackle	gamble	kindle	scramble	tackle	
candle	gentle	mantle	simple	tangle	
chuckle	grumble	marble	single	thimble	
circle	handle	mumble	sparkle	tingle	

Long vowel + consonant + *–le*

able	bugle	fable	ladle	rifle	stable	table
bible	cable	gable	noble	sable	staple	title
bridle	cradle	idle	ogle	sidle	stifle	trifle

Sight Words

Add 10 sight words of your or the students' choice (see Appendix A for possibilities).

Pretest

middle	paddle	jungle	riddle	sizzle
sample	fable	noble	title	buckle

Posttest

nibble	twinkle	fizzle	bugle	scribble
idle	cable	handle	marble	ripple

fell in a puddle · · · blowing a bubble
tipping the table · · · preferred the red candle

Add words or phrases that include selected sight words.

Spell Together

■ **Doubling rule for words with *–le* endings:** When a consonant plus *–le* follows a short vowel, the consonant is usually doubled.

ON THE BOARD

Group A	Group B	Group C
battle	ladle	stumble
juggle	fable	handle
paddle	trifle	sparkle

1. Read the words in Group A.
   - "Do you hear a long or a short vowel sound in these words?" (short)
   - "Look at the words. Is the consonant before *–le* doubled?" (yes)
2. Read the words in Group B. Repeat the questions under 1.

3. Lead a discussion of the rule. Emphasize the following:
   - When the consonant follows a short vowel, the consonant is doubled.
   - When the consonant follows a long vowel, the consonant is not doubled.
   - When the consonant follows another consonant, as in Group C, the rule does not apply.

Patterns and hints: *–cle* or *–cal*?

–cle is a noun ending
bicycle   uncle   circle   article   miracle

–cal is an adjective ending
musical   magical   vertical   practical   physical

A speedy arrangement

1. Write each of the following word beginnings and endings on a separate card. Make enough sets of cards for each group of about five students to have a full set.

Word beginnings					Word endings				
mar–	ri–	lit–	top–	pic–	–tle	–kle	–ple	–ble	–fle
mid–	gig–	un–	sta–	a–	–dle	–cle	–ple	–ble	–gle
rat–	chuc–	jug–	ta–	muf–	–fle	–ble	–kle	–gle	–tie
cra–	spar–	gob–	ti–	sni–	–kle	–dle	–tle	–ble	–fle
tem–	spin–	ca–	driz–	wig–	–ple	–dle	–ble	–zle	–gle

2. Divide the class into teams with about five students on each team.
3. Pass out a set of word beginnings and endings to each team.
4. At a given signal, each team must match up all word beginnings and endings to form correctly spelled words. Each team should list its words on the board or on a sheet of paper.
5. The first team to correctly use all the cards wins. Reassign the sets to the teams for another round. If necessary, use the word lists to make more sets of word parts and endings.

Listen for your classification

1. Have each student write one of the following headings on a sheet of paper:

   Sounds People Make   Words That Could Describe Water
   Words That Could Describe Young Animals

2. Have students listen as you read the following suggested words.
3. Read the words again slowly, and have the students write down those words that could relate to the heading they selected.
4. Have students write short paragraphs using their groups of words.
5. Read or post their paragraphs.
6. As a variation, you can dictate the words and have the students classify them in any way they can justify. After they have written a paragraph, they can share and discuss their classification with the class.

SPELLING RULES

Suggested words

Rearrange the words when dictating.

people: grumble, giggle, chuckle, mumble, babble*
water: dribble, trickle, bubble, sparkle, sprinkle
animals: little, gentle, cuddle, nibble, nuzzle

---

*Babble can also fit in the "water" category.

■ **Cinquain:** Cinquain was developed in the United States in the early 1900s. It is a form of poetry that followed haiku and was called cinquain from the French word for five (*cinq*) because it had five lines.

> ## ON THE BOARD
>
> Line 1: 1 word—title   Tab_____
> Line 2: 2 words describe the title   Gathering place
> Line 3: 3 words express an action   Nib_____ on an ap_____
> Line 4: 4 words express a feeling   Gig_____ with all the family
> Line 5: 1 word—another word for the title   Support
>
> ---
>
> Answers: table, nibble, apple, giggle

Cinquain can also be created by counting syllables:

    Line 1: 2 syllables (noun)
    Line 2: 4 syllables (adjectives)
    Line 3: 6 syllables (verbs)
    Line 4: 8 syllables (four-word phrase)
    Line 5: 2 or 3 syllables (a synonym for topic)

1. Remind the students of the doubling rule when adding the ending *–le* to a word.

2. Have the students complete the cinquain on the board by adding *–le* in the blanks.

3. Have the students write their own cinquains. You might also show them both forms, counting words or counting syllables.

Write and Spell on Your Own

Independent practice exercises for the objectives targeted in this unit are located in the corresponding Write and Spell on Your Own section of this book (see pp. 361–365).

© 2007, 2000, 1984 by Frances Bloom and Deborah Bloom Coates

UNIT 28 | -y

Focus

Spelling: To understand and apply the following rules:

1. When a consonant + -y follows a short vowel, the consonant is usually doubled.
2. When a consonant + -y follows a long vowel or another consonant, the consonant is not doubled.

Writing development: adjectives
Writing style: creative

Word List

Short vowel + consonant + -y

baggy	chilly	fatty	glassy	kitty	rally	stubby
belly	choppy	ferry	gritty	lobby	scurry	sunny
berry	chubby	flabby	groggy	marry	shabby	tabby
buddy	chummy	fluffy	happy	merry	shaggy	tally
buggy	clammy	foggy	hilly	messy	shinny	tarry
bunny	crabby	folly	hobby	muddy	shoddy	witty
caddy	curry	frilly	huffy	penny	silly	
canny	daddy	funny	hurry	petty	skinny	
carry	dizzy	fuzzy	jelly	poppy	sloppy	
chatty	dressy	giddy	jetty	puffy	snappy	
cherry	dummy	giggly	jolly	puppy	soggy	

Long vowel + consonant + -y

baby	duty	hazy	navy	shady	smoky	wavy
cozy	flaky	holy	pony	shaky	spiny	wily
crazy	gravy	lady	puny	shiny	tidy	
crony	grimy	lazy	scaly	slimy	tiny	

Consonant + consonant + -y

angry	corny	fancy	hardy	musty	shifty	thrifty
army	crispy	flimsy	hasty	nasty	skimpy	ugly
burly	curly	frisky	hefty	party	stingy	windy
candy	dandy	grumpy	husky	plenty	tardy	
catchy	dusty	gusty	marshy	rusty	thirsty	
chunky	empty	handy	musky	shanty	thirty	

Sight Words
Add 10 sight words of your or the students' choice (see Appendix A for possibilities).

Pretest

jolly	hobby	pony	messy	thirty
dandy	lady	army	ugly	tiny

Posttest

skimpy	dizzy	shaky	frilly	hasty
crabby	shiny	hefty	shaggy	marshy

a messy table   a jolly jingle
riding on a pony   jogging with my buddy

Add words or phrases that include selected sight words.

Spell Together
Discuss the similarity to the doubling rule for consonant + -le as presented in Unit 27. If necessary, review this rule.

- **A doubling rule for words with –y endings:** When a consonant plus –y follows a short vowel, the consonant is usually doubled.

ON THE BOARD

Group A	Group B	Group C
fun ny	po ny	fris ky
hap py	ha zy	dus ty
mud dy	la dy	cris py

1. Read the words in Group A.
   - "Do you hear a long or short vowel in these words?" (short)
   - "Look at the words. Is the consonant before –y doubled?" (yes)
2. Read the words in Group B.
   - "Do you hear a long or short vowel in these words?" (long)
   - "Look at the words. Is the consonant before –y doubled?" (no)

3. Lead a discussion of the rule.

- When the consonant follows a short vowel, the consonant is doubled.
- When the consonant follows a long vowel, the consonant is not doubled.
- When the consonant follows another consonant, as in Group C, the rule does not apply.

4. Present these exceptions to the rule: *body, study, copy, pity.*

■ **Patterns and hints: short vowel, add a letter:** It may be helpful to sum up Units 21, 22, and 25 through 28 by pointing out that changes in spelling often occur after a short vowel. *Example:* "As demonstrated on the board, a single consonant may be doubled or an extra consonant may be added after a short vowel."

ON THE BOARD

A		B		C
Long Vowel Sound	to	Short Vowel Sound	=	Add a Consonant
bake		back		k to ck
beach		batch		ch to tch
wage		wedge		ge to dge
mile		mill		l to ll
pining		pinning		n to nn
rifle		raffle		fle to ffle
holy		holly		ly to lly

---

1. Dictate the following words:

take	rake	like	file	pile	scraped
shiny	hoping	griping	moping	tile	base

2. For each word you dictate have students, in turn, do the following, adding to the lists on the board:

a. Write the word in Column A.

b. Change the long vowel to a short vowel and write the new word in Column B.

c. Note the spelling change in Column C.

■ **Word hunt for –*y* endings**

1. Divide the class into four or five teams.

2. Have the teams find as many words that end in –*y* (as a word ending, not just a letter) as they can in 10 minutes. They may use a dictionary, classroom books, or posters. Each team lists its –*y* ending words on a separate sheet of paper.

3. Give each team 15 more minutes to make up a story with their words.

4. The group that uses the most correctly spelled –*y* words wins.

5. As an optional activity, have the students develop individual word lists in three columns:

   Column A: short vowel before –y ending

   Column B: long vowel before –y ending

   Column C: consonant before –y ending

■ **A wishful dream, an ad lib story**

   1. Read words from the –y word list and have students select 16 adjectives. As students make their choices, list them on the board.

   2. Read the following story and fill in the blanks with the list of selected adjectives in the same order that they were listed on the board.

It was early one _____ morning when I heard a _____

noise at my window. I jumped out of my _____ bed and

opened the _____ window. My _____ wish had

come true. A _____ puppy, a _____ kitty, and a

_____ pony were all playing in my _____ yard. I pulled

on my _____ shirt and _____ pants and ran out to see

them. They were all so _____. My _____ mom and

_____ dad must have read my _____ mind. I reached

out to pet them and WHOOSH............ I awoke out of my _____

dream!! Maybe they will be there again tonight.

   3. Students can make up their own ad lib stories to share with a partner.

Write and Spell on Your Own

Independent practice exercises for the objectives targeted in this unit are located in the corresponding Write and Spell on Your Own section of this book (see pp. 367–370).

UNIT 29 | More Endings

Focus

Spelling: To understand and apply the following rule: Words ending in silent *e* usually drop the *e* before an ending that begins with a vowel and retain the *e* before an ending that begins with a consonant.

Writing development: suffixes, free verse
Writing style: creative

Word List

Endings that begin with a vowel (*-ed, -er, -ing, -ion*)

aging	diving	joked	saving	stroked
braking	dodger	liking	scared	taping
budging	edging	liner	scraper	tattled
carver	facing	lunged	shaking	tiling
chimed	filing	piling	skated	traded
circling	forged	priced	sliding	voting
creation	framing	quacked	smiled	wading
curing	glaring	racing	snored	wiping
dating	glider	raked	staging	zoned
diner	grudging	rated	striding	

Endings that begin with a consonant (*-ful, -ly, -ment*)

amusement	gamely	lamely	pavement	timely
arrangement	graceful	largely	peaceful	tuneful
careful	hateful	likely	safely	useful
disgraceful	homely	lovely	settlement	wasteful
excitement	hopeful	movement	tasteful	

Sight Words

Add 10 sight words of your or the students' choice (see Appendix A for possibilities).

Pretest

timely	curing	liking	hateful	wading
careful	edging	shaking	pavement	amusement

Posttest

graceful	circling	settlement	glider	voting
tattled	useful	budging	homely	hopeful

controlled the pricing   sliding down a hill

a likely tale   a tuneful song

Add words or phrases that include selected sight words.

Spell Together

■ **Drop *e* and add an ending:** Explain that words ending in silent *e* usually drop the *e* before an ending that begins with a vowel and retain the *e* before an ending that begins with a consonant.

ON THE BOARD

Group A

use + ing = using

settle + ed = settled

complete + ion = completion

Group B

use + ful = useful

settle + ment = settlement

complete + ly = completely

---

1. "Look at the groups of words on the board."
2. "How are the endings in Group A alike?" (begin with a vowel)
3. "How are the endings in Group B alike?" (begin with a consonant)
4. "Did adding an ending change the spelling of the base word in Group A?" (Yes, the final *e* was dropped.)
5. "Did adding an ending change the spelling of the base word in Group B?" (no)
6. Discuss the rule for dropping the *e* before an ending that begins with a vowel.
7. If necessary, use the word list to add more examples for each group on the board. Write the base word on the board and have students, in turn, add appropriate endings.

■ **Patterns and hints:** Discuss instances where the *e* stays before an ending:

- In order to retain the soft sounds of *c* and *g*, do not drop the *e* in words ending in –*ce* or –*ge* when adding an ending that begins with *a, o,* or *u.*

change—changing   *but* changeable

trace—tracing   *but* traceable

SPELLING RULES

- Keep the *e* in words ending in *–oe* when adding *–ing.*

  hoe—hoed   *but* hoeing

  shoe—shoed   *but* shoeing

  canoe—canoed   *but* canoeing

- Keep the *e* if the meaning of the word changes when the silent *e* is dropped.

  singe—singeing   *not* singing (sing)

  dye—dyeing   *not* dying (die)

- Keep the *e* in *acre* and *mile.*

  acre + age = acreage   mile + age = mileage

Ending rummy: This is a game for two to four players.

1. Have the players copy the following words onto file cards cut in half:

age	date	frame	lunge	replace	store
amuse	engage	gaze	move	save	stroke
arrange	fade	grace	nudge	scare	waste
base	disgrace	hate	nurse	scrape	trade
charge	forgive	hope	peace	skate	use

2. Have them make five cards for each of the following endings: *–ed, –ing, –ful, –able, –ment.* (They will have 25 ending cards.)

3. The object of the game is to make three new words by using three base words and three endings.

4. The dealer shuffles the word and ending cards together, deals six cards to each player, puts the remaining cards on the table in a pile face-down, and then turns one card up next to the pile.

5. Each player first tries to form words from the cards in his or her hand.

6. The players, in turn, then try to form new words by either taking the upturned card or a new card from the pile. The player then discards a card from his or her hand, face-up, to the upturned stack.

7. A player who can form three words from the cards in his or her hand calls "rummy" and spells the words correctly to win. Players must remember when to add or drop the *e.*

Ending bee

1. Divide the class into two teams.

2. Give each team a list of silent *e* words.

3. The first player on Team A reads a word from his or her list.

4. The first player on Team B must add an ending to the word and write the new word on the board.

5. If the first player on Team B cannot think of a word, adds an incorrect ending to the word, or misspells the word, that player is out of the game. Then another player from Team B attempts the word, until someone is successful.

6. Alternate turns by having the successful player on Team B read a word to the next player on Team A, and so on.

SPELLING RULES

7. The team with the most players still in the game after a predetermined time wins.

Suggested words

Add any other silent *e* words you wish.

Team A

age	dare	frame	joke	settle
budge	dodge	glide	large	taste
chime	fade	hate	move	tune

Team B

brake	date	home	like	safe
care	edge	hope	love	trade
cube	glare	large	peace	waste

■ **Free verse:** Discuss free verse. "Free verse gives you the freedom to form your own kind of poetry. There are very few rules. You can create your own style and rhythm to express your feelings and thoughts. The following words were used to create a poem."

ON THE BOARD

dive—divers—diving   dance—dancers—dancing

tune—tuneful

My eyes sparkle
at the sight
of divers diving,
as they dive
into deep water,
and of dancers dancing,
as they dance
to a tuneful tune.

Have the students add endings to the following words to create their own free verse.

circle   slide   lunge   smile

Write and Spell on Your Own

Independent practice exercises for the objectives targeted in this unit are located in the corresponding Write and Spell on Your Own section of this book (see pp. 371–374).

UNIT 30 | *y* to *i, i* Before *e*

Focus

Spelling: To understand and apply the following rules:

1. When adding an ending to words that end in *y* preceded by a consonant, change the *y* to *i* except when the ending begins with *i*.

2. Spell *i* before *e* except after *c* or when pronounced like /ā/.

Writing development: mnemonics
Writing style: creative

Word List

Words for Rule 2 are listed under Spell Together activity 2.

Final *y* preceded by a consonant

Example: copy—copied

allies	copied	enemies	jolliest	pitiful
angrier	coziest	fancier	laziest	shinier
applied	crazier	flashier	luckily	skinnier
armies	crispier	glorious	merriest	sloppiest
beautiful	defied	haziest	merrily	sneakier
busiest	denied	healthier	moodier	studious
carried	dreamier	heaviest	noisiest	tastiest
chummier	dustier	hurried	pettier	various

Except when the ending begins with *i*

applying	copying	denying	studying
carrying	defying	hurrying	

Final *y* preceded by a vowel

Example: buy—buying

attorneys	destroys	joyous	prayer
boys	dismays	payable	relayed
brays	employed	played	strayed
delaying	journeyed	player	

Sight Words

Add 10 sight words of your or the students' choice (see Appendix A for possibilities).

Pretest

sunnier	weight	heaviest	carried	sloppiest
copying	field	dustier	studying	chummier

Posttest

skinnier	beautiful	dismayed	belief	jolliest
enjoying	straying	merrily	buying	neighbor

hurrying to the skating rink   paid for a pony ride
copied the puzzle   played with a puppy

Add words or phrases that include selected sight words.

Spell Together

■ **Add an ending to words ending in *y***

ON THE BOARD

Base word	A	B	C
empty	emptiness	emptier	emptying
busy	busily	busier	busying
pity	pitiful	pitiable	pitying
worry	worrisome	worried	worrying

1. "What do the underlined words have in common?" (They end in *y*.)
2. "What happened to the *y* in Columns A and B?" (It changed to *i*.)
3. "What happened to the *y* in Column C?" (It did not change.)
4. Lead students to observe that when you add an ending to words ending in *y* preceded by a consonant, the following occurs:
   - The *y* changes to *i* when the ending begins with a consonant.
   - The *y* changes to *i* when the ending begins with a vowel.
   - The rule does not apply if the ending begins with *i*.
5. "This rule also applies to forming the plural of a noun that ends in *y*."

   berry—berries   city—cities   pony—ponies

SPELLING RULES

6. Discuss these exceptions:

One-syllable adjectives:

shy—shyly—shyness   dry—dryly—dryness
sly—slyly—slyness   wry—wryly—wryness

Irregular exceptions:
lay—laid   pay—paid
slay—slain   say—said

■ ***i* before *e*?** Some words are spelled *ie* or *ei*. The rule that applies is easily remembered with the examples and rhyme that follow.

Spell *i* before *e*

belief	fiend	grief	pierce	shriek	wield
chief	fierce	niece	priest	siege	yield
cashier	friend	piece	relief	thief	
field	frontier	pier	shield	tier	

Except after *c*

ceiling	conceive	deceive	receipt
conceit	deceit	perceive	receive

Or when sounding like /ā/

deign	feint	neighbor	skein	veil	weight
eight	freight	reign	sleigh	vein	

Exceptions
One or two mnemonic sentences will help students remember these exceptions: *The weird sheik seized time for leisure. Did either of the foods have protein or caffeine?*

either	neither	seize	sheik	caffeine
leisure	protein	seizure	weird	

Mnemonic
Students usually find the following rhyme helpful in remembering the rule for *i* before *e:*

Spell *i* before *e*
except after *c,*
or when sounding like /ā/
as in *neighbor* and *weigh.*

SPELLING RULES

■ **An exceptional exception:** Students can use the following example to write their own phrases or sentences to illustrate a spelling rule.

<u>**ON THE BOARD**</u>

<u>Spell i before e:</u>	My niece, the chief,
<u>except after c:</u>	hit the ceiling
<u>or when sounding like a:</u>	when her neighbor lost her sleigh.

<u>Words you can use</u>

belief	fierce	friend	relief	field
ceiling	conceit	deceive	receipt	either
eight	neither	seize	weird	

■ **Pick an ending**

<u>**ON THE BOARD**</u>

Base words		Endings	
angry	hurry	–er	–ing
stray	carry	–ful	–est
play	pretty	–ly	–able
shiny	enjoy	–ment	–ed

1. Have the students pick an ending for each base word.
2. Have them select some of the words they made to finish this story.

A Heavy Load

"Hurry up!" cried Harry. "I am not able to carry this any farther."

"I'm coming," giggled Sally, as she jumped over the low fence.

■ **War game:** This is a game for two players.

1. Have the players write the 30 words on the Suggested Words list on cards and number each card in the right-hand corner with a number from 1 to 10. (There should be three cards with each number.) For a longer game, add additional words from the word list or any other *y* words, and number the cards accordingly.

2. One player shuffles the cards and deals them all out (15 apiece). Players should not be allowed to look at each other's cards.

3. Each player places a card on the desk, face-up, at the same time.

4. The player with the higher number can keep both cards if he or she is able to add an ending to the word on each card and spell and write the words with those endings.

Example:

Player 1

7
cloudy

Player 2

3
beauty

Player 1 writes *cloudier* and *beautiful* and keeps both cards.

5. If both cards have the same number, the players say, "War." They each place three cards on the table, face-down, and add a fourth card, face-up. The player with the higher number takes all the cards if he or she can correctly add endings to all of the words in the piles.

6. If a player adds an ending incorrectly or otherwise misspells a word, the other player can challenge the spelling. If the challenger spells the word correctly, he or she keeps the card.

7. The winner is the player with the most cards after a designated time or the one who wins the entire deck.

Suggested words

cloudy	destroy	buy	happy	berry	buddy
nasty	study	apply	peppy	tiny	beauty
crazy	busy	stubby	envy	flimsy	stray
buggy	frosty	marry	enjoy	pony	supply
hurry	duty	stay	fry	hasty	joy

Write and Spell on Your Own

Independent practice exercises for the objectives targeted in this unit are located in the corresponding Write and Spell on Your Own section of this book (see pp. 375–377).

PART 4

Complementary Skills

I have many flowers, he said,
but the children are the most beautiful flowers of all.

—Oscar Wilde

UNIT CS1 | Prefixes and Suffixes

■ **Root words, prefixes, and suffixes:** Define and discuss root words: "A *root word,* also called a *base word,* is a word or part of a word that conveys the word's essential meaning. Syllables can be added to root words to form new words or to change the meaning of the root. A syllable added to the front of a word is called a *prefix,* and a syllable added to the end of a word is called a *suffix.*"

Example: enjoyable   *en–* is the prefix

                          –joy– is the root word

                          –able is the suffix

> **ON THE BOARD**
>
> unlike   freely   disagreement   misfit

1. Have a student find and circle the words within words on the board.
2. Say, "*Like, free, agree,* and *fit* are root words."
3. Add the following words to the words on the board and have students, in turn, circle the root word in each:

   slowly   helpful   misspelled   eventful   evaluation

4. Have students, in turn, identify the prefixes and suffixes in all the words on the board.

■ **Prefix + root = new word:** "A prefix is a letter or group of letters that comes before a root word and changes or modifies the meaning of the root word."

> **ON THE BOARD**
>
> midweek   export   prepaid   subnormal

1. Have a student underline the root in each word on the board and circle the prefix.

2. Explain, "*Mid–, ex–, pre–,* and *sub–* are prefixes. If you know the meanings of the prefix and the root word, you have a clue to the meaning of the whole word."

mid– = middle	*midweek* = middle of the week
ex– = out of, from	*export* = out of or from the port
pre– = before	*prepaid* = paid before
sub– = under, below	*subnormal* = below normal

3. "If you can spell the prefix and the root word, you should be able to spell the whole word."

ON THE BOARD

mis–   dis–   re–   inter–   semi–

Most dictionaries list prefixes separately. Have the students use a dictionary to find the meaning of each prefix on the board. Students can work singly or in pairs to see who can compile the longest list of words for each prefix.

■ Patterns and hints

Ante– or *anti–, inter–* or *intra–*?
Knowing the meaning of a prefix helps you remember its spelling.

ante = before

antebellum = before the war

anteroom = waiting room, room before the main room

anti = against

antisocial = against or disliking society

antiaircraft	antibody	antifreeze	antitoxin
antibiotic	anticlimax	antiseptic	antitrust

inter = between

interstate = between states

intermarry	international	intersection
intermingle	interracial	

intra = within

intrastate = within the state

intramural	intravenous

Add the whole prefix
Keep the *s* when adding *dis–* or *mis–* to a root word that begins with *s.*

dissatisfy	disservice	misshapen	misspend
dissect	dissimilar	misspell	misstep

Use a single *s* if the root word does not begin with *s*.

disagree	disarm	misfit	mistrust
disappear	dishonest	misprint	misuse

Keep the *n* when adding *un–* to a root word beginning with *n*.

unnatural	unnecessary	unnoticed	unnumbered

Use a single *n* if the root word does not begin with *n*.

uneasy	unequal	unknown	unsafe

- **Rules for spelling suffixes:** Review the following rules for adding a suffix to a root word:

  - Drop *e*—Drop the final *e* before a suffix beginning with a vowel:

    like—likable   use—usable

  - Change *y* to *i*—When adding a suffix to words ending in *y* preceded by a consonant, change the *y* to *i*, except when the suffix begins with *i*:

    rely—reliable—relying

- **Root + suffix = new word:** "A suffix is a letter or group of letters that comes at the end of a word and changes the meaning of the root word." Discuss the meanings of various suffixes and show how they change the meanings of root words.

Suffix	Definition	Root word	Root + suffix	Definition of new word
–ify	to make	solid	solidify	to make solid
–ment	state of	excite	excitement	state of being excited
–ness	state of	kind	kindness	state of being kind
–less	without	worth	worthless	without worth
–able	capable of	accept	acceptable	capable of being accepted
–ful	full of	force	forceful	full of force
–ly	in the manner of	free	freely	in the manner of freedom
–er	increase in degree	hot	hotter	more heat
–est	superlative of adjectives	lucky	luckiest	most lucky

■ **Suffixes and word structure:** The following points can be interesting for students who understand the basics of grammar.

- A suffix can change the tense of a verb or the comparative form of an adjective:

  walk—walked—walking   hot—hotter—hottest

- A suffix can change a word from one part of speech to another.

  Verb to noun: I will *run* in the race. I am the best *runner.*

  Adjective to noun: Jim is *happy. Happiness* is a good feeling.

  Noun to adjective: We hope for *peace.* We want a *peaceful* world.

  Verb to adjective: I *depend* on you. You are *dependable.*

  Noun to verb: I like *harmony.* They *harmonize* well.

  Adjective to adverb: I am *safe* here. I drive *safely.*

■ **Patterns and hints**

–ly or –ally?
Add *–ly* to words ending in *l.*

accidental—accidentally	general—generally
actual—actually	individual—individually
continual—continually	natural—naturally
exceptional—exceptionally	personal—personally
final—finally	successful—successfully

Add *–ally* to words ending in *ic.*

academic—academically	fantastic—fantastically
automatic—automatically	scholastic—scholastically
basic—basically	systematic—systematically

–sede, –ceed, or –cede?
Use *–sede* only for *supersede.*

Use *–ceed* only for *exceed, proceed,* and *succeed.*

Use *–cede* only for the following eight words:

accede	cede	intercede	recede
antecede	concede	precede	secede

–cle or –cal?
–cle is an ending for nouns, as in *bicycle, icicle,* and *uncle.*

–cal is an ending for adjectives, as in *physical, tropical,* and *vertical.*

-able or *-ible*?

Use *-able* in the following instances:

- if the root is a complete word:

  avoid—avoidable   change—changeable

  break—breakable   favor—favorable

- if the root word ends in a long vowel sound:

  abominate—abominable   demonstrate—demonstrable

- if the suffix follows hard *c* (to retain the hard sound of *c*):

  amicable   applicable   despicable   practicable

Use *-ible* in the following instances:

- if the suffix follows *ns* or *ss:*

  accessible   dismissible   responsible

  defensible   permissible   sensible

- if *-ion* can be added to the root word:

  collect—collection—collectible

  corrupt—corruption—corruptible

Latin prefixes and suffixes: Many English words have come to us from other languages, such as Latin, Greek, French, and Spanish. Students who are interested in the origins of words may enjoy forming words that use the following Latin prefixes and suffixes.

Prefix	Root	Suffix
re- = again, back	*-audi-* = hear	*-ion* = state of, act of
con- = with	*-ject-* = throw	*-ence* = state of, act of
contra- = against	*-cede-* = go, yield	*-ible* = able to be
de- = down	*-dict-* = say, tell	*-ary* = belonging to,
dis- = apart	*-tract-* = draw, drag	connected with
in- = not, in, into	*-scribe-* = write	
pre- = before, in advance	*-flex-* = bend	
	-vers- = turn	
	-spect- = look	

Some of the word parts in the preceding lists are combined to form the words below. Each word is followed by the literal Latin meaning and a dictionary definition in parentheses.

concede: go with (admit to be true)

audition: act of hearing (power or sense of hearing; tryout for a play)

reject: throw back (throw away)

detract: drag down (make of less worth)

COMPLEMENTARY SKILLS

describe: write down (write or tell about)
reflex: bend back again (automatic response)
revert: turn back (to come or go back)
prescribe: write in advance (to order or direct)
contrary: connected with being against (opposite)
precedence: going before (going before in time or importance)
inflexible: not able to bend (not easily bent, rigid)

■ Linkage (link a prefix, a root, and a suffix)

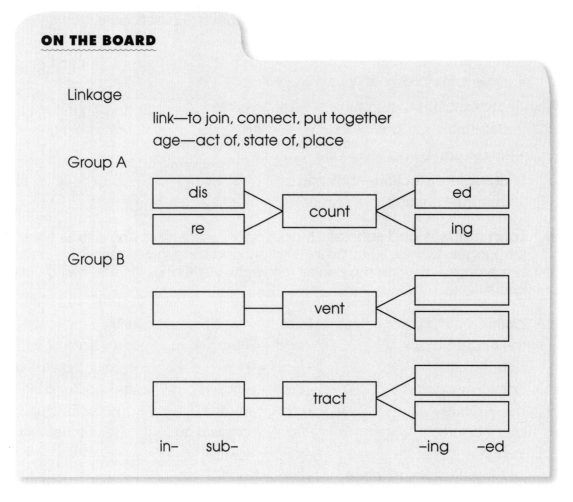

ON THE BOARD

Linkage

link—to join, connect, put together
age—act of, state of, place

Group A

| dis | | | ed |
| re | count | | ing |

Group B

| | vent | | |
| | | | |

| | tract | | |
| | | | |

in-   sub-   -ing   -ed

1. Read the word *linkage* and the definitions for *link* and the suffix *–age*.
2. Discuss the linking together of word parts to form new words.
3. Have a student link the word parts in Group A to make these words: *discounted, discounting, recounted, recounting.*
4. Ask a student volunteer to fill in the empty links in Group B with the prefixes and suffixes listed on the board, making sure the linkages make actual words.
5. Have another student write the words that can be made from each set of links: *invented, inventing, subtracted, subtracting.*
6. Have students refer to lists of prefixes, suffixes, and root words to construct their own links (see p. 183).

■ **Prefixes and suffixes make words grow**

ON THE BOARD

antidisestablishmentarianism

Have the students try to break the word into smaller words and put it back together again:

establish
establishment
disestablishment
disestablishmentarian
disestablishmentarianism
antidisestablishmentarianism

"Now try the same thing with *supercalifragilisticexpialidocious.*"

■ **Prefix and suffix list:** The list of prefixes and suffixes on the following pages can be used for additional activities.

Prefix	Meaning	Example
a–	on, in	afoot, ablaze
ab–	away from	abnormal, absent
ad–	to, toward	admit, adopt
ambi–, amphi–	on both sides	ambidextrous, amphibian
ante–	before, in front	antecedent, anteroom
anti–	against	antiseptic, antifreeze
auto–	self	automobile, automatic
be–	make, on, around	belittle, befriend
bi–	double, two	bicycle, bimonthly
circum–	around	circumference, circumlocution
com–, con–	with, together	complete, connect
contra–, counter–	against	contradict, counteract
de–	reduce, undo	devalue, deface
deci–	ten	decimal, decimeter
demi–	half	demitasse, demigod

COMPLEMENTARY SKILLS

Prefix	Meaning	Example
dis–	not, apart	disagree, disjoint
ex–	out of, away from	export, exception
extra–	beyond	extraterrestrial, extraordinary
fore–	in front of, before	foreground, forefather
hemi–	half	hemisphere
homo–	same	homonym, homogenize
hydro–	water	hydrometer, hydroplane
hyper–	too much, above	hyperactive, hypersensitive
in–, il–, im–, ir–	not, in, within	induct, illegal, implant, irresponsible
inter–	between	international, interstate
intra–	within	intramural, intrastate
kilo–	one thousand	kilogram, kilometer
mal–	bad, ill	malfunction
micro–	small, tiny	microsurgery, microfilm
mis–	wrong	misspell, misbehave
mono–, mon–	single, alone	monoplane, monosyllable
multi–	many	multinational, multivitamin
non–	not	nonstop, nonprofit
poly–	many	polygraph, polygon
post–	after	postwar, postscript
pre–	before	prejudge, precede
pro–	before, forward	project, proceed
quadr–	four	quadruped, quadraphonic
re–	back, again	rebuild, reflex
semi–	half	semifinal, semicircle
sub–	under	subway, submit
tri–	three	triplane, triangle

COMPLEMENTARY SKILLS

Suffix	Meaning	Example
–able, –ible	capable, fit for	agreeable, collectible
–age	act or state of	salvage, leakage
–al, –ial	like	fictional, official
–ance, –ence	state of, quality of	dependence, performance
–ant	one who	occupant, assistant
–ar	like, relating to	circular, spectacular
–ary	connected with	budgetary, parliamentary
–ate	cause to become	activate, domesticate
–dom	state, condition of	wisdom, kingdom
–ed	past	jogged, helped
–en	made of, to make	wooden, lighten
–er	degree of comparison	smarter, faster
–est	most	newest, oldest
–ful	full of	restful, helpful
–fy, –ify	to make	beautify, magnify
–hood	state of being	boyhood, womanhood
–ic	like, made of	poetic, historic
–ing	act of	running, learning
–ion	act or state of	correction, deception
–ish	like, relating to	childish, foolish
–ism	condition, quality of	heroism, capitalism
–ist	a person who does	cyclist, artist
–ity	state of, degree	humanity, unity
–itis	inflammation of	appendicitis, bronchitis
–ive	relating to	active, decorative
–ize	to make, cause to become	motorize, memorize
–less	without	painless, helpless
–let	small	booklet, droplet
–ly	like, in a manner	queenly, suddenly
–ment	state or condition	excitement, amazement
–meter	device for measuring	thermometer, speedometer

COMPLEMENTARY SKILLS

Suffix	Meaning	Example
–ness	state of, condition	kindness, goodness
–or	one who, that which	actor, elevator
–ous, –ious	full of	furious, poisonous
–ship	quality of, state of	leadership, relationship
–some	like, full of	lonesome, troublesome
–ward	toward	northward, backward
–y	action of, like, full of	muddy, wintry, inquiry

Write and Spell on Your Own

Independent practice exercises for the objectives targeted in this unit are located in the corresponding Write and Spell on Your Own section of this book (see pp. 381–385).

UNIT CS2 | Plurals

■ **The simple plural:** Define and discuss the simple singular and plural forms. The *singular* is a word form used to show only one of something, as in *hat, book, bird,* and *hand.* The *plural* is a word form used to show more than one, as in *hats, books, birds,* and *hands.* Direct students' attention to the board, saying, "These are simple plurals. You form the plural of most nouns simply by adding an *–s.*"

ON THE BOARD

I need five pens, four books, three desks, and six folders.

■ **Irregular plurals:** There are several types of exceptions to the basic "add *–s*" rule.

Add *-es* to words ending in *ss, x, z, ch,* and *sh.*

ss	x	ch	sh
class—classes	box—boxes	arch—arches	rash—rashes
cross—crosses	fox—foxes	beach—beaches	wish—wishes
dress—dresses	prefix—prefixes	inch—inches	**z**
glass—glasses	tax—taxes	latch—latches	buzz—buzzes
pass—passes	wax—waxes	patch—patches	waltz—waltzes

Point out that one can hear an extra syllable in the plural form of the preceding words.

Nouns ending in *y*

• If preceded by a consonant, change *y* to *i* and add *–es.*

ally—allies	city—cities	jelly—jellies
army—armies	enemy—enemies	library—libraries
berry—berries	family—families	memory—memories
bully—bullies	ferry—ferries	party—parties
cemetery—cemeteries	fly—flies	penny—pennies
century—centuries	hobby—hobbies	quantity—quantities

- Except for proper names

  Harry—Harrys   Kelly—Kellys   Mary—Marys

- If preceded by a vowel just add –s.

abbey—abbeys	donkey—donkeys	pulley—pulleys
alley—alleys	journey—journeys	ray—rays
attorney—attorneys	key—keys	turkey—turkeys
boy—boys	monkey—monkeys	valley—valleys
chimney—chimneys	play—plays	volley—volleys

Some nouns that end in *f* or *fe* change to *v* or *ve* and add *–s* or *–es.*

calf—calves	life—lives	thief—thieves
elf—elves	loaf—loaves	wife—wives
half—halves	self—selves	wolf—wolves
knife—knives	sheaf—sheaves	
leaf—leaves	shelf—shelves	

Exception: handkerchiefs

The pronunciation of the plural form of the word reflects the change from *f* to *v* (calf—calves).

Nouns ending in *o*

- If preceded by a consonant, usually add *–es* to form the plural.

echo—echoes	hero—heroes	tomato—tomatoes
embargo—embargoes	mosquito—mosquitoes	torpedo—torpedoes
desperado—desperadoes	motto—mottoes	veto—vetoes
fresco—frescoes	potato—potatoes	

- Exceptions that relate to music are usually of Italian origin.

alto—altos	concerto—concertos	solo—solos
banjo—banjos	contralto—contraltos	soprano—sopranos
basso—bassos	piano—pianos	virtuoso—virtuosos
canto—cantos	quarto—quartos	

- Other exceptions

  photo—photos   silo—silos

- If preceded by a vowel, usually add *–s* to form the plural.

cameo—cameos	patio—patios	rodeo—rodeos
embryo—embryos	radio—radios	
folio—folios	ratio—ratios	

- **Plurals that change a word's spelling:** The following irregular plurals involve changes to the root word rather than the addition of a suffix.

  - The spelling of the word itself changes and no *s* is added.

child—children	louse—lice	ox—oxen
foot—feet	mouse—mice	woman—women
goose—geese	man—men	

  - *is* can change to *es* to form the plural.

analysis—analyses	hypothesis—hypotheses	synopsis—synopses
antithesis—antitheses	oasis—oases	thesis—theses
axis—axes	parenthesis—parentheses	

  - *us* can change to *i* to form the plural.

alumnus—alumni	focus—foci	radius—radii
bacillus—bacilli	fungus—fungi	terminus—termini

Compounds

  - Compound nouns that are hyphenated or made up of two words form the plural by adding –*s* to the principal word.

son-in-law—sons-in-law	major general—major generals
attorney-at-law—attorneys-at-law	

  - If a compound noun is one word, the plural is usually formed by adding –*s* to the end of the word.

cupful—cupfuls	handful—handfuls

Letters and numbers

  - Capital letters and numbers (either spelled out or in figures) form the plural by adding –*s*.

three Bs	ones and twos	3s and 4s
the 1880s	PTAs	CODs

  - Abbreviations with periods and lowercase letters used as nouns form the plural by adding an apostrophe and an –*s*.

M.D.'s	Ph.D.'s	a's and b's

  - To avoid misreading, the capital letters *S, A,* and *I* form the plural by adding an apostrophe and –*s*.

S's	A's	I's

Singular form—plural form: Some nouns do not change in the plural form.

deer	gross	moose	sheep	traffic
fish	grouse	reindeer	spaghetti	trout

■ **Variant spellings:** Some dictionaries list two spellings for the plural of a word. The first is usually the preferred spelling. The following are examples of such words:

appendixes—appendices	mackerel—mackerels
bass—basses	memorandums—memoranda
buffalo—buffaloes	moneys—monies
cargoes—cargos	scarves—scarfs
calicoes—calicos	staffs—staves
dominoes—dominos	stilettos—stilettoes
dwarfs—dwarves	tornadoes—tornados
fish—fishes	volcanoes—volcanos
halos—haloes	wharves—wharfs
hooves—hoofs	zeros—zeroes
indexes—indices	

■ **Plural word hunt:** Have students try to find five nouns that begin with each letter of the alphabet and write them in plural form. They can observe or recall objects around them or can use books and dictionaries to generate words. Students can work alone or in pairs to collect the 130 words.

■ **Plural story:** List a group of nouns on the board. Have students, alone or in pairs, make up a story using as many nouns in the plural form as they can. The list should include words that will form simple and irregular plurals.

As an optional activity, have students count the plurals they use in their stories. Score one point for simple plurals (add –s to each word) and two points for irregular plurals (add –es or change the spelling of the word).

Suggested words

ape	baby	class	fish	library	piano
arch	banjo	deer	fox	mouse	radio
ax	beach	ditch	handful	party	wolf

■ **Spelling plurals**

1. Divide the class into two teams.
2. Dictate a singular noun to the first player of one team. Select nouns that form both simple and irregular plurals. You can use the suggested words listed for the previous activity. Enlarge the list by adding words that are suitable for your grade level and include representative words from each of the classes of irregular plurals.
3. The player must spell the word in the plural form and write it on the board. If the student spells the word correctly, the team earns one point. If the spelling is incorrect, the first player on the other team erases the word and tries to spell it correctly.
4. Continue until all the players on both teams have had a turn. The team with the most points wins.

Write and Spell on Your Own

Independent practice exercises for the objectives targeted in this unit are located in the corresponding Write and Spell on Your Own section of this book (see pp. 387–388).

COMPLEMENTARY SKILLS

Apostrophes for Contractions Versus Possessives

The apostrophe is a mark (') used to show the following:

- contractions—a shortening of a word, a word group, or number by leaving out a sound, letter, or number. The apostrophe stands in for the missing letters or digits.

  he's for *he is*   class of *'88* for *class of 1988*

- possessives—the case of a noun or a pronoun that shows possession (belonging)

  the *student's desk* for the *desk of the student*

Contractions

ON THE BOARD

I'm coming.

She's ready.

That's mine.

1. "A contraction is a shortened form of one or more words that is written and spoken as one word. An apostrophe is a mark used to show that a letter or letters are missing."
2. Read the sentences on the board. Have students, in turn, underline each contraction and write the words from which it is formed.
3. Contrast contractions and abbreviations.

   - An *abbreviation* is used only in writing. The abbreviation is read and spoken as a whole word.

     Mr.—Mister   ft.—feet   lb.—pound

   - A *contraction* is used in both speaking and writing. The contracted form is pronounced differently from the original words.

     didn't —did not   I'm —I am   won't —will not

■ **Hear one, say two, spell one:** Dictate the following phrases. Have students, in turn, do the following:

1. Listen to the phrase and repeat and spell the contraction out loud.
2. Say the two words from which the contraction is formed.
3. Write the contraction on the board.

Suggested phrases

She's here now.	Don't close the door.
You shouldn't go.	It isn't ripe.
We can't leave.	Here's my book.
We're on our way.	What's for dinner?
Where's the boat?	Let's go now.
They haven't finished.	We'd love to come.
They'll call you soon.	They'd like to play.
I'd like to drive.	You've won the prize.

Word List

Use the following contractions for additional activities and exercises.

's
Replace the *i* in *is* with an apostrophe.

he is—he's	that is—that's	what is—what's
she is—she's	it is—it's	when is—when's
here is—here's	who is—who's	where is—where's
there is—there's	how is—how's	

n't
Replace the *o* in *not* with an apostrophe.

are not—aren't	do not—don't	must not—mustn't
cannot—can't	had not—hadn't	was not—wasn't
could not—couldn't	have not—haven't	should not—shouldn't
did not—didn't	is not—isn't	would not—wouldn't

'd
Replace *woul* in *would* with an apostrophe.

I would—I'd	you would—you'd	who would—who'd
he would—he'd	they would—they'd	
she would—she'd	we would—we'd	

've

Replace the *ha* in *have* with an apostrophe.

I have—I've	they have—they've	could have—could've
you have—you've	we have—we've	should have—should've

'll

Replace the *wi* in *will* with an apostrophe.

I will—I'll	we will—we'll	what will —what'll
he will—he'll	you will—you'll	where will—where'll
she will—she'll	that will—that'll	who will—who'll
they will—they'll	there will—there'll	

're

Replace the *a* in *are* with an apostrophe.

you are—you're	they are—they're	we are—we're

Miscellaneous

let us—let's	I am—I'm
of the clock—o'clock	will not—won't

Possessives

ON THE BOARD

the book of the student =

the student, his book

the student's book

1. Read the phrases on the board.
2. "Both phrases tell us that a book belongs to a student. The student possesses a book. The phrase *the student, his book* sounds awkward, but *his,* placed before the object, was once used to show possession; *hi* was replaced by an apostrophe, and we now say, '*the student's book.*'"
3. "We have used the apostrophe in contractions. It is also important to be able to use the apostrophe to form the possessive."

■ Apostrophe or apostrophe + *s*

- Add apostrophe plus *s* to the singular form of the noun. Add only the apostrophe if the plural form of the noun ends in *s*.

Singular possessive	Plural possessive
one dog—the dog's bone	two dogs—the dogs' bone
one sister—her sister's car	two sisters—her sisters' car
Amy—Amy Dickens's uncle	Amy and Jane—the Dickenses' uncle

Exceptions: Jesus' birth, Moses' journey

- Add apostrophe plus *s* if the plural form of the noun does not end in *s*.

  the children's toys   the geese's feathers   the women's tools

■ Possessive pronouns

- Do not add an apostrophe to possessive pronouns ending in *s*.

  his   hers   its   ours   theirs   whose   yours

- Add apostrophe plus *s* to the following indefinite pronouns:

  another's   anybody's   everybody's   one's   other's

■ Multiple possessives

- Add apostrophe plus *s* to the last person named if two or more people together possess an item or a group of items.

  Fran and Bill's boat   Jane and Jim's pictures

- Add apostrophe plus *s* to each person if each person possesses a separate item.

  Fran's and Bill's boats   Jane's and Jim's pictures

■ Abbreviations: Add apostrophe plus *s* after the period in an abbreviation.

John Jones Sr.'s grandchildren   Clean Gas Co.'s new rates

Write and Spell on Your Own

Independent practice exercises for the objectives targeted in this unit are located in the corresponding Write and Spell on Your Own section of this book (see pp. 389–391).

Abbreviations

Titles

Mr.—Mister
Mrs.—Mistress
Ms.—Miss or Mistress
Dr.—Doctor
M.D.—Doctor of Medicine
Ph.D.—Doctor of Philosophy

Pres.—President
V.P.—Vice President
Gov.—Governor
Sec.—Secretary
Treas.—Treasurer

Jr.—Junior
Sr.—Senior
Gen.—General
Adm.—Admiral
Sgt.—Sergeant

Time

Jan.—January
Feb.—February
Mar.—March
April—(no abbr.)
May—(no abbr.)
June—(no abbr.)

July—(no abbr.)
Aug.—August
Sept.—September
Oct.—October
Nov.—November
Dec.—December

Sun.—Sunday
Mon.—Monday
Tue.—Tuesday
Wed.—Wednesday
Thurs.—Thursday
Fri.—Friday
Sat.—Saturday

sec.—second
min.—minute
hr.—hour
wk.—week
mo.—month
yr.—year

A.M.—before noon (ante meridiem)
P.M.—after noon (post meridiem)
A.D.—in the year of our Lord (anno Domini)
B.C.—before Christ
DST—daylight savings time

Measurement

bu.—bushel
cu.—cubic
doz.—dozen
ft.—foot, feet
gal.—gallon

in.—inch
lb.—pound
mi.—mile
mph.—miles per hour
no.—number

oz.—ounce
pt.—pint
qt.—quart
tbs.—tablespoon
tsp.—teaspoon

yd.—yard
ht.—height
wt.—weight

Note that metric measurements do not use periods.

cc—cubic centimeter   kg—kilogram   mg—milligram
cm—centimeter   km—kilometer   mm—millimeter
g—gram   l—liter   m—meter

Places

Ave.—avenue   St.—street   Rd.—road
Blvd.—boulevard   Co.—company   P.O.—post office
R.R.—railroad   Bldg.—building   Hwy.—highway

Spell Together

■ **Make it shorter**

> **ON THE BOARD**
>
> Meet me on Sun., Oct. 9, 2000, at 2 P.M. at 213 High St.
>
> Bring one pt. of milk, two doz. eggs, and three pkgs. of cookies.

1. Have a student read the message on the board and underline the abbreviated words.

2. Define and discuss abbreviations: "An abbreviation is a word that is spoken as a whole word but is written in a shortened form."

> **ON THE BOARD**
>
> gallon __**gal.**__   inch _____   president _____
>
> foot _____   height _____   teaspoon _____

1. Have students volunteer to cross out the letters you would eliminate to write the abbreviations of the words on the board. Note that the abbreviation is followed by a period.

   Exceptions:

   • Metric system abbreviations are unpunctuated.

   meter—m   kilogram—kg

- Two-letter state abbreviations used by the U.S. Postal Service are not followed by periods.

  Maryland—MD   California—CA

2. List abbreviations containing letters that do not appear in the original word.

  lb.—pound   oz.—ounce   no.—number

Activities with abbreviations

1. Have students compile lists of abbreviations in one or more of the following categories:

   a. time (ex. hour—hr.)
   b. measurement (ex. inch—in.)
   c. title (ex. doctor—Dr.)
   d. states (ex. Maryland—MD)
   e. places (ex. Avenue—Ave.)

2. List the initials of famous people, places, or organizations. How many can the students identify?

   JFK—John Fitzgerald Kennedy   IBM—International Business Machines
   FDR—Franklin Delano Roosevelt   ABC—American Broadcasting Company
   IRS—Internal Revenue Service   CBS—Columbia Broadcasting System
   UN—United Nations   NBC—National Broadcasting Company
   U.S.A.—United States of America   FBI—Federal Bureau of Investigation
   U.K.—United Kingdom   CIA—Central Intelligence Agency
   D.C.—District of Columbia   Two-letter state abbreviations

3. Students can write messages to each other using as many abbreviations as they can.

4. The classified section of a newspaper contains many abbreviations. Have students read the employment and real-estate ads and rewrite them without the abbreviations. Students can also write their own ads for items they would like to sell or trade.

5. Select the abbreviations you would like your students to learn. Have them match a column of abbreviations to a column of nonabbreviated words.

6. Introduce acronyms. An *acronym* is a new word made from the initial letters of a term, phrase, or organization. Acronyms are not spelled with periods. Many of the initials of organizations presented in number 2 above are acronyms.

   AWOL   Absent Without Official Leave
   AID   Agency for International Development
   FAA   Federal Aviation Administration
   FEMA   Federal Emergency Management Agency
   HUD   Department of Housing and Urban Development
   INTERPOL   International Criminal Police Organization
   JAG   Judge Advocate General

NAFTA	North American Free Trade Agreement
NASA	National Aeronautics and Space Administration
NATO	North Atlantic Treaty Organization
NOW	National Organization for Women
OPEC	Organization of Petroleum Exporting Countries
SEC	Securities and Exchange Commission
START	Strategic Arms Reduction Talks
UNICEF	United Nations Children's Fund
UNESCO	United Nations Educational, Scientific, and Cultural Organization
WHO	World Health Organization

■ **Patterns and hints**

1. Radio and television stations, well-known organizations, companies, government agencies, and unions may be abbreviated without periods.

   WABC   IBM   WU   HUD   AFL-CIO   GE   IRS   FBI

2. Spell out *United States* when used as a noun but abbreviate when used as an adjective.

   citizen of the United States—U.S. citizen

Write and Spell on Your Own

Independent practice exercises for the objectives targeted in this unit are located in the corresponding Write and Spell on Your Own section of this book (see pp. 393–394).

Write and Spell on Your Own

PART 1

Spelling Sounds

UNIT 1 | /a/

Read the Words

Read each word. Focus on /a/ as in *cat*.

lap	dad	wax	pal	cat	bag
fat	rat	cab	zap	bat	sat
nag	can	van	sad	cap	rap

Complete a Word

Make a short *a* (/a/) word by adding beginning consonants.

____**b**___ag   _____an   _____ap   _____ax

_____at   _____am   _____ad   _____ab

Make a short *a* (/a/) word by adding ending consonants.

ha__**t**____   fa_____   pa_____   ba_____

ra_____   sa_____   ca_____   ma_____

Write and Spell on Your Own

Words in the Bag

Make as many words as you can by using the letters below and the letter *a*.

Write the words in the bag.

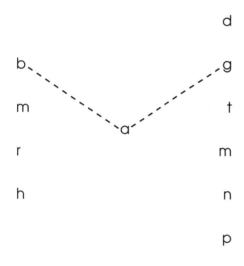

bag

Use some of the words in the bag to write three sentences.

_____

_____

_____

Challenge: A String of Words

Change one letter at a time to make a new word. Keep the /a/ in each word.

bad　　**bag**　　**tag**　　___a___　　___a___　　___a___

___a___　　___a___　　___a___　　___a___　　___a___　　___a___

___a___　　___a___　　___a___

© 2007, 2000, 1984 by Frances Bloom and Deborah Bloom Coates

Write and Spell on Your Own

Wow!

Use the pictures to help you fill in the blanks with short /a/ words.

I had a c_____,

a very sad c_____.

His tail did not w_____

and he had no h_____.

He went to my d_____.

On Dad's head was a h_____.

The c_____ s_____ on Dad's l_____.

The cat saw Dad's h_____.

"Wow!" said the c_____.

"I can get Dad's h_____!"

Now Dad is s_____.

The cat has his h_____.

Write and Spell on Your Own

Rhyme Time

Find a word to rhyme with *at*.

1. The fat cat saw the _____**rat**_____.

2. The lad will pat his _____.

3. The hat is on the _____.

4. I saw Pat with his _____.

Complete a Rhyme

Use the answers to complete the rhymes below.

A fat _____**cat**_____

saw a _____

on a _____.

Said the _____,

"I will hit the _____

with my _____."

But the _____

got under the _____.

© 2007, 2000, 1984 by Frances Bloom and Deborah Bloom Coates

Write and Spell on Your Own

A Hat Full of Words

Find some words and make some words.

1. How many words can you find in the hat? You should find 20 or more words. Write the words you found in the spaces below:

_____ _____ _____ _____ _____

_____ _____ _____ _____ _____

_____ _____ _____ _____ _____

_____ _____ _____ _____ _____

2. Fill each empty space with a consonant to make your own words.

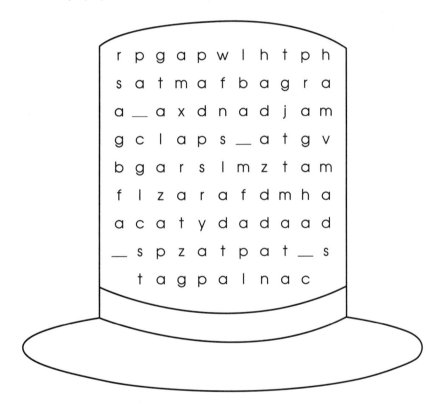

```
r  p  g  a  p  w  l  h  t  p  h
s  a  t  m  a  f  b  a  g  r  a
a __ a  x  d  n  a  d  j  a  m
g  c  l  a  p  s __ a  t  g  v
b  g  a  r  s  l  m  z  t  a  m
f  l  z  a  r  a  f  d  m  h  a
a  c  a  t  y  d  a  d  a  a  d
__ s  p  z  a  t  p  a  t __ s
   t  a  g  p  a  l  n  a  c
```

Use the words in the hat to complete the sentences.

1. Dad had a _____.

2. The _____ is in a _____.

3. The _____ had a _____.

Write and Spell on Your Own

/a/ **Puzzle**

Complete the puzzle with /a/ words using the clues below.

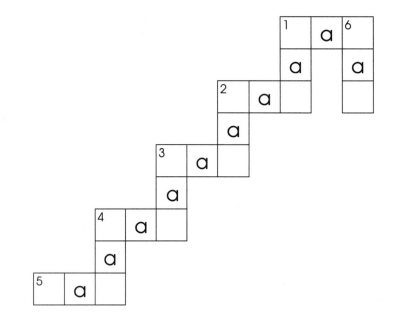

Across

Down

1. __a__

2. __a__

3. __a__

4. __a__

5. __a__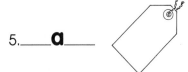

1. __a__

2. __a__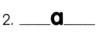

3. __a__

4. __a__

6. __a__

Write and Spell on Your Own

UNIT 2 | /i/

Read the Words

Read each word. Focus on /i/ as in *big*.

bid	fix	lip	jig	pit	dip
fin	nip	tin	six	yip	in
dig	hid	pin	zip	wig	rim

Complete a Word

Make a short *i* (/i/) word by adding a beginning consonant in each blank.

_____ig   _____ip   _____im   _____id

_____it   _____ix   _____ib   _____in

Make a short *i* (/i/) word by adding ending consonants.

hi_____   wi_____   bi_____   fi_____

ri_____   li_____   di_____   ni_____

Write and Spell on Your Own

/a/ or /i/?

Put an *a* or an *i* in the box to make a word.

1. c [ ] n   d [ ] g   l [ ] t

2. m [ ] p   h [ ] p   m [ ] n

3. j [ ] m   p [ ] g   r [ ] b

4. c [ ] t   r [ ] n   d [ ] p

5. r [ ] t   s [ ] d   v [ ] n

Write and Spell on Your Own

Change a Letter

See how many new words you can make by changing the last letter of the following words. You can find at least two words to write on every line.

1. bag __**bad, ban, bat**_____

2. fin _____

3. hip _____

4. dim _____

5. hat _____

6. ran _____

7. man _____

8. wit _____

A String of Words

Change one letter at a time to make a new word. Keep the /i/ in each word.

pin   **pit**   **sit**   ___ i ___   ___ i ___   ___ i ___

___ i ___   ___ i ___   ___ i ___

Word Shapes

Match words and shapes to make a rhyme.

A big fat pig

had a ___**wig**___

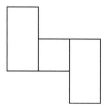

and a rag

in a _____

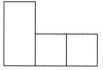

and a pin

in a _____

and a lid

that he _____.

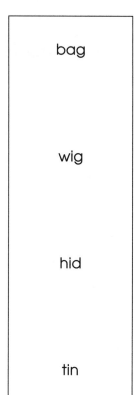

bag

wig

hid

tin

Tick-Tack-Tuck

Tuck a letter in the empty corners to complete the words in the squares.
Each letter must make a word both across and down.

l	i	t
i	TICK TACK TUCK	i
d	i	**p**

r	i	
i	TICK TACK TUCK	i
	i	g

	i	t
a	TICK TACK TUCK	a
d	i	

h	i	
i	TICK TACK TUCK	a
	a	p

© 2007, 2000, 1984 by Frances Bloom and Deborah Bloom Coates

Write and Spell on Your Own

Categories

A. Pick the short *i* (/i/) word that goes with each group of words.

1. large, tall, great _____ **big** _____

2. on, under, over _____

3. top, cover, cap _____

4. tear, cut, break _____

| rip |
| big |
| in |
| lid |

B. Unscramble the letters to make a word.

hpi   xis   gpi   pli

_____   _____   **pig**   _____

C. Put the words you made in the correct group.

1. cow, horse, chicken _____

2. three, eight, four _____

3. nose, eye, cheek _____

4. elbow, knee, ankle _____

Write and Spell on Your Own

/i/ Puzzle

Across

2. Not her, but _____.

3. Not out, but _____.

5. Not small, but _____.

Down

1. Not to lose, but to _____.

2. Not to miss, but to _____.

4. Not to break, but to _____.

Who Can Do the Opposite?

Write a complete sentence to tell "Who can do it?"

1. If I break the bat, who can fix it?

_____ can _____ the bat.

2. If I lose the game, who can win it?

_____ can _____.

3. If I miss the ball, who can hit it?

_____.

© 2007, 2000, 1984 by Frances Bloom and Deborah Bloom Coates

Write and Spell on Your Own

UNIT 3 | /o/

Read the Words

Read each word. Focus on /o/ as in *hot*.

cod	fox	lot	mom	ox	pod
pop	jog	sod	tot	lob	cop
bob	hop	sox	sop	bog	cog

Complete a Word

Make a short *o* (/o/) word by adding beginning consonants.

_____ot   _____og   _____ob

_____ox   _____od   _____op

Make a short *o* (/o/) word by adding ending consonants.

jo_____   po_____   to_____   bo_____

ro_____   fo_____   do_____   mo_____

Write and Spell on Your Own

Unit 3: /o/

One or More Than One?

Write the correct word next to the picture.
Remember to add an *s* if you see more than one.

 1. _____

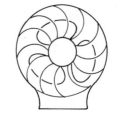 6. _____

 2. _____

 7. _____

 3. _____

 8. _____

 4. _____

 9. _____

 5. _____

 10. _____

SPELLING SOUNDS

© 2007, 2000, 1984 by Frances Bloom and Deborah Bloom Coates

Write and Spell on Your Own

Picture Puzzle

Complete the puzzle with *a, o,* or *i.* Then match the puzzle to the picture.

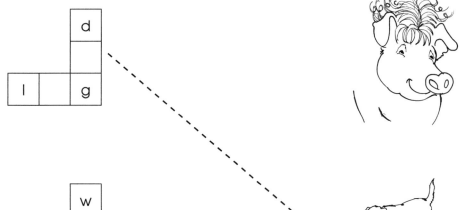

1.

	d
l	g

2.

	w
p	g

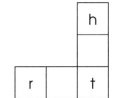

3.

	h
r	t

1. The _____ is on the _____.

2. The _____ is on the _____.

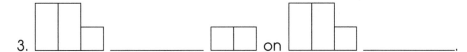

3. _____ on _____.

Write and Spell on Your Own

Solve the Riddles

Unscramble these /o/ words to help you solve the riddles.

opm   tpo   fxo   obx

1. You can open me
   and close me
   and put me away.
   You can put things in me.

   I am a __**box**__.

2. I will wash your floor
   and make it shine.
   You have to push me.

   I am a _____.

3. I look like a little red dog
   with a long bushy tail.
   I live in a den.

   I am a _____.

4. You can cook in me.
   I will get hot.
   I will shine when you wash me.

   I am a _____.

Tick-Tack-Tuck

Tuck a letter in the empty corners to complete the words in the squares.
Each letter must make a word both across and down.

h	o	**p**		c	o			r	o			h	o	
o	TICK TACK TUCK	o		o	TICK TACK TUCK	o		i	TICK TACK TUCK	i		i	TICK TACK TUCK	a
g	o	**t**			o	p			o				a	

Write and Spell on Your Own

© 2007, 2000, 1984 by Frances Bloom and Deborah Bloom Coates

Lunchtime

What did the dog have for lunch? Follow the maze to find out.

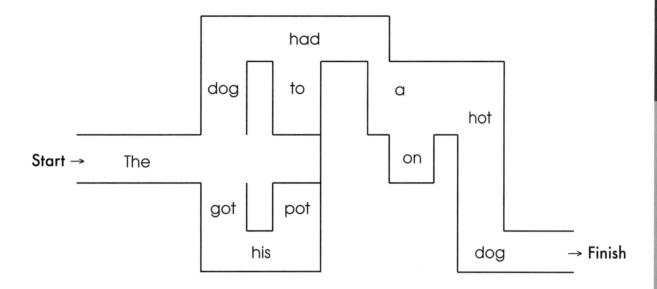

Complete the sentence to write your answer.

The dog

Write and Spell on Your Own

/o/ Puzzle

In this puzzle, there is an *o* in the middle of every word except one. Some words have two meanings. Watch for these words. They are used twice.

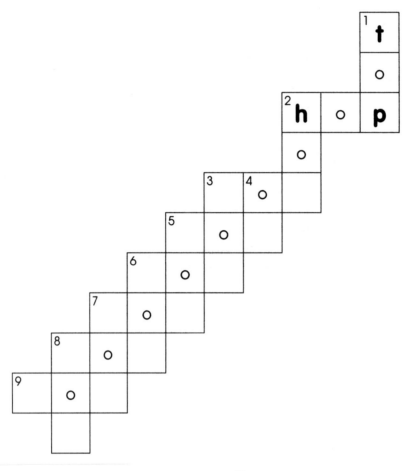

Across

2. jump on one foot
3. a dish for cooking
5. a stiff-sided container
6. sponge or string on a stick used to wash a floor
7. a bushy-tailed wild animal
8. a spinning toy
9. a pet that barks and wags its tail

Down

1. opposite of bottom
2. opposite of cold
3. a sudden burst; another name for Dad
4. a large animal that pulls loads
5. to fight in a ring
6. wipe or wash a floor
7. thick, cloudy air
8. a small child

Write a silly sentence that uses some of the /o/ words in the puzzle.

_____

_____

Write and Spell on Your Own

UNIT 4 | /u/

Read the Words

Read each word. Focus on /u/ as in *fun*.

bun	cub	cup	dud	gum	hug
nun	jut	lug	mud	pun	rut
tug	up	cud	pug	sum	tug

Complete a Word

Make a short *u* (/u/) word by adding beginning consonants.

_____un   _____ug   _____ut   _____um

_____ud   _____ub   _____up

Make a short *u* (/u/) word by adding ending consonants.

gu_____   bu_____   fu_____   hu_____

ju_____   mu_____   ru_____   cu_____

Write and Spell on Your Own

SPELLING SOUNDS

Different Letters—Different Words

Change the vowel to *u*.

Change the first letter of the word you made for more new words.

1. bad	2. not	3. cab
bud	_____	_____
cud	_____	_____
dud	_____	_____
mud	_____	_____

4. jig	5. fin	6. him
_____	_____	_____
_____	_____	_____
_____	_____	_____
_____	_____	_____

Bug in a _____?

Where is the bug?

Connect the letters in alphabetical order to see where the bug is.

Finish the sentence to tell where the bug is.

Where is the bug?

The ___ ___ ___ is ___ ___ the ___ ___ ___.

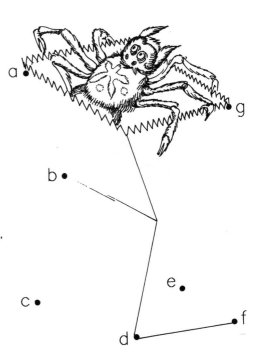

Write and Spell on Your Own

How Are They Alike?

Write the correct short *u* word next to each picture.

1. __bus__

2. _____

3. _____

4. _____

5. _____

6. _____

7. _____

8. _____

Write the words for things you find inside a house.

_____ _____ _____ _____ _____

Write the words for things you find outside a house.

_____ _____ _____ _____ _____

Tick-Tack-Tuck

Tuck a letter in the empty corners to complete the words in the squares.
Each letter must make a word both across and down.

h	u	**t**
u	TICK TACK TUCK	u
m	u	**g**

	u	b
u	TICK TACK TUCK	u
n	u	

c	a	
u	TICK TACK TUCK	i
	a	t

r	a	
i	TICK TACK TUCK	a
	u	g

Write and Spell on Your Own

What Is It?

1. first letter of

2. second letter of

3. third letter of

1. $\underline{\textbf{f}}$ $\underline{\textbf{u}}$ $\underline{\textbf{n}}$
      1   2   3

1. first letter of

2. second letter of

3. third letter of

2. _____ _____ _____
      1   2   3

1. first letter of

2. second letter of

3. third letter of

3. _____ _____ _____
      1   2   3

Use the words you made to complete this sentence.

It was _____**fun**_____ to _____ off of the _____.
          1   2   3

Now complete this sentence. Tell what is fun for you.

It is fun to _____.

Write and Spell on Your Own

Word Shapes

Please take the time
to match words and shapes to make a rhyme.

1. He hid a [n | u | t]

[i | n] the [h | u | t]

in

nut

hut

2.

in the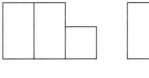

pot

is

It

not

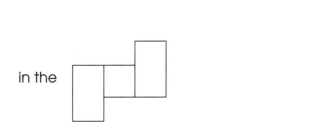

3.

the

Put

on

pot

top

the

Write and Spell on Your Own

Before, After, in Between

Write the letter of the alphabet that comes *before* each of these letters.

__c__ d   _____h   _____k   _____p

_____t   _____w   _____x   _____z

_____s   _____m   _____u   _____e

Write the letter in the alphabet that comes *after* each of these letters.

a__b__   y_____   q_____   d_____

b_____   f_____   v_____   n_____

c_____   r_____   g_____   l_____

Write the letter in the alphabet that comes *in between* each of these letters.

f__g__h   a_____c   j_____l   n_____p

g_____i   l_____n   v_____x   m_____o

d_____f   x_____z   r_____t   o_____q

ABC Mix-Up

Put the words in the following sentences in ABC order using the first letter of each word.

1. ran Zak to Pat _____

2. in cat the a van hid _____

3. yams cub up a digs big _____

Write and Spell on Your Own

UNIT 5 | /e/

Read the Words

Read each word. Focus on /e/ as in *pet*.

bed	get	jet	yes	red	vet
pep	net	met	hen	den	fed
bet	wed	let	web	hem	wet

Complete a Word

Make a short *e* (/e/) word by adding beginning consonants.

_____ed   _____eg   _____en   _____et

_____es   _____ep   _____eb

Make a short *e* (/e/) word by adding ending consonants.

pe_____   le_____   te_____   we_____

be_____   fe_____   ye_____   ve_____

Go to the Bank

A. Pick the short *e* (/e/) word that goes with each group of words.

1. pencil, paper, _____   red

2. blue, yellow, _____   jet

3. duck, goose, _____   leg

4. train, boat, _____   hen

5. arm, head, _____   pen

B. Complete each sentence with an /e/ word.

1. The floor gets w_____ when you mop it.

2. Five plus five equals t_____.

3. You can take your sick p_____ to the v_____.

4. I sleep in a big b_____.

Write and Spell on Your Own

Riddles

Finish each riddle with a short *e* word.

1. You can sleep in me.
   I'm soft and warm.

   I am a __**bed**__.

2. I am a color in a sunset.
   I am the color of a stoplight.

   I am _____.

3. A spider makes me.
   I trap bugs.

   I am a _____.

4. I can fly high in the sky.
   I can go very fast.

   I am a _____.

5. I am a number.
   I am 5 + 5.

   I am _____.

6. I take care of animals.
   I am a doctor.

   I am a _____.

Tick-Tack-Tuck

Tuck a letter in the empty corners to complete the words in the squares.
Make words both across and down.

h	e	m
e	TICK TACK TUCK	e
n	e	t

l	e	
e	TICK TACK TUCK	e
	e	n

p	e	
i	TICK TACK TUCK	o
	a	

w	i	
i	TICK TACK TUCK	u
	e	t

© 2007, 2000, 1984 by Frances Bloom and Deborah Bloom Coates

Write and Spell on Your Own

Hen in a Pen

Unscramble the rhyming short *e* words to complete the rhyming story.

nhe __**hen**__   pne _____   nem _____   tne _____

evt _____   twe _____   def _____   dbe _____

gbe _____   gle _____

There was an old ___**hen**___ who hated her _____ and so stayed out in

the cold. They called the _____. He said, "Don't let her get _____,

make sure she is _____, and put her to _____."

The men all did _____. They pulled on her _____, but still that old

_____ stayed out of the _____. Then finally the _____ stared

hard at the _____ and counted to _____ and off she went to her

_____.

What Would You Do?

1. Who would beg you to come in?

   _____ would beg me to come in.

2. What would you do if you did not want to come in?

   I would _____.

© 2007, 2000, 1984 by Frances Bloom and Deborah Bloom Coates

Write and Spell on Your Own

Analogies

Complete the analogies with short *e* words.

1. hand | arm
   foot | **leg**

5. hands | two
   fingers | _____

2. lead | pencil
   ink | _____

6. down | up
   no | _____

3. desert | dry
   ocean | _____

7. go | green
   stop | _____

4. girls | boys
   women | _____

8. bird | nest
   spider | _____

Write and Spell on Your Own

UNIT 6 | Short Vowel Review

Read the Words

Read each word. Focus on the vowel in the middle.

bag	bat	dad	nag	yak	wax
bin	hip	fix	jig	pip	wig
bob	fox	pod	cog	lob	rot
jug	pug	gut	nun	did	rut
pep	yen	bet	hem	vex	wed

Change the Vowel

How many new words can you make?

1. pot   **pat**   **pet**   **pit** _____

2. bag _____ _____ _____ _____

3. hut _____ _____ _____

4. bed _____ _____ _____

5. jog _____ _____ _____

6. pin _____ _____ _____

Write and Spell on Your Own

Three from One

Complete the triangle by adding one consonant to the vowel to make three new words.

New Words

1.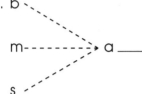
b
m ----→ a ___
s

___**bad**___

___**mad**___

___**sad**___

2.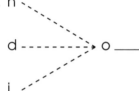
h
d ----→ o ___
j

_____

_____

_____

3.
t
h ----→ e ___
m

_____

_____

_____

4.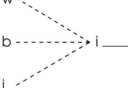
w
b ----→ i ___
j

_____

_____

_____

5.
b
h ----→ u ___
t

_____

_____

_____

Write and Spell on Your Own

Pick a Vowel

Replace the symbols in each sentence with the letters they stand for.

a = △   e = ▢   i = ◯   o = ◇   u = ⬡

1. B▢n h◯d the b◇x under the t⬡b.

2. J◯m h△d a b◯g b△g of g⬡m.

3. T▢n m▢n g◇t the f◇x into the p▢n.

4. B◇b d◯d n◇t see h◯s ch⬡m.

Challenge: No Symbols!

Just think of a vowel that will complete the sentence. If you can think of a silly sentence that makes sense, just go for it!

1. J___m h___d the h___t under the r___g.

2. The b___g s___t on t___p of the b___g w___b.

Write and Spell on Your Own

Make It Rhyme

Write a synonym for each word in the parentheses.

1. Look at the cat

   run for his _____. (cap)

2. Can a _____ (hog)

   dance a jig?

3. Over the mop

   we will _____. (jump)

4. He fell on his hip

   and his shirt he did _____. (tear)

5. I stuffed the old rag

   into the _____. (sack)

6. Do you think a pup

   can drink from a _____? (mug)

Make Your Own Rhyme

Use each group of words to make your own rhyme.

1. sun   run   fun

   __Let's run in the sun__

   __And have some fun.__

2. jug   bug   rug

   _____

   _____

3. fox   sox   box

   _____

   _____

© 2007, 2000, 1984 by Frances Bloom and Deborah Bloom Coates

Write and Spell on Your Own

Antonym Sentences

Complete each sentence with a word that is the opposite of the word in *italics*.

1. I'm *cold,* but you're ____**hot**____.

2. Mary said *no,* but Tom said _____.

3. Turn the water *off,* and turn the lights _____.

4. The dog is *thin,* and the cat is _____.

5. I'm *happy,* but you are _____.

6. Sometimes we *lose,* and sometimes we _____.

7. What goes _____ must come *down.*

8. When I go *out,* you can come _____.

9. My hands are *dry,* but my feet are _____.

10. You can *stand,* and I will _____.

Scrambled Sentences

Unscramble the words to make a sentence.

1. on rug the wet got The pup

   _____

2. mop get a Bud ran to big

   _____

3. wet rid that Mom of got rug

   _____

How Are They Different? How Are They Alike?

Classify the following words into two groups. All of the words in each group should be alike in some way.

ham	cat	bun	nut	jam	pig
fox	gum	bug	dog	rat	yam

_____ _____   _____ _____

_____ _____   _____ _____

_____ _____   _____ _____

Tick-Tack-Tuck

Tuck a letter in the empty squares to complete the words. Make words both across and down.

r	**a**	t
i	TICK TACK TUCK	**a**
d	**i**	p

b		g
	TICK TACK TUCK	
n		t

h		d
	TICK TACK TUCK	
t		g

p		n
	TICK TACK TUCK	
t		p

Write and Spell on Your Own

UNIT 7 | /sh/ /ch/ /th/ /wh/

Change a Letter—Change a Word

Add a letter to change each consonant into a consonant digraph. Write the new word in the blank.

Digraphs

sh as in *ship, shop, gosh*   ch as in *chip, chat*

th as in *this, that, with*   th as in *thin, thug, bath*

wh as in *whip, when*

1. bat**h**   **bath**   9. ___hen   _____

2. ___hat   _____   10. ___hip   _____

3. ___hop   _____   11. ___hem   _____

4. ___hut   _____   12. pat___   _____

5. mat___   _____   13. ___his   _____

6. ___hen   _____   14. ___hot   _____

7. ___hum   _____   15. gas___   _____

8. wit___   _____   16. ___hug   _____

Scrambled Synonyms

Unscramble the letters in Column B to find the synonyms for the words in Column A. (*Hint:* All the scrambled words have a consonant digraph.)

A	B	Synonym
1. money	ashc	**cash**
2. plate	idsh	_____
3. store	shpo	_____
4. boat	siph	_____
5. close	tuhs	_____
6. slim	inth	_____
7. arithmetic	htam	_____
8. trail	paht	_____
9. talk	caht	_____
10. hut	edsh	_____
11. run	hads	_____
12. quiet	uhsh	_____
13. flake	ihcp	_____
14. hope	iswh	_____
15. clunk	uhtd	_____

Write and Spell on Your Own

One Small Wish

Complete each word with *sh, ch,* or *th* and find out what would make the following wishes.

1. A _____ip would wish for a cookie.

2. A la_____ would wish for an eye.

3. A di_____ would wish for some food.

4. A ba_____ would wish for some soap.

5. A _____in would wish for a face.

6. A _____op would wish for customers.

7. A _____ug would wish for a choo-choo train.

8. A ga_____ would wish for a bandage.

9. A sa_____ would wish for a dress.

10. A fi_____ would wish for a pond.

11. A _____ip would wish for an ocean.

What would you wish for?

_____

_____

My Wish

Write a letter to a friend. Tell your friend which of the following you would wish for and why.

a chum   a bath   a fish   a shop   cash

Write and Spell on Your Own

Questions

Complete the following questions with a *wh* question word. Answer the questions with a complete sentence.

1. __**What**__ is your name? _____

2. _____ is your birthday? _____

3. _____ do you live? _____

4. _____ of the U.S. presidents do you most admire?

_____

5. _____ subject is easiest for you?

_____

6. _____ of your subjects do you like the least?

_____

7. _____ makes you feel happy?

_____

8. _____ would you like to visit?

_____

9. _____ is your best friend?

_____

Use the *wh* question words to make up your own questions.

You can do the following:

1. Ask an older person about your town 20 years ago.

2. Ask your parents about their childhoods.

3. Ask your teacher about his or her experiences in your school.

4. Interview a classmate running for a school office.

5. Use the results of the questions to write a class newspaper.

Write and Spell on Your Own

Where Is Dad?

Connect the words in alphabetical order to see where Dad is.

Where is Dad? Dad is on a _____.

chop •   • fish

Start: ash •   bath •   hush •   • mesh

zap •

which •   • this

Tick-Tack-Tuck

Tuck a consonant digraph in the empty corners to complete the words in the squares. Make words both across and down.

wh	i	**ch**
e	TICK TACK TUCK	i
n	a	p

	r	a
u	TICK TACK TUCK	o
	u	t

	i	s
e	TICK TACK TUCK	a
m	a	

	o	p
u	TICK TACK TUCK	a
m	a	

Write and Spell on Your Own

Consonant Digraph Puzzle

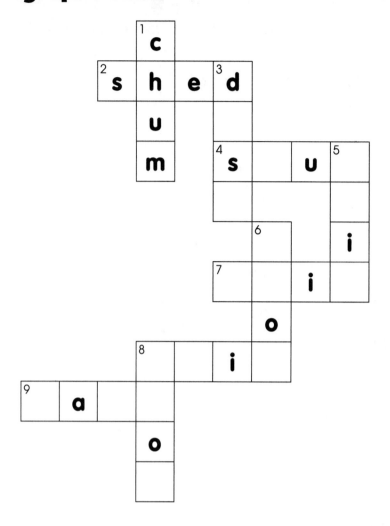

Across

2. a small building used to store things
4. opposite of open
7. a part of your face under your mouth
8. a large boat
9. red spots on the skin

Down

1. a friend
3. a plate for food
5. opposite of fat
6. to cut or break with a hard blow
8. a store

Write and Spell on Your Own

UNIT 8 | Beginning *l* and *r* Blends

Read the Words

Read each word. Focus on the sounds at the beginning.

glad   flex   club   flat

blip   glen   slop   plum

Expand a Word: *l* Blends

Add different letters to the front of each word to make three new words. Write your new words in the blanks.

1. **blush**

   flush   lush

   slush

3. _____

_____ led

_____

2. _____

_____ lap

_____

4. _____

_____ lip

Blend a Word: *l* Blends

Blend the beginning consonants of two words to make one new word.

1. sap
lap **slap**

2. sit
lit _____

3. lash
cash _____

4. lot
pot _____

5. lip
sip _____

6. led
bed _____

Write and Spell on Your Own   **247**

© 2007, 2000, 1984 by Frances Bloom and Deborah Bloom Coates

Spelling Words

Read each word. Focus on the sounds at the beginning.

broth   crab   drip   frog

grid   prop   shrub   fresh

Blend a Word: *r* Blends

Blend the beginning consonants of the two words to make one new word.

1. bag

   rag _____ **brag** _____

2. bat

   rat _____

3. rash

   cash _____

4. tip

   rip _____

5. rip

   dip _____

6. rap

   tap _____

7. ban

   ran _____

8. rot

   tot _____

Change a Word: *r* Blends

Make a new word by adding a consonant or *sh* before the *r*. You can make more than one new word for some of the words.

1. _____rib

2. _____rim

3. _____rush

4. _____rug

5. _____rash

6. _____red

7. _____rag

8. _____rip

Write and Spell on Your Own

Simon Says

Fill in each blank with an *r* or an *l* to complete the commands.

1. G____ab a partner.

2. C____ap your hands.

3. G____ip the bat.

4. F____ash the light.

5. B____ush your hair.

6. T____im your nails.

7. F____ip the pancake.

8. P____an a party.

What Can You Do?

Fill in the blank with a vowel and an *l* or an *r* for a blend.

1. Can you s_____m the lid on the trashcan?

2. Can you g_____b a big green f_____g?

3. Can you make a big c_____sh on a drum?

4. Can you p_____n a school t_____p?

Scrambled Sentences

Put the words in alphabetical order to make sentences.

Remember:

- A sentence starts with a capital letter.
- A sentence ends with a period (.) or a question mark (?).

1. drag mud can a bug

   A bug can drag mud. _____

2. if win clap they

   _____

3. Fred my did sled get

   _____

4. shrubs bird a nest can on

   _____

5. hold can a toys baby small

   _____

6. the shut tiny Brad trunk can

   _____

Write and Spell on Your Own

UNIT 9 | More Beginning Blends, Ending Blends

Read the Words

Read each word. Focus on the blend at the beginning or end.

Beginning blends

scab	scat	smog	snag	span	splash
stag	smash	stub	swam	swish	strip

Ending blends

bask	bond	dent	depth	fact	fund
gulf	gust	husk	mast	munch	pact
punt	romp	shaft	tenth	vent	zest

Blend a Word

Blend the final consonants of each pair of words to make a new word.

1. run

   rut ____**runt**____

2. Ben

   bet _____

3. an

   at _____

4. bus

   but _____

5. bran

   brad _____

6. scan

   scat _____

7. lam

   lap _____

8. cam

   cap _____

9. ban

   bad _____

10. clam

    clap _____

11. tram

    trap _____

12. ram

    rap _____

Write and Spell on Your Own

Expand a Word

Add one or more letters to each word to build a new word. The synonyms next to each box will help you.

Example:

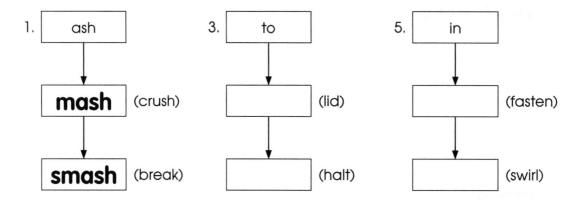

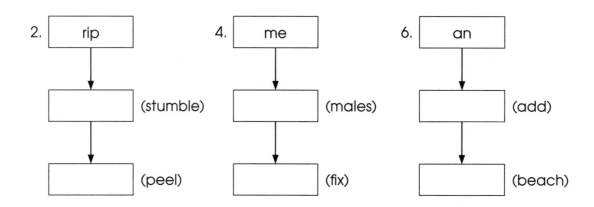

Write and Spell on Your Own

What Would You Do If ...?

Unscramble these words. Remember, each has a consonant blend.

ntpa   shsma   pumj   spalhs   tspi

_____   _____   _____   _____   **spit**

misw   erts   srucb   ndme   ptso

_____   _____   _____   _____   _____

Use the unscrambled words to tell what you would do if the following things happened. The first one has been done for you.

What would you do if ...

1. you had a bug in your mouth? ____**spit**____

2. you fell out of a boat? _____

3. you tore your pants? _____

4. you had to get over a big puddle? _____

5. you want to get your friend wet? _____

6. you got a pot very dirty? _____

7. you just dropped a cup? _____

8. you hiked ten miles? _____

9. you were running very fast? _____

10. you came to a red light? _____

Homonyms—Same Word, Different Meanings

These words have two meanings:

bump   brush   rest   last   club   band   land   hand   trip   film

Fill in the blanks in each sentence with the correct word. (Use the same word twice.)

1. Will the milk I bought ___**last**___ night ___**last**___ all week?

2. Fred bought a new _____ to _____ the cats.

3. The airplane will _____ when we see _____.

4. The _____ of the men are tired and want to _____.

5. Please _____ me the pencil with your left _____.

6. We won't go on the _____ if you _____ and hurt yourself.

7. I lost my rubber _____ when the _____ marched by.

8. You can join our _____ if you hit the ball with the _____.

9. I would like to _____ a movie for the _____ festival.

10. Did you _____ your head when you hit the _____ in the road?

Pick Two

Pick two words. For each word, write a sentence that uses two meanings of the word in it.

sand   clamp   bump   stand   plant

_____

_____

Write and Spell on Your Own

UNIT 10 | Dual-Blend Words

Read the Words

Read each word. Focus on the beginning and ending blends.

blanch	blimp	brash	clinch	drift	flinch
grasp	prompt	shrimp	squint	thump	trend

Expand a Word

Fill in the boxes with words that build from the words shown.

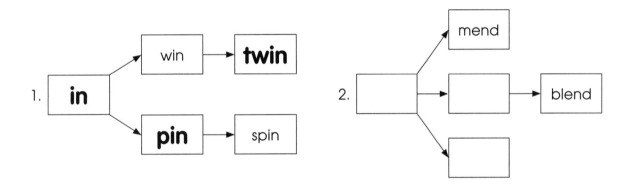

1. in → win → **twin**
   in → **pin** → spin

2. ☐ → mend
   ☐ → ☐ → blend
   ☐ → ☐

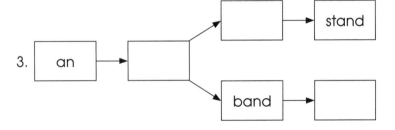

3. an → ☐ → ☐ → stand
   ☐ → band → ☐

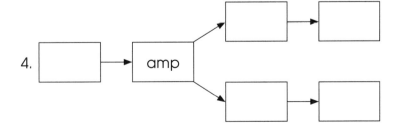

4. ☐ → amp → ☐ → ☐
   ☐ → ☐

Write and Spell on Your Own

SPELLING SOUNDS

Words Within Words

A. The letters in each of these words can make at least five different words. Can you find them?

1. blend __bend, lend, end, bed, led, bled__

2. grunt _____

3. scant _____

4. tramp _____

5. clamp _____

B. Now write each group of words in alphabetical order. (Watch for the second and third letters.)

1. __bed, bend, bled, end, led, lend__

2. _____

3. _____

4. _____

5. _____

Write and Spell on Your Own

One to Two

There are two words in each word. One word begins with a consonant blend, and the other ends in a consonant blend. Can you find them? (Check your dictionary if you are not sure of a word.)

Example: tramp = tram ramp

1. plump _____ _____

2. branch _____ _____

3. cramp _____ _____

4. slump _____ _____

5. clamp _____ _____

6. scamp _____ _____

Try to use each group of words in a sentence.

Example: The *tramp* sat on the *tram* as it went up the *ramp.*

1. _____

2. _____

3. _____

4. _____

5. _____

6. _____

Write and Spell on Your Own

Not the Same

Underline the word in each line that does not have the same meaning as the other words.

1. drop   grasp   fall   loosen

2. slim   thin   plump   slender

3. save   spend   scrimp   keep

4. tardy   late   prompt   slow

5. blend   separate   split   divide

6. skip   stand   hop   jump

7. join   clasp   split   fasten

Write each of the underlined words in a complete sentence.

1. _____

2. _____

3. _____

4. _____

5. _____

6. _____

7. _____

Write and Spell on Your Own

Spelling Arithmetic

1. Cross out the boxes with sums that do not equal 10.
2. Unscramble the remaining letters to make a word.

8 + 2	5 + 4	3 + 8	9 − 6	12 − 3	4 + 5	5 + 5	8 + 7	1 + 11
L	**Y**	**B**	**L**	**A**	**H**	**E**	**J**	**E**

9 − 5	15 − 5	1 + 4	8 + 4	10 − 2	6 + 4	3 + 2	14 − 7	20 − 10
W	**D**	**V**	**X**	**T**	**N**	**O**	**S**	**B**

Tick-Tack-Tuck

Tuck the blends in the empty squares to make three words across and one diagonally. Use the blends above each square. Use each blend only once.

mp—nd—st

bl	i	**mp**
bl	a	**st**
bl	e	**nd**

nd—nt—mp

st	u	
st	a	
st	a	

ft—mp—sp

cr	a	
cr	i	
cr	a	

sp—nt—nd

gr	a	
gr	a	
gr	u	

Write sentences using as many words as you can from each square.

1. _____

_____

2. _____

_____

3. _____

_____

4. _____

_____

Write and Spell on Your Own

Synonym Crossword

Use synonyms to complete the puzzle.

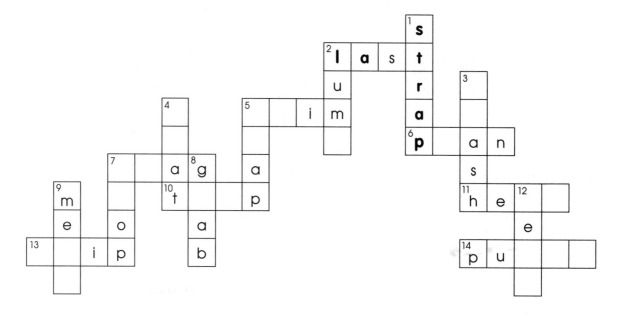

Across

2. end
5. thin
6. plot
7. pull, tug
10. stumble
11. aid
13. cut
14. beat, strike

Down

1. fasten, bind
2. a bump, a piece
3. break into pieces
4. even, level
5. break suddenly
7. let fall
8. snatch
9. patch, repair
12. give a loan

© 2007, 2000, 1984 by Frances Bloom and Deborah Bloom Coates

Write and Spell on Your Own

UNIT 11 | Compounds

Read the Words

Read each compound word.

bobcat	cobweb	hubcap	humbug
chitchat	hotshot	upshot	whiplash
filmstrip	handclasp	hobgoblin	withheld

True or False?

Name the two pictures to make a compound word. Then mark the sentences true or false.

1. + = **catfish**

   I can say "meow."   true   (false)

2. + = _____

   I can stop trains.   true   false

3. + = _____

   I am a lamp made out of the sun.   true   false

4. + = _____

   I am a bag full of hands.   true   false

5. + = _____

   I am a pen full of pigs.   true   false

Write and Spell on Your Own

An ABC Story

SPELLING SOUNDS

A. Combine two words in the first sentence to make a compound word to complete the second sentence.

1. My pig likes the mud in his pen.

   It might be fun to play in his _____.

2. I will set the table in the sun.

   I like to watch a _____ after dinner.

3. My new hat came in a pretty box.

   I'll keep my hat in a _____.

B. Put the words you made in alphabetical order in the blanks below.

bobcat, cobweb, _____, _____,

_____, suntan, zigzag

C. Use the alphabetized words to fill the blanks in the story.

Oh my! Oh my! A large _____ must have come into my room.

He put a giant _____ behind my bed and a _____

on the floor. My room looks like a _____.

Should I clean my room or watch the _____? I think I will just put

lotion on my _____ and watch the stars _____

across the sky.

D. Write about how you avoid cleaning your room.

_____

_____

_____

Write and Spell on Your Own

Compound Puzzle

Put the words in Group A in alphabetical order. Write the words in order in front of the words in Group B to make common words.

A	B		A	B
cob	**bath** tub	sand	_____ bag
dust	_____ nap	snap	_____ box
bath	_____ web	sun	_____ pen
gum	_____ rag	hand	_____ box
cat	_____ pan	pig	_____ shot
dish	_____ drop	hat	_____ set

Use the compound words you made in the crossword puzzle.

Across

2. a picture in an album
3. a container to sweep dust into
6. a place for pigs
8. something to bathe in
10. a sandy place for children to play
11. a home for a spider

Down

1. a quick nap
3. a cloth for washing dishes
4. time of setting of the sun
5. a woman's bag
7. a chewy candy
9. a container for hats

Write and Spell on Your Own

UNIT 12 /ar/

Read the Words

Read each word. Focus on the /ar/ sound as in *far*.

arm   barn   darn   hard   lard

marsh   scar   sharp   snarl   yard

Complete a Word

How many words can you make that end in these letters?

1. ar   **far tar** _____

2. arm   _____

3. art   _____

4. arch _____

5. ark   _____

6. ard   _____

7. arp   _____

8. arsh _____

9. arn   _____

Write and Spell on Your Own

Pick One

1. Find and complete the words that can be spelled with *ar*.

2. Complete the remaining words with a vowel.

   dr___p   b___k   fl___g   y___d

   b___n   d___k   cr___sh   gr___b

   tr___p   sh___p   sm___t   pl___n

3. Use the *ar* words you made to finish this story. Write on the back or on a separate sheet of paper if you need more space.

   A Dark Yard

   "Oh no!" yelled Mark as he and his dog ran to the barn.

   _____

   _____

   _____

   _____

A Sandy Mystery

What did Sandy find at the beach? (Use the following clues to fill in the blanks.)

a ___ ___ ___ ___ ___ ___ ___ ___
    1   2   3   4   5   6   7   8

1. The first letter is in *paste* but not in *tape*.
2. The second letter is in *smart* but not in *rams*.
3. The third letter is in *taste* but not in *test*.
4. The fourth letter is in *trend* but not in *dent*.
5. The fifth letter is in *frame* but not in *mare*.
6. The sixth letter is in *trims* but not in *smart*.
7. The seventh letter is in *sharp* but not in *parch*.
8. The eighth letter is in *haste* but not in *seat*.

Write and Spell on Your Own

How Are They Alike?

Unscramble these *ar* words.

acr   rahd   rnya   trat   amfr

_____   _____   _____   _____   **farm**

Use the unscrambled words to answer the following questions.

1. How are a horse, a cow, and a pig alike?   **farm animals**

2. How are a sweater, a scarf, and mittens alike? _____

3. How are a lemon, a lime, and a grapefruit alike? _____

4. How are a rock, metal, and cement alike? _____

5. How are a Ford, a Chevrolet, and a Buick alike? _____

Opposites

Complete each sentence with an /ar/ word that is the opposite of the underlined word.

1. The nut is as _____ as a rock.   soft

2. Barb is as _____ as a tack.   dull

3. The gum is as _____ as a lemon.   sweet

4. The cave was as _____ as the night.   light

5. The jet was as _____ as a star.   near

Write and Spell on Your Own

Analogies

Complete the following analogies with *ar* words.

1. silk   soft

   rock   __**hard**__

2. hands   gloves

   neck   _____

3. cat   meow

   dog   _____

4. end   begin

   finish   _____

5. people   house

   horse   _____

6. foot   leg

   hand   _____

7. bread   bag

   jelly   _____

8. high   low

   near   _____

Counting Syllables

How many syllables are in the following words?

1. march _____
2. shipyard _____
3. yard _____
4. hardship _____

5. star _____
6. starch _____
7. artist _____
8. tar _____

9. overcast _____
10. undergo _____
10. bombard _____
12. understand _____

How many syllables are in the following sentences?

1. Someone parked the car. __**5**__

2. Bill has two scarves. _____

3. The horses are in the barn. _____

4. I heard the harp. _____

Write and Spell on Your Own

Barn Search

How many *ar* words can you find in the barn? Words go across and down. Write the words you found in the spaces below. If you look carefully, you may find more than 20 words. Write the words you found in the spaces below:

```
        e  j  c  b  p  j  k  j  l  h  o
      d  f  a  m  a  r  c  h  g  n  p
       q  m  r  s  r  t  b  a  r  n
      r  s  p  a  r  k  t  u  x  z  v
   w  a  h  a  r  d  s  b  t  a  r
   m  k  a  s  l  a  u  c  y  h  t
   f  g  r  c  a  r  d  o  a  z  s
   v  a  s  b  i  k  j  w  r  h  m
   r  c  h  e  x  d  s  l  d  g  a
   n  s  t  a  r  c  h  n  o  y  r
   y  o  d  p  p  v  a  s  w  a  t
   m  f  a  r  m  a  r  s  h  f  z
   r  u  g  t  x  f  p  d  e  z  b
```

_____   _____   _____   _____

_____   _____   _____   _____

_____   _____   _____   _____

_____   _____   _____   _____

_____   _____   _____   _____

Write and Spell on Your Own

Words Within a Word

How many *ar* words can you make out of the following words? List them in the blanks. How many other words can you find? List these on a separate sheet of paper.

farmyard

yardstick

dogcart

_____

_____

_____

_____

_____

_____

_____

_____

_____

_____

_____

_____

_____

_____

_____

partnership

barnyard

farmhand

_____

_____

_____

_____

_____

_____

_____

_____

_____

_____

_____

_____

_____

_____

_____

© 2007, 2000, 1984 by Frances Bloom and Deborah Bloom Coates

Write and Spell on Your Own

UNIT 13 | -ng, -nk

Read the Words

Read each word. Focus on the /ng/ or /nk/ sound as in *sing* and *sink*.

cling	ping	zing	gong	prong
hung	lung	sprung	brink	mink
clank	dank	shank	conk	honk
clunk	flunk	slunk	throng	shrink

Complete the Links

Add or subtract any letter from each word to complete the link.

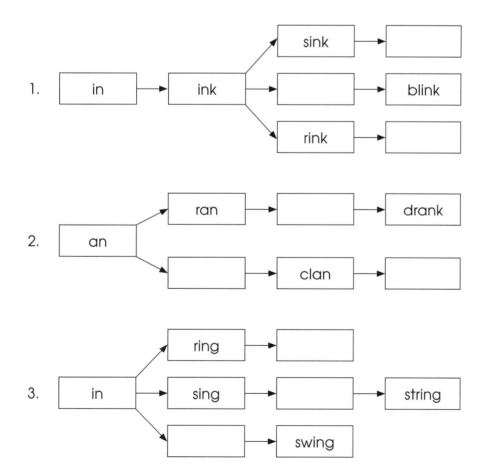

Write and Spell on Your Own

Spelling Analogies

Complete each group of words with a word that ends in *-ing, -ong, -ank,* or *-ink.*

1. shrank   shrink

   thank   **think**

2. sang   sing

   rang   _____

3. wink   wing

   kink   _____

4. clank   clink

   sank   _____

5. hang   hung

   sang   _____

6. slink   link

   stank   _____

7. sting   stung

   string   _____

8. bring   ring

   swing   _____

9. chunk   hunk

   spunk   _____

Haiku

Complete each haiku with an *-ink, -ank, -unk,* or *-ing* word. Remember to count the syllables.

> **Rule**
> Line 1 has five syllables, line 2 has seven syllables, and line 3 should have 5 syllables.

1. Push me one more time.

   I will go high in the sky.

   I fly on my **swing**.

2. I saw one eye close.

   Does that mean that he likes me?

   Did he _____ at me?

3. I see nothing here.

   A page with no words on it.

   A page that is _____.

4. It falls in water.

   Deep down under the surface.

   Rocks will always _____.

5. I climb to the top.

   I get to sleep way up high.

   I like my _____.

Write and Spell on Your Own

Fact or Opinion?

A. Think of a word ending in *-ng* to fill in both blanks. Remember to add an *s* for more than one. Then read each sentence and decide if it is a fact or an opinion. Circle the correct answer.

1. Both of your diamond _____ are beautiful.	Fact	Opinion
This _____ is made out of gold.	Fact	Opinion
2. The woman is strumming five _____ on the banjo.	Fact	Opinion
That is the most colorful ball of _____.	Fact	Opinion
3. Our school chorus sang three pretty _____.	Fact	Opinion
There are six _____ in our book.	Fact	Opinion
4. The airplane has two _____.	Fact	Opinion
The _____ on that bird are very graceful.	Fact	Opinion

B. These sentences are facts. Use the underlined word in each to write another sentence that is an opinion.

1. I heard him <u>honk</u> his horn two times.

_____

2. Mom put the toys in the <u>trunk</u> of the car.

_____

These sentences are opinions. Use the underlined words to write another sentence that would be a fact.

1. The stuff in Jed's room looks like <u>junk</u>.

_____

2. The trim on that dress should be <u>pink</u>.

_____

C. When the newspaper staff states their opinion, it is called an editorial. Pick one of the following topics to write an editorial about:

1. Your opinion on grades and report cards in school.
2. Your opinion on the time that school should start in the morning.

Write and Spell on Your Own

UNIT 14 | -ed

Read the Words

Read each word. Focus on the *-ed* at the end.

/ed/	chanted	melted	twisted
/t/	brushed	clanked	marked
/d/	armed	snarled	darned

Change a Word

Add *-ed* to each word. Put it in the column that matches the sound of *-ed*.

blush	bark	tramp	last	prompt	dust
spank	brand	darn	starch	blink	spill
film	arm	harm	farm	hand	drift

/t/	/d/	/ed/
blushed		

Write and Spell on Your Own

Make a Sentence

Add *-ed* to the following words and use them in sentences.

start   jump   bump   march   plant   harm

1. _____

_____

2. _____

_____

3. _____

_____

4. _____

_____

5. _____

_____

6. _____

_____

Write and Spell on Your Own

Sounds of -ed

smashed	printed	harmed	helped	darned
rested	snarled	flashed	landed	

A. Circle each word in the list above that has the sound of /ed/, as in *blasted*. Use the words you circled to complete the following sentences.

1. Jim ____**printed**____ his name carefully in his new book.

2. The men _____ after the long hike in the woods.

3. The jet _____ safely in spite of the storm.

B. Underline each word above that ends with the sound of /d/, as in *farmed*. Use the words you underlined to complete the sentences.

1. The fruit trees weren't _____ by the storm.

2. When the kites crashed in the air, the strings became _____.

3. The holes in my socks should be _____.

C. Put a check mark (✓) next to each word above that ends with the sound of /t/, as in *stamped*. Use the words you checked to complete the sentences.

1. The glass was _____ by the falling branch.

2. We all _____ plan for the party.

3. The lightning _____ and the thunder roared.

Write and Spell on Your Own

Haiku

Complete the last line of each haiku. Use the circled word in the line you write.

> **Remember:**
> first line = five syllables
> second line = seven syllables
> third line = five syllables

A white world of snow.

The bright sun warmed everything.

_____

(melted)

A giant black dog.

Do you think it was friendly?

_____

(barked)

The horses ran fast.

Up and down the hills they went.

_____

(rested)

I saw my big toe

Poking through my old red sock.

_____

(darned)

I jumped on the sled.

The sleeve on my new coat ripped.

_____

(mended)

Write and Spell on Your Own

Memories

Use the past tense of the word in italics in a sentence to tell about what you remember. (You can make up whatever you like.)

I remember when...

1. *blink*   I __**blinked**__ when the king rushed by.

2. *thank*   I _____ them for _____.

3. *blush*   I _____ when _____.

4. *trust*   I _____ him to _____.

5. *plant*   I _____ the _____.

6. *march*   I _____ to _____.

7. *punch*   I _____.

8. *rest*   I _____.

9. *help*   I _____.

10. *bump*   I _____.

What Do You Remember?

1. Write about your favorite memory.

    _____

    _____

2. Write about your scariest memory.

    _____

    _____

3. Write about your first memory.

    _____

    _____

Write and Spell on Your Own

Review Puzzle

Across

3. put in the ground to grow
6. opposite of light
8. applaud
10. a picture taken with a camera
12. empty space on page
13. unhappy; filled with sorrow
16. make potatoes soft and mushy
18. run at a slow pace
19. a safe place to keep money
20. opposite of bottom
21. crosspiece of a ladder
23. past tense of dent

Down

1. a drawing to get you someplace
2. opposite of dull
4. opposite of fat
5. opposite of first
7. a ruler who wears a crown
8. part of the face below the mouth
9. a chum or friend
10. opposite of sunrise
11. close or shut with a bang
12. past tense of brush
14. run with speed;
    a twenty-yard _____
15. past tense of darn
17. opposite of soft
18. trash; rubbish
22. opposite of lose

© 2007, 2000, 1984 by Frances Bloom and Deborah Bloom Coates

Write and Spell on Your Own

PART 2

Spelling Choices

UNIT 15 /ī/

Spell Long /ī/ Words

List the words below in the correct column.

bride	sly	slight	pride	dine	hire	spry	fright
pry	flight	fight	sky	try	tight	blight	why
quite	line	spy	might	nine	shy	crime	right

i–e		y			igh	
bride	**line**	_____	_____	_____	_____	_____
_____	_____	_____	_____	_____	_____	_____
_____	_____	_____	_____	_____	_____	_____
_____	_____	_____	_____	_____	_____	_____

1. Write five sentences using as many of the above words as you can in each sentence.

   _____

   _____

   _____

   _____

   _____

2. Challenge! Write three sentences using one word from each group (*i–e, y, igh*) in each sentence.

   _____

   _____

   _____

SPELLING CHOICES

Word Play

kit	right	bit	shin	twin	dye	by	pin
site	whip	hit	mite	rid	dim	hid	quit

1. Pick the words you can change by adding an *e* at the end. Write them here.

   kit–kite _____ _____ _____

   _____ _____ _____

   _____ _____ _____

2. Use two pairs in sentences (the word with *e* at the end and the word *without*).

   kit–kite—Mom gave me a kit to make a kite.

   _____

   _____

   _____

   _____

Write and Spell on Your Own

Expand a Word

Add or subtract a letter to make a new word.

Hint: The word in the last box ends in *e.*

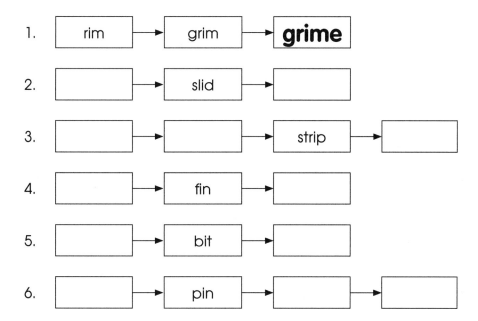

1. rim → grim → **grime**

2. [ ] → slid → [ ]

3. [ ] → [ ] → strip → [ ]

4. [ ] → fin → [ ]

5. [ ] → bit → [ ]

6. [ ] → pin → [ ] → [ ]

Condense a Word

Drop a letter in each word to make a new word in the next box.

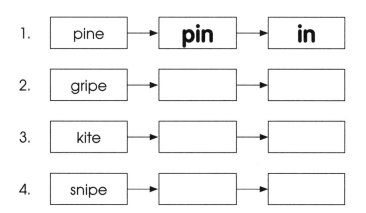

1. pine → **pin** → **in**

2. gripe → [ ] → [ ]

3. kite → [ ] → [ ]

4. snipe → [ ] → [ ]

SPELLING CHOICES

Add an e

Add an *e* to one of the words in each sentence and use that word to fill in the blank.

1. I bit off a piece of candy before he got a __**bite**__.

2. I bought a kit to make a _____.

3. I hurt my shin when I tried to _____ the car.

4. The twin tied up the plants with some _____.

5. I can't find my _____ in this dim light.

6. I slid down the steep _____.

Add a Letter, Change a Word

Add a letter to each word in italics and unscramble the word to make a long *i* word.

1. Add an *r* to *fight* and get a word that means fear. ___**fright**___

2. Add a *w* to *lid* and get savage. _____

3. Add an *i* to *men* and get what belongs to me. _____

4. Add an *r* to *tie* and get what a car wheel needs. _____

5. Add an *i* to *red* and get a trip in a car. _____

6. Add an *e* to *lip* and get a big heap. _____

Write and Spell on Your Own

Make Sense out of Nonsense

Reorder the letters in the word in *italics* and write a sensible phrase.

1. a forest of *spine*   **a forest of pines**

2. take a five *lime* hike   _____

3. catch a *vile* fish   _____

4. have a good *mite*   _____

5. the best time of your *file* _____

6. a *pier* banana   _____

7. a pretty *slime* on her face _____

8. grow grapes on a *vein*   _____

SPELLING CHOICES

Idioms for Every Occasion

Complete each idiom with a long *i* word (/ī/).

1. You bought two new cars. Did you **strike** it rich?

2. Please help me. It's a matter of _____ and death.

3. He won't hurt you. His bark is worse than his _____.

4. You are bothering me. Please get off _____ back.

5. You keep teasing me. Are you trying to pick a _____?

© 2007, 2000 by Frances Bloom and Deborah Bloom Coates

Analogies

Complete each analogy with a long *i* word.

1. sad	frown		6. hear	deaf	
happy	**smile**		see	_____	
2. yellow	lemon		7. man	adult	
green	_____		boy	_____	
3. apples	trees		8. 25	quarter	
grapes	_____		10	_____	
4. fish	swim		9. night	dark	
birds	_____		day	_____	
5. boat	water				
jet	_____				

© 2007, 2000, 1984 by Frances Bloom and Deborah Bloom Coates

Sentence Stretchers

Include a long /ī/ word to complete the analogies.

1. Apples grow on trees and grapes __**grow**__ __**on**__ __**vines**__.

2. 25 cents is a quarter and 10 cents _____ _____ _____.

3. Fish like to swim and birds _____ _____ _____.

4. Oceans are wet and deserts _____ _____.

Write and Spell on Your Own

Opposites

Complete each sentence with the antonym (opposite word) of the word in *italics*.

Hint: The antonyms are all long *i* (/ī/) words.

1. Sometimes I *laugh* so hard that I _____.

2. Irene's shoes got *wet,* but her feet stayed _____.

3. The pencil is *yours,* but the pen is _____.

4. Some cats sleep all *day* and hunt all _____.

5. If I *lose* my paper will you try to _____ it?

6. My shirt is _____, but my pants are *loose.*

7. I think I'm _____, and you're *wrong.*

8. The boys will sing the *low* parts, and the girls will sing the _____ parts.

9. I can make the *dull* ring very _____ if I polish it.

10. People shouldn't try to *tame* _____ animals.

An Opposite Day

What if you woke up one morning and everything was opposite? Use any of the opposite pairs to describe your opposite day.

_____

_____

_____

_____

Write and Spell on Your Own

SPELLING CHOICES

What If?

Use a long *i* word to complete each phrase. "What would do if ...?"

1. a giant came into your room?   _____**hide**_____ under the bed

2. you just took a bath?   _____ myself with a towel

3. the house was dark?   turn on a _____

4. you were next to a pool?   _____ into the water

5. you were a bird?   _____ high in the sky

What Would You Do?

Include a long *i* in the answer to the following questions.

1. What would you do if you lost your kitten?

_____

2. What would you do if you got a new horse?

_____

3. What would you do if you got your own car?

_____

4. What would you do if your homework was hard?

_____

5. What would you do if your dad gave you a bright red apple?

_____

6. What would you try to do if you knew you could not fail?

_____

© 2007, 2000, 1984 by Frances Bloom and Deborah Bloom Coates

Write and Spell on Your Own

UNIT 16 /ā/ /ār/

Spell Long a Words

List each word below in the correct column.

stray	make	vein	may	mail	jail	sleigh
great	hay	lame	clay	veil	drain	stain
cake	pain	aim	break	late	steak	weigh
trail	date	shade	play	pay	game	eight
blade	freight	day	stay	whale	safe	sail

ay	ai	eigh	ea	ei	a–e
_____	_____	_____	_____	_____	_____
_____	_____	_____	_____	_____	_____
_____	_____	_____	_____		_____
_____	_____	_____			_____
_____	_____				_____
_____	_____				_____
_____	_____				_____
_____	_____				_____
					_____
					_____

Write silly sentences, using words from two or three columns in each sentence.

_____

_____

Write and Spell on Your Own

Word Play

weigh   tap   pan   mail   tail   scram   break   lam

mad   scrap   trap   plan   span   fad   pear   eight

1. Pick the words you can change by adding an *e* at the end.

_____

   Use two pairs in sentences.

_____

_____

2. Pick the words that have homophones.

_____

   Use two homophone pairs in sentences.

_____

_____

Plus or Minus an e

Add or subtract an *e* to or from one of the words in each sentence and use that word to fill in the blank.

1. The _____ ran at a fast rate.

2. We were _____ when you made us wait.

3. Do you _____ to travel by plane?

4. The clown wore a cap and a _____.

5. Amy's pal was _____ after she was sick.

6. Did Craig gape at the _____ in the tent?

7. The latest fad is to allow your shirt to _____.

8. Can you _____ off the scrap of tape?

9. You might _____ the tape to make it play.

10. Jane _____ make a cane out of that branch.

Write and Spell on Your Own

Homophones with Long a

Complete each sentence with a homophone for one of the words in the sentence.

1. If you brake too quickly, the glasses will _____.

2. I will tell you a tale about a cat with no _____.

3. Faith started to stare at the woman on the _____.

4. The bus _____ to the state fair was one dollar.

5. It's hard to wait when you are trying to lose _____.

6. The new grate will be _____ for grilling steaks.

7. A new sail for our boat is on _____ at the store.

8. A very plain looking man is flying the _____.

9. Gail looked very pale after she carried the heavy _____.

10. It's hard to hold the horse's reins when it _____.

Flying Mystery

What does my airplane carry?   **f** __ __ __ __ __ __
1 2 3 4 5 6 7

1. The first letter is in *flake* but not *lake.*

2. The second letter is in *spray* but not *pays.*

3. The third letter is in *glade* but not *glad.*

4. The fourth letter is in *pail* but not *lap.*

5. The fifth letter is in *great* but not *rate.*

6. The sixth letter is in *hail* but not *ail.*

7. The seventh letter is in *weight* but not *weigh.*

Write and Spell on Your Own

Stretch a Word

How many new words can you make by adding one or more letters to the words listed below?

Challenge! How many homophones can you find for the words you make?

	New Words	Homophones
1. lay	**clay, play, slay, delay, relay**	**slay, sleigh**
2. air		
3. ail		
4. aid		
5. ale		
6. ate		

Sentence Stretchers

Use a homophone for the underlined word to stretch each sentence.

1. It is not <u>fair</u> to pay a big _____ on the bus.

2. The <u>sail</u> we bought was on _____.

3. We <u>ate</u> _____.

4. <u>Where</u> can _____?

5. What is the best <u>way</u> to _____?

6. The <u>maid</u> _____.

© 2007, 2000, 1984 by Frances Bloom and Deborah Bloom Coates

Write and Spell on Your Own

Haiku

Use the spelling choices to complete each haiku.

1. Use *ay* or *a–e*.

The sun is so bright!

We pl___ ___ a g___m___ and get hot.

Please find us some sh___d___.

2. Use *ay, ai,* or *a–e*.

I s___ ___l as d___ ___ f___d___s.

The sunset fl___m___s around me.

I am s___f___ in my boat.

3. Use *ay, ai, a–e,* or *eigh*.

Her shiny gr___ ___ m___n___,

Her t___ ___l flowing behind her,

She n___ ___ ___ ___s for her h___ ___.

Make your own last line for the following haikus.
Remember: The last line has five syllables.

4. Use *a–e* or *ay*.

I love to pl___ ___ ball,

Feel home pl___t___ under my feet.

_____

5. Use *ai* or *ay*.

The r___ ___ndrops fall hard.

The sn___ ___l goes into his shell.

_____

Homophone Puzzle

Solve the puzzle with a homophone for each word listed.

Across

2. rein
3. pain
4. steak
5. wait
8. eight
9. plain
14. tail
15. hail
16. brake

Down

1. grate
4. sale
5. weigh
6. tale
7. vane
10. ail
11. ate
12. stair
13. pail

Write and Spell on Your Own

UNIT 17 /ō/

Spell Long o Words

List each word below in the correct column.

grown	loan	note	doe	thrown	flow	floe
load	quote	dome	soak	lone	though	gold
show	boast	vote	slope	throne	told	dough
hoe	groan	foe	coast	glow	stove	oath

ow	o–e	oe	oa	old	ough
grown	_____	_____	_____	_____	_____
_____	_____	_____	_____	_____	_____
_____	_____	_____	_____	_____	_____
_____	_____	_____	_____	_____	_____
_____	_____	_____	_____	_____	_____
		_____	_____		
		_____			

Find three pairs of homophones in the list above. Use each pair of homophones in a sentence. Write your answers on a separate piece of paper.

Write and Spell on Your Own

SPELLING CHOICES

Word Play

glob	pole	slop	throne
whole	hop	shop	throw
rod	road	not	crop
dough	mop	spot	grown

1. Pick the words you can change by adding an *e* at the end.

_____

Use in sentences.

_____

_____

_____

_____

2. Pick the words that have homophones. Write the homophones.

whole–hole _____

_____

_____

Use two of the homophone pairs in sentences.

_____

_____

_____

Write and Spell on Your Own

SPELLING CHOICES

Fact or Opinion?

1. Fill the blank with a long *o* antonym of the word in parentheses.
2. Is the sentence a fact or an opinion? Circle F or O.

		Fact	Opinion
(hide)	1. You will sell your art if you __**show**__ it.	F	(O)
(sink)	2. Cork will _____ in water.	F	O
(catch)	3. Joe can _____ a ball better than Frank can.	F	O
(shrink)	4. The plants will _____ two inches each week.	F	O
(fast)	5. A trip on a _____ boat can be fun.	F	O
(hot)	6. _____ drinks taste good in the summer.	F	O
(bought)	7. Dad _____ his car last week.	F	O
(high)	8. _____-fat milk is very tasty.	F	O
(new)	9. My _____ shoes are dark brown.	F	O

Opinions—Pro and Con

Write your opinion and the opposite opinion on one of the following topics.

1. Kids spend too much time watching TV.
2. School should be in session 12 months a year.
3. Schools should have P.E. classes every day.

_____

_____

_____

Write and Spell on Your Own

Rhyming with Long o

Complete each sentence with a long *o* word that rhymes with the word in parentheses. (The spelling of the rhyming word may be different.)

(home) 1. Tony decided to _____ the countryside.

(cold) 2. Mom _____ me to walk the dog.

(load) 3. The cyclist _____ his bike down the _____.

(coat) 4. We'll _____ for a class president today.

(foam) 5. If I have a cold I'll stay _____.

(hose) 6. Please remember to _____ the door.

(so) 7. A female deer is called a _____.

(tone) 8. When we need money we ask for a _____.

Long o to the Rescue

Make each sentence make sense by replacing one word in it with an /ō/ word.

/ō/ Word

1. They dug a deep hill to bury the treasure. _____

2. Trucks travel on a track. _____

3. Cook the vegetables on the dryer. _____

4. Let's go sailing in the car. _____

5. Yolanda stubbed her ear when she jumped over the log. _____

6. It is always hot in the winter. _____

7. I want a double-dip ice-cream salad. _____

8. We hope it will rain so we can go sledding. _____

Write and Spell on Your Own

Home by Jove

Fill in the blanks with *oa, ow, o–e,* or *ough* to read the verse.

Th_____ in winter she'd c_____st

on her sled through the sn_____

to thr_____ a stone

at the Ice King's thr_____,

she loved even more

summer's cold-free zone.

Without even a c_____t

she'd doze and fl_____t

lying prone in her b_____t

while the hot sun sh_____,

or troll for fish

bel_____ the b_____t

and catch a fine bass

to p_____ch on her st_____,

and eat it with t_____st

sharing it all

with her old dog, Jove.

© 2007, 2000, 1984 by Frances Bloom and Deborah Bloom Coates

Write and Spell on Your Own

Anagrams

> **Rule**
>
> Anagrams are words made by rearranging all the letters in a word to make another word. No letter can be used twice or left out.
>
> *Examples:* *pale* to *leap*   *part* to *trap*   *step* to *pets*

Solve the puzzle with an anagram for each word.

Across

5. now
7. worth
8. lope
9. notes

Down

1. wolf
2. poles
3. bore
4. stove
6. tone

1. Write four sentences. Use a word from the puzzle and its anagram in each sentence.

_____

_____

_____

_____

2. Find your own anagrams. Try looking through word lists for ideas. Use the words for a message in code.

   Examples: I will *prod* the *grin* in the *gum.* = I will *drop* the *ring* in the *mug.*

_____

_____

Write and Spell on Your Own

Step up or Down

Fill in the corners of the steps to make long *o* words both across and down.
Do not use any word more than once.

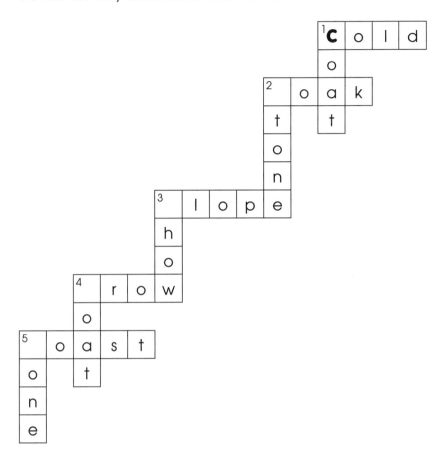

Puzzle for oa and ow Words

Across

3. We can row ashore in my _____.
5. The old papers were _____ out.
6. We need some _____ to play with our sleds.
7. Can we have buttered _____ with our breakfast?

Down

1. You should wear a hat and _____ on a cold day.
2. You can _____ out the candle when the lights are on.
3. Did you ever hunt with a _____ and arrow?
4. Rhoda has a cold and a sore _____.
6. Wash your hands with _____ and water.

Write and Spell on Your Own

Find and Add

Find a word in the sentence that you can change by adding an *e*. Use the word to fill in the blank.

Example: The *tote* was too big for the little *tot*.

1. Do you think Jake will _____ if his mom makes him mop the floor?

2. I _____ you didn't hop on the flowers.

3. Jill did not think she could sing the high _____ in the song.

4. When Bess hid in the shed, she saw Bill _____ the ball in the grass.

5. I hope to invent a kit that will make a _____ fly without wind.

6. I think we will get rid of the pumpkin if we get a _____ home.

7. If you put the glass _____ in the tub, it will sink.

8. Dave _____ a drink for Fred and was mad when he saw him pour it in the sink.

Challenge

Change the final consonant of each of the following words to *e* and write a sentence using both words. If necessary, add an *s* to make a word plural.

pill   fill   mill   bass

_____

_____

_____

_____

© 2007, 2000, 1984 by Frances Bloom and Deborah Bloom Coates

Write and Spell on Your Own

UNIT 18 /ē/ /ēr/

Spell Long e Words

List the words below in the correct column.

steer	feet	leisure	shady	meal	field	gleam
baby	squeal	seal	greed	wheat	screen	either
seize	chief	belief	meet	shield	lady	

ee	ea	ie	ei	y
_____	_____	_____	_____	_____
feet	_____	_____	_____	_____
_____	_____	_____	_____	_____
_____	_____	_____	_____	_____
_____				

Word Play

Make 1 + 1 = 1. Combine one word from Group A with one word from Group B to make one word.

Group A		Group B		New Word
street		while		_____
leap		coast		_____
speed		way		_____
tea	**+**	car	**=**	_____
bee		cup		_____
sea		hive		_____
mean		frog		_____

Write and Spell on Your Own

Switching Letters

A. Shift the consonants to make a new long *e* word. Use both words in a sentence.

Example: peal to leap: The loud peal of the bells made me leap.

1. flea to _____ : _____

2. eat to _____ : _____

3. deal to _____ : _____

4. read to _____ : _____

5. east to _____ : _____

6. teach to _____ : _____

B. Put the final *e* before the *a* to make a new long *e* word. Use both words in a sentence.

Examples: ate to eat or tea and pale to peal or leap

1. lane to _____ : _____

2. mate to _____ : _____

3. stale to _____ : _____

4. sale to _____ : _____

5. male to _____ : _____

6. same to _____ : _____

© 2007, 2000, 1984 by Frances Bloom and Deborah Bloom Coates

Write and Spell on Your Own

Finding Homophones

Write a phrase using two long *e* words that are homophones and have the same meaning as the sentence.

Example: Don't take that hard metal that isn't yours. **Don't steal the steel.**

1. Look at the ocean.

   _____

2. Look quickly at the top of the mountain.

   _____

3. Make the back of your foot feel better.

   _____

4. A little insect bites your dog and gets away.

   _____

5. Smash the plant with the round red root.

   _____

How Are They Alike?

Fill the blanks in the following words with *ee, ea,* or *ey.* Then put them into two groups: animals or things we grow.

p_____ch   b_____n   sh_____p   w_____d   monk_____

d_____r   b_____t   s_____l   b_____   wh_____t

Animals	Things we grow
_____	_____
_____	_____
_____	_____
_____	_____
_____	_____

Write and Spell on Your Own

What Would You Do? Compare and Contrast

A. Fill the blanks of the following words with *ee, ea,* or *ie.* These words describe what you do when you show your feelings.

ch_____r   squ_____l   pl_____d   w_____p   scr_____m   shr_____k

B. 1. Which words tell what you do when you are excited? _____

2. Which words tell what you do when you are afraid? _____

3. Use these words to compare how you act when you are excited and when you are afraid.

_____

_____

Either ... or—Neither ... Nor

A. Complete the sentences with a long *e* antonym for each word in italics. Combine both sentences with *either ... or,* and write the new sentence on a separate piece of paper.

Example: Is the baby *awake?* Is the baby *asleep?*
The baby is *either* awake *or* asleep.

1. Is the lake *shallow?* Is the lake _____?

2. Is the sun in the *west?* Is the sun in the _____?

3. Is your shirt *dirty?* Is your shirt _____?

B. Combine both sentences with *neither ... nor,* and write the new sentence on a separate sheet of paper.

Example: This dress is not *expensive.* This dress is not *cheap.*
This dress is *neither* expensive *nor* cheap.

1. That is not the *king.* That is not the _____.

2. The book is not *there.* The book is not _____.

3. Joan's room is not sloppy. Joan's room is not _____.

Write and Spell on Your Own

The Queen and the Flea

Fill the blanks with *ee, ea,* or *ey* to complete the story.

Far away,

on the edge of the s_____,

there lived a great qu_____n

who loved to be fr_____.

She loved to climb tr_____s,

and r_____d about l_____ves.

She would hike up st_____p trails

and sit on high p_____ks.

She had no fear of the d_____r

and would ch_____r

when a monk_____ came n_____r.

One day a fl_____

came and sat on her knee.

He felt great gl_____.

He wanted to scr_____ch

but no one could h_____r.

He asked the qu_____n

to teach him to scream.

"Alas," said the qu_____n,

"your voice is very small to h_____r,

but it still can calm fears.

When you sp_____k out with gl_____

we all can f_____l fr_____."

Write and Spell on Your Own

Rhyming Long e

1. Underline the long *e* word in each sentence.
2. Find a rhyming long *e* word to complete the puzzle.

Across

1. You'd <u>feel</u> better if your arm would ____**heal**____.

5. The thorn on the weed made my finger _____.

6. We'll have holiday cheer at the end of the _____.

7. Don't _____ when we play hide and seek.

9. Let's plan to _____ on Main Street.

11. I need to _____ the hungry cat.

12. We each had to give a four-minute _____ to the class.

14. Turn up the _____ to warm your feet.

Down

2. We <u>need</u> to find someone to ____**lead**____ the parade.

3. I seem to _____ a lot when I nap in the afternoon.

4. Sheep can't _____ over a high fence.

5. The police chief gave a talk that was _____ and to the point.

8. I will _____ trying to drive up the steep hill.

10. Mom can _____ you how to make a good peach pie.

13. _____ saw the bee fly into the room.

Write and Spell on Your Own

UNIT 19 /ow/

Spell /ow/ and /ou/ Words

> **Rule**
> The /ow/ sound is usually spelled *ow* at the end of the word or before a final *l* or *n.*

List the words below in the correct column.

prowl	fowl	vow	plow	sow	spout	brow
pouch	chow	proud	town	down	howl	jowl
crouch	mound	scowl	gown	oust	found	

ou	ow	owl	own
_____	_____	_____	_____
_____	_____	_____	_____
_____	_____	_____	_____
_____	_____	_____	_____
_____	_____	_____	_____
_____	_____	_____	_____
_____			

Write and Spell on Your Own

Word Play

Fill in the blanks with *ow* or *ou.*

Group A	Group B	
br **OW** n	c_____ch	t_____n
r_____nd	_____l	gr_____nd
st_____t	cl_____d	m_____th
pr_____d	cl_____n	c_____
l_____d	g_____n	sc_____t

Write three sentences using a word from Group A to describe something in Group B.

_____

_____

_____

Change a Word

Add a letter to the beginning or end of the long *o* word to make a new /ow/ word. Use the clue to figure out the new word.

/o/ word		/ow/ word	Clue
1. row	to	**brow**	your forehead
2. tow	to	_____	a city or village
3. own	to	_____	dress or robe
4. low	to	_____	to break up and turn over soil
5. crow	to	_____	a king's headdress
6. grow	to	_____	snarl or grumble

 © 2007, 2000, 1984 by Frances Bloom and Deborah Bloom Coates **Write and Spell on Your Own**

What Do I Do?

Unscramble the words to find the answers to the sentences. All answers are /ow/ words.

nwrof   psuot   glrow   owb   lohw   tupo   oprwl   lwpo

1. I am a wolf. I __**howl**__.

2. I am a mean dog. I _____.

3. I am a grumpy child. I _____.

4. I am an actor. I _____.

5. I am an unhappy boy. I _____.

6. I am a farmer. I _____.

7. I am a whale. I _____.

8. I am a burglar. I _____.

Homonyms

Match the word in *italics* to its definition. You can use a dictionary.

_____ 1. The man will *bow* to the woman.   A. a kennel for stray animals

_____   A wave broke on the ship's *bow*.   B. fastened, tied

_____ 2. I will *count* to ten.   C. forward part of a ship

_____   The *count* lived in a castle.   D. name numbers in order

_____ 3. I got my dog at the *pound*.   E. leap

_____   He will *pound* the stake.   F. bend the body in greeting

_____   I gained five *pounds*.   G. nobleman

_____ 4. He's *bound* with a rope.   H. strike heavily

_____   She'll *bound* out of school.   I. measure of weight

Write and Spell on Your Own

Compound It

See how many compound words you can make by combining any two of the following words.

down   bound   snow   fit   town   side   wit

in   out   cast   south   sun   smart   law

Example: south + bound = southbound

Use two of the compound words you made in one sentence.

_____

Complete an /ow/ Story

Fill in the blanks with *ow* or *ou*.

One day a cl_____n came to _____r school. She had a r_____nd, red nose and

a big m_____th. She wore a fl_____er in her shirt and floppy br_____n shoes on

her feet. But the cl_____n wasn't happy. She had a big fr_____n on her face. The

children sat very still and didn't make a s_____nd. They didn't know h_____ to

cheer up a cl_____n.

   One small boy walked right up to the cl_____n. He said, "You shouldn't

p_____t. You should be pr_____d of your job. You make me laugh and h_____l,

and you never make a s_____nd." The boy b_____ed to the cl_____n and went

to sit d_____n. The cl_____n had f_____nd a friend in _____r t_____n.

Write about what you would do to cheer up a clown.

_____

_____

_____

Write and Spell on Your Own

A Poetic Shape

It's fun to create your own forms for poetry. These poems have a syllable count for each line.

Poetry Form

Line 1—One syllable
Line 2—Three syllables
Line 3—Five syllables
Line 4—Seven syllables

Line 5—Five syllables
Line 6—Three syllables
Line 7—One syllable

Fill the blanks in the poems with *ow* or *ou* to complete each poem.

Cl_____ds

At sund_____n

Seem high in the sky,

They are r_____nd and soft and white

Float high off the gr_____nd.

H_____ I love

Cl_____ds.

H_____

Can you gr_____l

And not make a s_____nd?

Though you p_____t and fr_____n and sc_____l,

You can somehow gr_____l

With_____t s_____nd.

H_____?

Pick a topic, count the syllables, and make up your own poetic shape.

Write and Spell on Your Own

/ow/ Puzzle

Fill in the blanks with /ow/ words to complete the puzzle.

Across

1. Say _____ if I hurt you.

5. Don't _____ at the baby.

6. _____ team won the game.

8. He tripped on the big, _____ wheel.

10. If you slip on the ice, you may fall _____.

11. A large _____ of people were at the ball game.

12. A lifeguard tries to make sure you won't _____.

Down

1. Did you throw _____ the old flowers?

2. I saw a white, puffy _____ outside the airplane window.

3. Thunder makes a _____ sound.

4. You have pretty _____ eyes.

5. Lemons have a very _____ taste.

7. Dig a deep hole in the _____ to plant the tree.

9. Mother said to wash the dishes right _____.

11. Did you ever milk a _____?

Write and Spell on Your Own

More Anagrams

> **Rule**
>
> Anagrams are made by rearranging all the letters in a word to make another word. A letter cannot be used twice or left out.

These anagrams review sounds you have already learned.

A. Reorder the letters of the underlined word to fill the blank in the sentence.

Examples: I would like to <u>eat</u> the cookie when I drink a cup of <u>tea</u>.
Were you able to <u>trace</u> where the <u>crate</u> came from?
Please <u>save</u> the broken parts of the <u>vase</u>.

1. It is <u>mean</u> to make fun of someone's n_____.

2. I would walk <u>miles</u> for her s_____.

3. The dog's <u>master</u> carried him across the swiftly flowing s_____.

4. He used the p_____ to ski down the <u>slope</u>.

5. We were <u>charmed</u> to see the way they m_____ in the parade.

6. It is too _____ to read that long <u>tale</u>.

7. The hearty _____ was not made for just the <u>male</u> members of the club.

8. The <u>wrong</u> plants were _____ in that garden.

9. The <u>tone</u> of his _____ was very harsh.

10. Did you <u>lose</u> the _____ of your shoe?

B. 1. Find an anagram for each of the following words:

flow _____   hint _____   worth _____

much _____   shrub _____

2. Use each pair of anagrams in a sentence.

_____

C. Try to find more anagrams to share with your classmates.

Write and Spell on Your Own

UNIT 20 /aw/

Spell /aw/ Words

List the words below in the correct column.

awl	gawk	prawn	hall	squawk	sought
stalk	fault	fraud	fall	haunch	daughter
ought	dawn	tall	balk	fought	slaughter
stall	walk	vault	naughty	maul	

aw	**au**	**all**	**alk**	**augh**	**ough**
_____	_____	_____	_____	_____	_____
_____	_____	_____	_____	_____	_____
_____	_____	_____	_____	_____	_____
_____	_____	_____	_____	_____	_____
_____	_____	_____	_____	_____	_____

Spell It *aw* or *au*?

Fill in the missing letters *aw* or *au*.

Remember: /aw/ is spelled *aw* at the end of a word or before a final *l* or *n*.

cl**aw**	h____nt	b____l	y____n	v____lt
g____nt	j____	p____	t____nt	br____n
dr____n	str____	th____	cr____l	fr____d
l____nch	j____nt	fl____	dr____	fl____nt
spr____l	l____	p____nch	t____t	l____n

1. Find two words that are part of an animal's leg. Use them in a sentence.

_____

2. Find two words that involve opening your mouth. Use them in a sentence.

_____

SPELLING CHOICES

Add a Letter and What Do You Have?

Unscramble the word in italics and add a letter. You will have a new /aw/ word.

1. Add a letter to *law* and get the cry of a baby. **bawl**

2. Add a letter to *slam* and get little. _____

3. Add a letter to *fan* and get a young deer. _____

4. Add a letter to *wart* and get something to drink your milk through. _____

5. Add a letter to *tuna* and get what a ghost does. _____

Think of an Antonym

Complete the second sentence with an /aw/ word that is the opposite of the word in *italics* in the first sentence.

1. My younger brother is *short.* I am very _____**tall**_____.

2. Claudia forgot to *cook* the steaks. They were still _____.

3. My brother *threw* me a fast ball. I _____ it easily.

4. I *learned* all my new words. I then _____ them to my sister.

5. We *sold* our old car last week. We _____ a new one yesterday.

6. Paul was very *good* all week. But on Saturday, he was very _____.

Write and Spell on Your Own

Analogies

Complete the analogies with /aw/ words spelled *all, aw, augh,* or *ough.*

1. *Pitcher* is to *catcher* as *threw* is to _____**caught**_____.

2. *Little* is to *big* as *short* is to _____.

3. *Person* is to *fingernail* as *cat* is to _____.

4. *Bird* is to *nest* as *horse* is to _____.

5. *Night* is to *day* as *dusk* is to _____.

6. *Boy* is to *girl* as *son* is to _____.

7. *Paper* is to *scissors* as *wood* is to _____.

8. *Whale* is to *large* as *mouse* is to _____.

9. *Storekeeper* is to *customer* as *sold* is to _____.

Anagrams

Unscramble the letters.

Words about school

gthhtuo _____

khalc _____

alhl _____

ahutgt _____

Words about babies

lawrc _____

llsma _____

gterdauh _____

albw _____

Use some of these words to write a story about a school for babies.

_____

_____

_____

Write and Spell on Your Own

UNIT 21 | /k/

Spell /k/ Words

List the words below in the correct column or columns.

struck   school   task   crust   fix   yoke

quail   whack   ache   shark   cake   express

drake   quack   hulk   chrome   camp   block

strike   quench   chemist   quite   brisk   hike

ck	ke	k	c
____	____	____	____
____	____	____	____
____	____	____	____
____	____	____	____
	____		

qu	ch	x
____	____	____
____	____	____
____	____	____
____	____	____

Write and Spell on Your Own

Ways To Spell /k/

Complete the words with a spelling for the sound /k/.

> **Remember:** /k/ is usually spelled *ck* after a short vowel, as in *clock; ke* after a long vowel, as in *like;* and *k* after a consonant, as in *dark.*

spar**k**_____   cra_____   bri_____   fa_____   sul_____   pa_____

jo_____   hul_____   de_____   mar_____   cho_____   spo_____

sma_____   bris_____   bi_____   ca_____   tru_____   yo_____

Pick two things from the list you would like to have. Use them in a sentence that tells why you want them or what you would do with them.

_____

Analogies

1. *Car* is to *road* as *train* is to _____**track**_____.

2. *Four wheels* are to *car* as *sixteen wheels* are to _____.

3. *Hat* is to *head* as *scarf* is to _____.

4. *Home* is to *healthy* as *hospital* is to _____.

5. *Steak* is to *broil* as *cake* is to _____.

6. *Slither* is to *snake* as *waddle* is to _____.

Write and Spell on Your Own

Say and Do

Unscramble the following words to answer the questions. (All the words end in *k*, *ck*, or *ke*.)

icckkott   rbka   kkic   krae   ukclc   ackqu   kbuc   lkic

What do we say?		**What do we do?**	
1. ducks	**quack**	1. donkeys	**kick**
2. dogs	_____	2. kittens	_____
3. clocks	_____	3. wild horses	_____
4. chickens	_____	4. gardeners	_____

A Conversation

Pick two animals. Write what they might say to each other if they could talk.

_____

_____

_____

_____

_____

SPELLING CHOICES

Write and Spell on Your Own

> **Remember the following rule:**
>
> When you hear /k/ at the end of a word, it is spelled
>
> > *ck* after a consonant
> >
> > *ke* after a long vowel sound
> >
> > *k* after a vowel digraph (two vowels together)

Which *k* Am I?

Fill in the blanks with *k, ck,* or *ke.*

1. Kaitlin went to the la_____ in the park to feed her pet du_____.

2. I will as_____ the coo_____ to ba_____ a ca_____ for the party at the

   ban_____.

3. Justin told the tru_____ driver not to po_____ the sna_____ with his sti_____.

4. Jennifer qui_____ly rode her tri_____ horse to the barn to as_____ the

   bla_____smith to fix the horse's shoe.

5. Joshua would li_____ to have a panca_____ for brea_____fast.

6. The si_____ clown had a stuffy nose and an aching ba_____ and could only

   spea_____ in a whisper.

7. Michelle will pi_____ up her fris_____y puppy and ta_____ him to play in the

   par _____.

Write and Spell on Your Own

Homonyms

Use each of the following words twice to complete the phrases below.

back   milk   block   bark   like   rock   park   check

1. __**back**__ up the car

2. _____ the cow

3. _____ covers a tree

4. play in the _____

5. dogs can _____

6. _____ near the curb

7. I _____ to eat

8. scratch my _____

9. a glass of _____

10. it looks _____ rain

11. pay by _____

12. _____ the pass

13. sink like a _____

14. a wooden _____

15. _____ the baby to sleep

16. _____ in to the hotel

Keep Stretching

Pick three of the above phrases. Stretch each one into one or two sentences. See if you can combine two phrases into one sentence.

_____

_____

_____

_____

_____

What Compound Am I?

Add *ke* or *ck* to make words:

ba_____   lu_____   bla_____   sti_____   si_____   ni_____   sha_____

Use the words to make the compound words in the following sentences. The hints in parentheses will help you.

Example: bare **back**_____   (I don't ride with a saddle.)

1. pot_____   (What will we have for dinner?)

2. chop_____   (I love Chinese food.)

3. _____smith   (Does your horse need new shoes?)

4. hand_____   (I'm pleased to meet you.)

5. _____name   (My friends shortened my name.)

6. home_____   (I miss my family.)

Words Within a Word

How many /k/ words can you find in these compound words?

clambake: **cake,**_____

bareback: _____

racetrack: _____

quicksand: _____

Write and Spell on Your Own

/k/ Puzzle

Solve the puzzle with words that end in *k, ck,* or *ke.*

Across

1. I'll wear a ___**mask**___ on my face for Halloween.

3. Don't _____ your car in front of my driveway.

5. I ate too much popcorn and felt _____.

7. It's very _____ outside tonight.

8. Jack's magic _____ had us amazed.

9. We always _____ the door when we leave the house.

10. Her _____ fur coat looks almost real.

Down

1. We get fresh ___**milk**___ from our cow.

2. When you play soccer, you _____ the ball with your foot.

4. Mark would be taking a _____ if he swam alone.

6. We need plaster to fill the thin _____ in the wall.

7. Nick likes to do his homework at a large, roomy _____.

8. We bought a new _____ for our tropical fish.

9. The _____ at our camp is large enough for swimming and boating.

Write and Spell on Your Own

UNIT 22 /ch//j/

Spell /ch/ and /j/ Words

List the following words in the correct column.

coach	large	porch	sketch	barge	change
nudge	trench	ridge	thatch	page	clutch
mulch	latch	twinge	smudge	trudge	hatch

ch	tch	ge	dge
_____	_____	_____	_____
_____	_____	_____	_____
_____	_____	_____	_____
_____	_____	_____	_____
_____	_____	_____	_____

Spell It *ch* or *tch*, *ge* or *dge*

Complete each word with *ch* or *tch*.

1. in**ch**____
2. sti_____
3. pa_____
4. wi_____

5. coa_____
6. cru_____
7. bran_____
8. ca_____

9. di_____
10. ma_____
11. scra_____
12. tren_____

13. stre_____
14. star_____
15. bun_____
16. mar_____

Complete each word with *ge* or *dge*.

1. bri**dge**
2. ca_____
3. char_____

4. bul_____
5. chan_____
6. ba_____

7. pa_____
8. fu_____
9. stran_____

10. wa_____
11. ju_____
12. le_____

Write and Spell on Your Own

Find the Homonyms

The following words have two meanings.

match   change   branch   bridge   march   charge   coach   inch

Find the word that goes with the two meanings.

1. make equal or the same; a thing used to start a fire   **match**

2. a unit of length; move by a small amount   _____

3. name of a month; walk in a parade   _____

4. extend from the main body of a thing; part of a tree   _____

5. train, teach; carriage   _____

6. a card game; a structure over water   _____

7. to make different; money in coins   _____

8. cost or price; restore current to a battery   _____

Find the Meanings

Use your dictionary to find two meanings of the following words.

edge _____

sage _____

hedge _____

judge _____

Use both meanings in a sentence.

_____

_____

_____

_____

Write and Spell on Your Own

Conversations

Complete the words in the conversation below with *ch* or *tch*.

TOM: I'm getting tired of sitting on this hard ben**ch**___.

FRED: Just watch that man pi_____ a fast ball.

TOM: I'd rather mun_____ some peanuts.

FRED: Oh! He missed that ball by one in_____.

TOM: It's almost time for lun_____.

FRED: Do you think the player will ca_____ that ball?

TOM: I need something to quen_____ my thirst.

FRED: I have a hun_____ that you are not enjoying the game.

TOM: What could make you think that?

Complete the words in the conversation below with *ge* or *dge*.

MIDGE: Did you read the front pa_____ of the paper?

GRETCHEN: Yes, a hu_____ lion got out of its ca_____.

MIDGE: It ran across the bri_____ and is hiding on the le_____.

GRETCHEN: That is a stran_____ place for a lion to hide.

MIDGE: I hope it doesn't char_____ at anyone.

GRETCHEN: I would try to do_____ it if it came towards me.

Write your own conversation using as many words as you can that end in *ch*, *tch*, *ge*, and *dge*.

_____

_____

_____

_____

Write and Spell on Your Own

SPELLING CHOICES

Verbs and Nouns with /ch/ and /j/

A. Complete each sentence with the following /ch/ words. These words are all verbs. Not all the words will be used.

march	fetch	mulch	sketch	scratch	hitchhike
pitch	pinch	catch	switch	punch	stretch

1. A person with an itch might   **scratch**

2. A large group of people in uniform might _____

3. Two boxers in a ring might _____

4. A player on a baseball team might _____

5. A dog playing with a ball might _____

6. A man who wanted a free ride might _____

7. A cat fighting with a dog might _____

8. An artist with a paper and a pencil might _____

B. Complete each sentence with a /ch/ or /j/ word that names a *person, place,* or *thing.* These words are all nouns. Not all the words will be used.

wage	stage	witch	crutch	judge	fudge
inch	cage	match	bridge	arch	bench

1. If you break your leg, you need a   **crutch**

2. If you act in a play, you stand on a _____

3. If you want to light a candle, you need a _____

4. If you take one twelfth of a foot, you have an _____

5. If you have a lion, you keep him in a _____

6. If you work, you will be paid a _____

7. If you go to court, you see a _____

8. If you want to scare someone, you could dress up as a _____

Write and Spell on Your Own

UNIT 23 /or/

© 2007, 2000, 1984 by Frances Bloom and Deborah Bloom Coates

Spell /or/ Words

List the following words in the correct column.

cork	snore	board	four	door
scorch	more	your	thorn	torch
core	roar	floor	wore	forlorn

or	our	oor	ore	oar
_____	_____	_____	_____	_____
_____	_____	_____	_____	_____
_____	_____	_____	_____	_____
_____	_____	_____	_____	_____
_____	_____	_____	_____	_____

Using Homophones Together

Write the homophone or homophones for each word.

or __**oar, ore**__   soar _____   pore _____

boar _____   for _____

Complete each sentence with a homophone pair.

1. The bird had a _____ wing and could not _____ high in the sky.

2. Nora is looking _____ _____ lost kittens.

3. You can either try to fix the motor _____ grab an _____ to

   paddle the boat.

4. I hope my pictures of the wild _____ do not _____ you.

5. I will _____ a glass of milk while you _____ over that difficult book.

Write and Spell on Your Own   335

What Comes Next?

Complete each sequence with the correct /or/ word.

1. whimper, snarl, __**roar**__

2. _____, medium, tall

3. two, _____, six, eight

4. _____, south, east, west

5. less, the same, _____

6. _____, wall, ceiling

7. knife, _____, spoon

8. _____, live, die

Pick one of the sequences. Write a sentence that includes all parts of the sequence.

Example: I have *less* lunch than Bob, *the same* as Tom, and *more* than Joe.

_____

_____

Analogies

1. *Cow* is to *beef* as *pig* is to ___**pork**____.

2. *Bike* is to *two* as *car* is to _____.

3. *Cook* is to *home* as *buy* is to _____.

4. *Dog* is to *bark* as *lion* is to _____.

5. *Canoe* is to *paddle* as *rowboat* is to _____.

© 2007, 2000, 1984 by Frances Bloom and Deborah Bloom Coates

Write and Spell on Your Own

An /or/ Puzzle

Solve the puzzle using words with the /or/ sound. Look for some compound words.

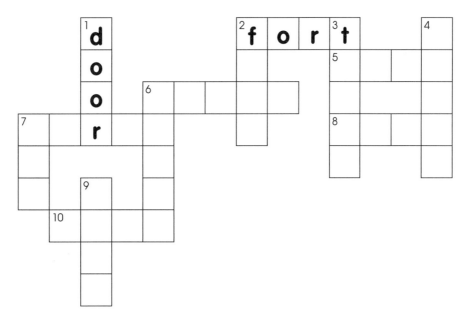

Across

2. They built a strong wall around the **fort** to keep the enemy out.

5. If you blow your _____ you will wake up the baby.

6. The schools were closed when we had a big snow _____.

7. Do you think Santa Claus lives at the _____ Pole?

8. We were scared when we heard the loud _____ of the lion.

10. After a long voyage, the ship returned to home _____.

Down

1. Please wipe your feet on the **door** mat.

2. Clouds seem to _____ interesting shapes and patterns.

3. Lorenz pricked his finger on the sharp _____ on the rosebush.

4. When you _____ while sleeping, the noise is loud and harsh.

6. I love strawberry _____ cake for dessert.

7. The men seemed neither very happy _____ very sad.

9. I am still hungry and would like some _____ pancakes.

SPELLING CHOICES

UNIT 24 /er/

Spellings for /er/

List each word below in the correct column.

colder	louder	heard	earth	early
curl	worm	world	bird	work
learn	church	chirp	stern	shirt
girl	curb	browner	winter	dirt

er	ir	ur	or	ear
colder	_____	_____	_____	_____
_____	_____	_____	_____	_____
_____	_____	_____	_____	_____
_____	_____	_____	_____	_____
_____	_____	_____	_____	_____

Match a word from one column with a word in another column to make a phrase. Write four phrases. *Example:* an early bird.

_____

_____

_____

_____

SPELLING CHOICES

Write and Spell on Your Own

Make New Words

How many *ir* words can you make using letters in the circle? How many *ur* words can you make using letters in the square? List the *ir* words and *ur* words on a separate sheet of paper.

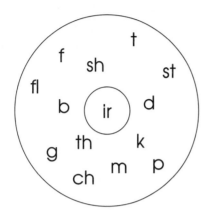
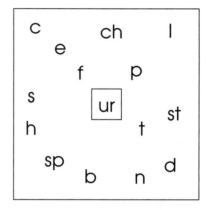

If you get 10 words from each figure you are GOOD; 15 words are GREAT; and more than 15 words make you SUPER!

/er/ Rhymes

Complete each sentence with an /er/ word that rhymes with the word in italics.

1. The *first* balloon I bought already _____.

2. You must *learn* not to _____ the toast.

3. I hope the robin will *perch* on the steeple of the _____.

4. I *heard* the song of the _____ in the woods.

5. The *first* section of the test was the _____ part.

6. Fern couldn't read the *third* _____ in the sentence.

7. It's your _____ to water the *fern*.

Write and Spell on Your Own

Analogies

Use /er/ words to complete the analogies.

1. *Late* is to *early* as *last* is to _____.

2. *Tie* is to _____ as *belt* is to *pants.*

3. *End* is to *beginning* as *death* is to _____.

4. *One* is to *three* as *first* is to _____.

5. *Food* is to *hunger* as *water* is to _____.

6. *Boy* is to _____ as *male* is to *female.*

Just *ir*

Across

2. after second
5. a tree with white bark
6. solid, not weak
7. a female child
8. a piece of clothing worn on the upper body

Down

1. mix, blend
3. mud or dust
4. a sound made by a bird
5. an animal with wings
6. before second

Write and Spell on Your Own

Pick an /er/ Sound

Complete the puzzle with *er, ir, or, ur,* or *ear.* Use a dictionary to check your choices.

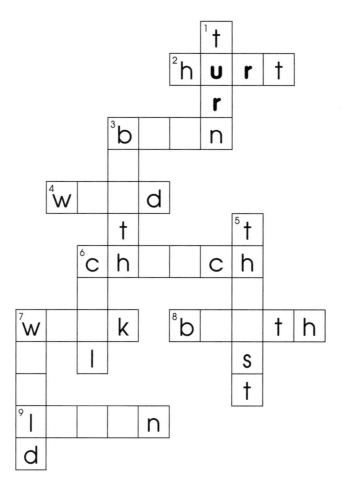

Write and Spell on Your Own

More Sounds

Homophone Pairs

Homophones are words that sound alike but have different spellings and meanings.

Example: to, two, too

A. Find a homophone for each of the following words:

knight _____   knead _____

no _____   right _____

new _____   wring _____

knot _____   through _____

B. Use the homophone pairs to complete the sentences.

1. You _____ to _____ dough to make good bread.

2. Mom _____ that Sally would want to buy a _____ dress for the party.

3. Did you _____ the _____ numbers when you copied the address?

4. I _____ that there are _____ more cookies in the cookie jar.

5. The brave _____ spent the stormy _____ alone in the forest.

6. The scout was _____ able to tie a square _____ correctly.

7. Do not let the _____ on your finger drop in the sink when you _____ out the wet swimsuit.

8. Tom was glad the window was open when he _____ the ball _____ it.

Secret Messages

Use the *x* and *y* coordinates to find the letters that spell the words in these messages. The *x* point is listed first in the parentheses.

Example: m = (5, 4)

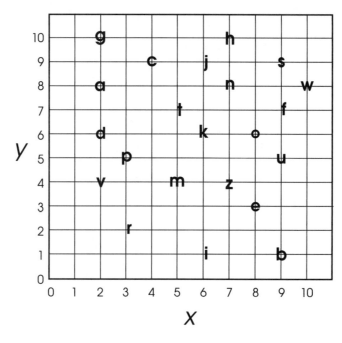

A. (5,4) (8,3) (8,3) (5,7)   (9,5) (9,9)   (2,8) (5,7)   (5,7) (7,10) (8,3)

___ ___ ___ ___   ___ ___   ___ ___   ___ ___ ___

(9,9) (5,7) (2,8) (5,7) (6,1) (8,6) (7,8)   (2,8) (5,7)   (7,8) (8,6) (8,6) (7,8)

___ ___ ___ ___ ___ ___ ___   ___ ___   ___ ___ ___ ___

B. (5,7) (7,10) (8,3)   (3,5) (3,2) (8,3) (4,9) (6,1) (8,6) (9,5) (9,9)

___ ___ ___   ___ ___ ___ ___ ___ ___ ___ ___

(4,9) (8,6) (6,1) (7,8)   (6,1) (9,9)   (6,1) (7,8)   (7,10) (6,1) (9,9)

___ ___ ___ ___   ___ ___   ___ ___   ___ ___ ___

(9,1) (8,6) (8,6) (5,7)

___ ___ ___ ___

Make up and exchange secret messages by using this coordinate system as a code.

Write and Spell on Your Own

SPELLING CHOICES

Proverbs

A. Match an old proverb with a new saying.

1. Haste makes waste. _____ A. If you try hard you will succeed.

2. A bird in the hand is worth two in the bush. _____ B. We often forget about things that are not right in front of us.

3. When the cat's away, the mice will play. _____ C. If you do something too quickly, you might not do a good job.

4. Out of sight, out of mind. _____ D. It is sometimes better to keep what you have than to try to get more.

5. Where there is a will, there is a way. _____ E. When no one is watching, people often goof off.

B. Pick two proverbs. Write about what they mean to you.

1. Better late than never.

2. His bark is worse than his bite.

3. Too many cooks spoil the broth.

4. A friend in need is a friend indeed.

_____

_____

_____

_____

Write and Spell on Your Own

PART 3

Spelling Rules

UNIT 25 | Double *f, l, s, z*

Spell Words with Double *f, l, s, z*

> **Rule:** If a one-syllable word with one short vowel ends in *f, l, s,* or *z,* the final consonant is usually doubled.

List the words below in the correct columns.

cliff	quell	dwell	lass	jazz
buzz	staff	bass	fuzz	stress
chess	scoff	thrill	spell	stuff

ff

_____

_____

_____

_____

ll

_____

_____

_____

_____

ss

_____

_____

_____

zz

_____

_____

_____

Write and Spell on Your Own

Double or Not Double?

Add a letter to the words that should end in a double letter.

1. swel ____

2. ham ____

3. dul ____

4. mes ____

5. gruf ____

6. kil ____

7. stil ____

8. cut ____

9. hat ____

10. buz ____

11. fus ____

12. sel ____

13. les ____

14. sun ____

15. pet ____

16. muf ____

17. cup ____

18. fit ____

19. rub ____

20. fiz ____

Which letters did you double? _____

How many syllables does each of these words have? _____

How many vowels do these words have? _____

Write two sentences using one word from each column in each sentence.

_____

_____

_____

_____

Write and Spell on Your Own

Pick an Ending

Make words by adding one of the following endings to each set of letters.
(The same ending must work for all three.)

–ell   –ess   –uff   –ill

Write the words you make in the blanks.

1. b   = __**bell**__   3. c   = _____

   sh + __**ell**__ = __**shell**__   fl + _____ = _____

   sm   = __**smell**__   bl   = _____

2. st   = _____   4. str   = _____

   ch + _____ = _____   l + _____ = _____

   dr   = _____   pr   = _____

Switch and Change

Start at the top. Change one letter at a time as you make new words to get
to the bottom word.

1. cash   3. bark   5. cape   7. test

   __**mash**__   _____   _____   _____

   __**mass**__   _____   _____   _____

   mess   mass   lass   pass

2. feed   4. list   6. flask   8. trust

   _____   _____   _____   _____

   _____   _____   _____   _____

   sell   kiss   class   _____

                                                  chess

SPELLING RULES

Spell and a Spell Cast

Homonyms

Remember that homonyms are words that look and sound alike but have two or more meanings.

---

1. Fill in the blanks in the story below with one of the homonyms.
2. Underline the definition used in the story. (Each word is used only once.)

Homonyms	Meanings
bluff	1. trick, deceive; 2. cliff with a broad face
spell	1. magic power; 2. period of time
staff	1. employees, assistants; 2. stick, pole
stuff	1. fill, pack; 2. matter, material
cuff	1. turned-back hem; 2. slap with the palm of the hand
well	1. in a satisfactory way; 2. hole dug in the earth to get water
press	1. push, force; 2. iron, smooth
cross	1. pass, step over; 2. cranky, irritable
miss	1. <u>fail to have or attend</u>; 2. title of an unmarried woman
bill	1. statement of what is owed; 2. mouth of a bird

Under a Spell on a Bluff

Camilla couldn't wait to go camping in the park. She hurried to get ready so she wouldn't **miss** her ride. She had to _____ her wrinkled shorts and sew a button onto the _____ of her shirt sleeve. Then she had to _____ her sleeping bag into a sack.

On a hike in the park, Camilla and her friends saw a bird with a bright red _____. The bird flew with the hikers as if it were trying to lead them somewhere. Camilla used a long _____ to help her walk up the steep hills. The hikers had to _____ a stream on a fallen log. They got cold water out of a deep _____. Then they all had a nap under a tree for a short _____. When they woke up, they were sitting on top of a beautiful _____. They thought they could see the whole world before them.

On a separate sheet of paper, answer the following questions:
1. What happened?
2. What do you think they saw?
3. How do you think they felt?
4. What do you think the bird was trying to show them?

© 2007, 2000, 1984 by Frances Bloom and Deborah Bloom Coates

Write and Spell on Your Own

Match a Double Ending

Complete the puzzle with a double *f, l, s,* or *z.*

A Scrambled Answer

"Don't make a mountain out of a _____."

1. Cross out the numbers that equal 12.
2. Unscramble the remaining letters to complete the saying.

| 24 – 12 | 6 + 7 | 7 + 5 | 19 + 5 | 6 + 6 | 3 + 9 |
| y | o | b | m | c | t |

| 9 + 5 | 18 – 6 | 15 – 4 | 4 + 8 | 18 – 6 | 12 + 7 |
| h | p | e | w | x | l |

| 17 – 5 | 5 + 6 | 3 + 9 | 9 + 6 | 7 + 4 | 20 – 8 |
| r | l | z | l | i | f |

Write and Spell on Your Own

UNIT 26 | Doubling Rule

Spell Words with the Doubling Rule

Rule: Double the final consonant of a one-syllable word when you add an ending that begins with a vowel.

1. drip + ing = **dripping**

2. dent + ed = _____

3. wet + est = _____

4. hand + ful = _____

5. big + est = _____

6. fresh + ly = _____

7. clear + ly = _____

8. quiz + ing = _____

9. sail + ing = _____

10. weigh + ing = _____

11. chop + ing = _____

12. rest + ful = _____

13. blast + ed = _____

14. steep + est = _____

Complete a Phrase

Complete each phrase with one of the following endings:

–ed –ful –ing –less –ment

1. chop_____ the logs

2. a braid_____ rug

3. a stun_____ dress

4. rip_____ his shirt

5. a late ship_____

6. flag_____ the train

7. knit_____ a sweater

8. a clean, spot_____ floor

9. wish_____ thinking

10. drop_____ in for tea

11. a play_____ puppy

12. flop_____ into bed

13. miss_____ the children

14. pat_____ the dog

15. a harm_____ prank

16. sand_____ the table

Write and Spell on Your Own

Use –ing and –ed

Complete each sentence by adding the suffix –ing or –ed to one of the following words:

boil   plug   order   win   forget   flap   stir   visit   enjoy   begin

1. Our team is ahead. We are __**winning**__ the game.

2. The bird _____ its wings and flew away.

3. You cannot make the tea until the water has _____.

4. I _____ the cake batter 50 times.

5. Bill _____ the hole to stop the leak.

6. We all _____ our trip to the park yesterday.

7. What are you _____ for dinner at the restaurant?

8. I hope I am not _____ to pack something that I need.

9. Today we are _____ a new unit about reptiles.

10. I _____ my friend at the hospital yesterday.

Then and Now

Add –ed and –ing to one of the following words to complete each sentence.

visit   clean   chop   plan   shop

1. We __**planned**__ a trip to the farm last week and are __**planning**__ to go to the beach tomorrow.

2. Dan is _____ his grandmother today and _____ his uncle yesterday.

3. Dad _____ enough firewood for this winter and is now _____ wood for next winter.

4. I _____ my desk last week and am _____ the rest of the room today.

On a separate sheet, write about something you did that you would do differently if you could do it over.

Write and Spell on Your Own

–est Can Exaggerate

Add *–est* to the following words to complete the sentences. Use each word only once.

hot   dark   big   sharp   sad   old   cold   flat   neat   hot   fat   plump

1. I have the ___**biggest**___ bike in my town.

2. The lost girl had the _____ face I have ever seen.

3. This is the _____ room in the house.

4. That is the _____ book in the school.

5. Kansas is the _____ state in the country.

6. My sharpener makes the _____ points on pencils.

7. Mom's electric percolator makes the _____ coffee.

8. Alaska is the _____ place in the United States.

9. My pig is the _____ at the fair.

10. This is the _____ day this summer.

11. My mom has the _____ desk.

12. I have the _____ pillow.

Do You Ever Exaggerate?

Add an ending to the following words to write some exaggerations of your own.

stiff   slim   mad   hard   light   wet

_____   _____   _____

_____   _____   _____

_____   _____   _____

SPELLING RULES

Accent and Add

Each of the words below has two syllables.

1. Put an accent (') mark before the part of the word you say the loudest.
2. Underline the words that end in one consonant, have one vowel before the last consonant, and have the accent on the second syllable.
3. Add the ending to each word and write the new word in the blank. The first one has been done for you.

1. <u>be 'gin</u> + ing   **beginning**

2. con trol + ing _____

3. re sent + ed _____

4. gar den +ing _____

5. pre fer + ed _____

6. ga ther + ed _____

7. of fer + ed _____

8. pre vent + ed _____

9. com mit + ing _____

10. re bel + ing _____

11. sub tract + ing _____

12. re veal + ing _____

13. ad mit + ed _____

14. for got + en _____

15. o mit + ed _____

16. pa trol + ed _____

17. gal lop + ing _____

18. re main + ing _____

Write and Spell on Your Own

Add the Second Syllable

Use one of the following words to complete the words in each phrase. You may need to add a consonant to some words.

fit   sent   lot   it   vent   quip   ploy   joy   pen   get   bid

Example: befitting a queen

1. pre_____ing our play

2. ex_____ing from the rear

3. en_____ed a good meal

4. pi_____ed a fast plane

5. em_____ed a new secretary

6. in_____ing a better mousetrap

7. e_____ing them with uniforms

8. o_____ing the door

9. for_____ing them to swim

10. for_____ing to write

A Scrambled Day

Rearrange the letters in the two words in the parentheses to make one new word that completes each sentence.

Did you ever have a day when ...

1. (drip, pet)   you _____ when you got out of bed?

2. (dell, sip)   you _____ your juice on the table?

3. (part, sped)   you _____ your bookbag on your back and couldn't get it off?

4. (prod, ped)   a boy _____ his books on your foot?

5. (beg, grad)   your best friend _____ about getting all A's?

6. (grid, pep)   you _____ your pencil so hard that it broke?

7. (met, led)   your ice cream _____ before you could eat it?

8. (pep, dots)   If you ever did, maybe you _____ everything and crawled back into bed.

Did you? On a separate sheet of paper, write about a scrambled day you might have.

Write and Spell on Your Own

Diamante

> **Diamante is a seven-line poem formed in a diamond pattern.**
>
> Line 1: one word (noun or a topic)
> Line 2: two words (adjectives)
> Line 3: three words (verbs ending in *–ing*)
> Line 4: four words (nouns or a phrase)
> Line 5: three words (verbs ending in *–ing*)
> Line 6: two words (adjectives)
> Line 7: one word (a noun or a synonym or antonym to line 1)

Remember the doubling rule and fill in the blanks with *–ing* to complete the diamante.

Basketball

Bouncy, orange

Throw_____, run_____, jump_____

Uniforms, baskets, players, coach

Pass_____, shoot_____, win_____

Round, hard

Game

Garden

Happy, excited

Plan_____, dig_____, plant_____

Roses, tomatoes, violets, lettuce

Grow_____, weed_____, pick_____

Pretty, tasty

Summer

Use the rule in the box to make up your own diamante poem.

Write and Spell on Your Own

Complete a Word

Complete each word with one of the following endings:

–ble   –cle   –fle   –gle   –ple   –tle   –kle   –zle   –ckle   –dle

> **Remember:** –*ck* always follows a short vowel.

Consonant before ending	Short vowel before ending	Long vowel before ending
1. gen _____	bu _____	ri _____
2. jun _____	ju _____	cra _____
3. trem _____	ba _____	sta _____
4. un _____	pe _____	la _____
5. bun _____	cri _____	a _____
6. an _____	ri _____	ma _____
7. jum _____	dri _____	ti _____
8. spar _____	ke _____	fa _____
9. ram _____	mu _____	ca _____
10. hum _____	da _____	tri _____
11. mar _____	bo _____	sti _____

> **Rule:** When a consonant plus –*le* follows a short vowel, the consonant is usually doubled.

SPELLING RULES

Keep the Ending

For each word listed, write four more words with the same ending. (The words don't have to rhyme.)

1. simple **pimple** **dimple** **ample** **crumple**

2. drizzle _____ _____ _____ _____

3. shuttle _____ _____ _____ _____

4. struggle _____ _____ _____ _____

5. muffle _____ _____ _____ _____

6. gable _____ _____ _____ _____

7. doodle _____ _____ _____ _____

Challenge!

Find two words that cross and blend.

1.
```
      t
      a
b  a  b  b  l  e
      l
      e
```

3.
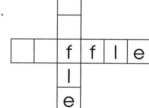

5.
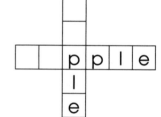

2.

4.
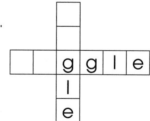

6.
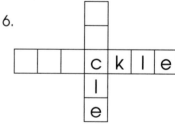

Write and Spell on Your Own

Can You Remember?

Complete the nursery rhymes with consonant + *–le* words.

1. Jack be __**nimble**__, Jack be quick,

   Jack jump over the __**candle**__ stick.

2. Hey _____, _____

   The cat and the _____,

   The cow jumped over the moon.

3. _____ Simon met a pieman going to the fair.

4. _____, _____ _____ star,

   How I wonder what you are.

5. _____ bells, _____ bells, _____ all the way.

   Oh, what fun it is to ride in a one-horse open sleigh.

6. Three _____ kittens have lost their mittens.

7. Rock-a-bye baby, on the treetop!

   When the wind blows, the _____ will rock.

8. One, two, _____ my shoe,

   Three, four, shut the door.

Reporter for the Mother Goose Daily Paper

A. Cub Reporter

   1. Pretend you plan to interview one of the nursery rhyme characters.

   2. Write the questions you will ask for your article.

   3. Write the newspaper article.

B. Ad Writer

   You have a product to sell. Create an advertisement using one of the nursery rhymes.

Write and Spell on Your Own

Cinquain

Cinquain is a five-line poem that follows a pattern.

Line 1: one word—title

Line 2: two words—description of the title

Line 3: three words—an action or actions

Line 4: four words—a feeling

Line 5: one word—another word for the title (a synonym)

Remember the doubling rule.

1. Fill the blanks with –*le* to complete the cinquain.

Horse

Nob_____, gent_____

Jumps, runs, races

Loves to nib_____ ap_____s

Stallion

2. Fill the blanks with –*le* to complete the first three lines of the cinquain. Use the rule above to finish the last two lines of the cinquain.

Cand_____

Waxy wick

Twink_____, spark_____, daz_____

_____

_____

Use the pattern to build your own cinquain. Use as many –*le* words as you can.

_____

_____

_____

_____

_____

Write and Spell on Your Own

Find a Word to Stretch

Add *–le* to one of the words in each sentence to fill in the blank and solve the puzzle. (Remember the doubling rule.)

Across

2. Even the little bug woke up when Bill blew his _____**bugle**_____.

3. When the rat ran across the roof, it sounded like a baby shaking a _____.

5. It was a steep climb to the top of the church _____.

6. Will you lend me a hand to fix the _____ on the pot?

7. Did the dust _____ on the old set of books?

Down

1. When Jim dances a jig, his entire body seems to _____.

2. Bob grabbed his bat and then went out to _____ the opposing team.

4. I need a _____ to sew a button on my shirt.

5. When you start the motor with a loud noise, you _____ the passengers.

7. The cowboy was sad because he could not find a _____ for the horse.

Write and Spell on Your Own

UNIT 28 | -y

Pick an Ending

Complete each word with one of the following endings:

–ly   –vy   –by   –dy   –ty   –py   –ny   –sy   –ky   –ry

> **Remember:** Following a short vowel, the final consonant is doubled.

Hint: There will be two answers that are exceptions to the rule.

1. cho _____
2. sha _____
3. thir _____
4. pe _____
5. si _____

6. smo _____
7. ug _____
8. bo _____
9. bu _____
10. emp _____

11. la _____
12. cur _____
13. stu _____
14. han _____
15. nas _____

How's the Weather?

You are a TV weather person. You need to write the weather report for the day. Add an ending to each of the following words to make words that could describe the weather.

–cy   –gy   –wy   –ny   –ly   –my   –zy   –dy   –ry

1. fo _____
2. su _____
3. chi _____
4. clou _____
5. mu _____

6. i _____
7. wint _____
8. sno _____
9. stor _____
10. ha _____

Write your weather report.

Write and Spell on Your Own

y Makes a New Word

Fill in the blanks by adding a *y* to one of the words in each sentence. Remember to double the consonant when necessary.

1. My **belly** knows that it is time to eat when the bell rings.

2. Please put your _____ old pants in the laundry bag.

3. There was a _____ bit of food in that tin can.

4. Danny broke his arm when he was in the _____.

5. It takes more than one _____ to buy a pen.

6. Is Sally's car big enough to _____ all of these people?

7. I banged my shin on the _____ bumper of your new car.

8. That _____ boy has a rash on his skin.

9. We have a slim chance of finding any _____ worms today.

10. _____ men tried to defend the fort.

11. Only part of our class is going to the _____.

12. I bought a grooming kit to keep my _____ brushed and clean.

13. I almost swallowed a bug as we rode in the _____.

14. Mom looked grim when I showed her my _____ pants.

15. Will the lad deliver the newspaper to the _____?

Write and Spell on Your Own

Opposites

> **Remember:** When a consonant + *y* follows a short vowel, the consonant is usually doubled.

Add a *y* to the underlined word to change a word in the sentence that doesn't make sense.

Example: A little pup plays like an old dog.
A little pup plays like a puppy.

1. Only a small piece of <u>tin</u> will fit in that very large box.

   _____

2. Tom said Jill was quiet as he saw her <u>chat</u> and giggle with her sister and the kids on the farm.

   _____

3. If we <u>skimp</u> on the food in the pot, we will all have a very big dinner.

   _____

4. The <u>dust</u> in the air settled on the table and made it look very clean.

   _____

5. We went to swim at the lake on a gloomy day when the <u>sun</u> was bright.

   _____

Add a *y* to each of the following words. Draw a line to its opposite.

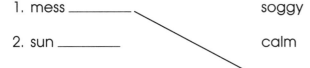

1. mess _____   soggy

2. sun _____   calm

3. wind _____   neat

4. crisp _____   clean

5. mud _____   cloudy

Make up two sentences using each word and its opposite. Write your sentences on a separate sheet of paper.

Write and Spell on Your Own

Make 1 + 1 = 1

Unscramble the letters from the two words to make one new word. Use the words in parentheses to figure out the new word. (If necessary, check the dictionary for meanings.)

Hints: All the words end in *y*.
Some words have a double consonant before the *y*.

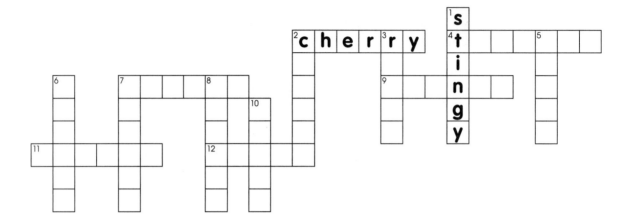

Across

2. cry + her (small fruit)
4. rift + thy (frugal)
7. shy + gag (rumpled)
9. sky + inn (scrawny)
11. spy + nap (lively)
12. dud + my (dirty)

Down

1. sty + gin (miserly)
2. sip + cry (crunchy)
3. us + try (corroded)
5. try + of (20 + 20)
6. ply + ten (more than enough)
7. sly + pop (messy)
8. pry + gum (grouchy)
10. dud + by (pal)

SPELLING RULES

© 2007, 2000, 1984 by Frances Bloom and Deborah Bloom Coates

Write and Spell on Your Own

UNIT 29 | More Endings

Add and Subtract

Long *e* word	Drop the *e* before adding *-ing*	To make a new word, make the vowel short and double the consonant
tape	**taping**	**tapping**
ride	_____	_____
scrape	_____	_____
plane	_____	_____
file	_____	_____
pine	_____	_____
hope	_____	_____
tile	_____	_____

Drop the e or Let It Be

1. Add the ending to each word.
2. Write the word in the column that matches the rule.

explode + ed	dazzle + ing	amuse + ment
complete + ion	like + ly	stride + ing
crumble + ly	use + ful	forgive + ing
mere + ly	create + ion	settle + ment
able + ly	noble + ly	care + ful

Before a vowel drop the *e*	Before a consonant keep the *e*	If a word ends in *-le*, drop *-le* and add *-ly*
exploded	**merely**	**crumbly**
_____	_____	_____
_____	_____	_____
_____	_____	_____
_____	_____	_____

SPELLING RULES

e—Use It or Drop It

Fill in each blank with a different form of the underlined word.

1. He likes to skate.

   He **skated** all the way home.

2. Today we can vote for class president.

   Who are you _____ for?

3. I tasted a new vegetable.

   It is fun to _____ new foods.

4. I can dive off the high board.

   We have _____ practice tomorrow.

5. The children were wasting our good paper.

   I try not to _____ anything.

6. Please smile for the photo.

   You were not _____ in the last photo I took.

7. Who was snoring last night?

   I certainly never _____.

8. He _____ his baseball cards.

   Will you trade baseball cards with me?

9. My cat's tail sticks straight up when she is scared.

   I wonder who is _____ my cat.

10. Glenda loves to arrange flowers.

    Her _____ looks pretty on the table.

11. Justin saved up enough money to buy a game.

    Now he is _____ to buy a book.

12. Kerry has finished her picture and has no use for the paints.

    Please give them to someone who might find them _____.

Write and Spell on Your Own

New Endings

1. Circle the words that are made from silent *e* words.

saved   turned   glared   liked   tuned   lunged

raked   planted   skipped   jumped   wiped   learned

exploded   timed   lined   dined   faded   stared

2. Write the silent *e* word for each circled word below.

_____   _____   _____   _____

_____   _____   _____   _____

_____   _____   _____   _____

_____

3. Write five sentences using a silent *e* word and the same word with an *–ing* ending.

Example: raked—rake
    We saw Bob raking the lawn with the new rake.

_____

_____

_____

_____

_____

_____

_____

_____

_____

_____

SPELLING RULES

Challenge: Add Endings

How many endings can you add to the words in the first column? (*Hint:* Only two of these words take more than three endings.) Remember the exceptions to the rule for dropping *e* before an ending beginning with a vowel.

Word	–ing	–ed	–able	–ous	–age
singe	singeing	singed			
venture	venturing	ventured		venturous	
1. change					
2. outrage					
3. canoe					
4. mile					
5. ridicule					
6. trace					
7. use					
8. store					
9. hoe					
10. dye					
11. acre					
12. waste					
13. continue					
14. courage					
15. adventure					

Write and Spell on Your Own

UNIT 30

y Math

1. Circle the word if the final *y* is preceded by a consonant.
2. Underline the word if the final *y* is preceded by a vowel.
3. Add the ending to the word.

> **Remember:**
> If the final *y* is preceded by a consonant, change the *y* to an *i*, except when the ending begins with an *i*.
> If the final *y* is preceded by a vowel, do not change the *y* to an *i*.

1. (deny) + ing = **denying** _____

2. angry + ly = _____

3. fancy + ful = _____

4. frisky + er = _____

5. enjoy + ed = _____

6. musty + est = _____

7. pity + ing = _____

8. happy + er = _____

9. buy + ing = _____

10. apply + ed = _____

11. boy + ish = _____

Complete a Story

A Friendly Neighbor?

"Look Keith!" shrieked Midge. "Do you see what I see? Look at what Mr. Reid did to his yard this time!"

Add suffixes to the following words to complete the story.

angry	moody	sloppy	jolly	busy	sly	tasty
healthy	play	pity	lazy	worry	noisy	

Include some of the following words.

sleigh	yield	fierce	friend	field	yield
either	weird	seize	chief	relief	receive

Write your story on a separate sheet of paper.

Write and Spell on Your Own

To *i* or Not To *i*

Add one of the following endings to the word on the left to complete each sentence.

−est   −er   −ed   −ly   −ing   −ful

rely   1. The dog _____ on its master for food.

betray   2. Jane was _____ a confidence when she told the secret.

apply   3. She _____ all the rules to solve the geometry problem.

beauty   4. The park looked _____ with all its flowers.

healthy   5. I am _____ than you.

pretty   6. That drawing is the _____ in the class.

merry   7. Molly walked _____ along the street.

busy   8. The ice-cream parlor was the _____ place in town.

employ   9. John was _____ by the owner of the busy store.

annoy   10. It is _____ to speak to a noisy audience.

Mix and Match *i* Before *e*

Pick one phrase from each group to make a sentence. How many combinations can you make?

i before *e*	except after *c*	sounding like /a/
My niece	got a receipt for	the eight dogs
The chief	has received	the freight
My friend	fixed the ceiling for	the sleigh
The thief	deceived	my neighbor

A Crossword Challenge Review

Across

1. Plump, fat
3. Used to make a canoe go
4. A bed for a baby
7. A glass or plastic container for juice or milk
8. Showing affection (add *-ing* to *love*)
10. Offended (add *-ed* to *repel*)
11. Neat, well kept
15. One who pilots a plane (add *-er* to *fly*)
16. A stick of wax with a wick burned for light
17. Making frightened (add *-ing* to *scare*)
18. Applauding (add *-ing* to *clap*)
19. Surrender, give up

Down

1. Snuggle (add *-le* to *cud*)
2. A fastening for a belt
5. A light rain
6. six + two =
7. Short, as in a short visit
9. Asked for (add *-ed* to *apply*)
12. Covered with a powdery film that settles on furniture and other surfaces (add *-y*)
13. A high piece of land, but lower than a mountain
14. Confined, as for a bird or other animal
16. The head of an Indian tribe

SPELLING RULES

Write and Spell on Your Own

PART 4

Complementary Skills

Expand with Affixes

You can expand a word by adding a prefix or a suffix. How many additional words can you make by adding a prefix or suffix (or both) to the words listed?

Prefixes: un–   re–   bi–   mid–   mis–   dis–

Suffixes: –er   –ed   –ly   –ful   –ing   –able   –ment

week _____

like _____

agree _____

kind _____

use _____

twist _____

load _____

match _____

lock _____

manage _____

place _____

service _____

Write and Spell on Your Own

Make a New Word

Find a word in the first sentence that can be used in the second sentence by adding a prefix, a suffix, or both. Use the word to fill in the blank in the second sentence.

Prefixes and suffixes to use:

re–   mis–   –able   –ed   –ing   –age   –ist   –est

Example: I should write a letter to my friend.
          The letter was silly and I decided to *rewrite* it.

1. I am a fast runner.

   The _____ runner won the race.

2. It was my good fortune to win the prize.

   Losing that great job was a _____.

3. You should enjoy seeing Jim in that comic role.

   The great acting and scenery made the play very _____.

4. You must study to get good grades.

   They spent the whole day _____ for the exam.

5. Did you notice that the glass was cracked?

   The tear in her dress was very _____.

6. It is only a mile to the road.

   Dad likes to keep a record of his _____ when he drives his car.

7. After Nancy studied, she knew she could spell all the words.

   Roy noticed that a few of the words in his new book were _____.

8. I love to go to the art museum.

   One day I will become a famous _____.

Two from One

Use the two root words and the prefix in each box to make two words to complete each sentence.

1. willing pack un

1. Tom was ___**unwilling**___ to ___**unpack**___ the suitcase.

2. The current mayor was _____ after a _____ of the votes.

2. re count elected

3. way sub marine

3. Uncle Bill has been underwater in a _____ and underground in a _____.

4. It is a _____ that the man was _____ in the newspaper.

4. quoted mis fortune

5. biography auto graph

5. I asked the author to _____ his _____.

6. Did you _____ of _____ the club?

6. dis banding approve

Prefix Phrases

Make two words equal one by adding a prefix to one of the words. Then write a phrase with each new word.

1. write again = ___**rewrite**___   ___**Rewrite the letters.**___

2. not numbered = _____   _____

3. judge incorrectly = _____   _____

4. pay before = _____   _____

5. within the state = _____   _____

6. after war = _____   _____

7. half a circle = _____   _____

8. not eaten = _____   _____

9. behave badly = _____   _____

10. make a friend = _____   _____

Write and Spell on Your Own

A New Part of Speech

> Different suffixes make different parts of speech.
>
> **Examples**
>
>   *–ment, –tion, –ness*—usually make *nouns*
>   *–less, –able, –ible, –ful*—usually make *adjectives*
>   *–ize, –fy, –ify*—usually make *verbs*
>   *–ly*—usually makes an *adverb*

Fill in the blank in the second sentence of each pair by adding one of the above suffixes to the italicized word in the first sentence.

Form an adjective or a noun:

1. Most birds *migrate* south in the winter.

   We will study about _____ in science class.

2. Would you like to *use* our old TV?

   It is _____ to us.

3. Our kittens *play* all the time.

   They are the most _____ animals I have ever had.

4. Steve will *reproduce* this map for you.

   He always makes a beautiful _____.

5. We *live* in an old farmhouse.

   It is not a _____ house in the winter.

6. Janet always looks *lonely*.

   _____ can be a sad feeling.

Form an adverb or a verb:

7. It is important to know the *alphabet*.

   Authors must _____ the index in a book.

8. Pam wanted to make a new *friend*.

   She was very _____ toward the new girl in school.

9. The answer to his question was *false*.

   People should never _____ information.

Write and Spell on Your Own

COMPLEMENTARY SKILLS

Linkage

Use the listed prefixes, suffixes, and root words to complete the links.

1. Write the words you make.
2. Use each word in a sentence that will show the meaning of the word.

Prefixes
inter–
dis–
re–
de–
un–
in–

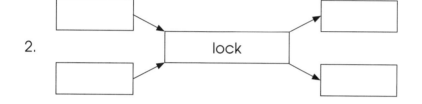

Suffixes
–ing
–ion
–ed
–able

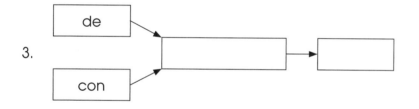

Root words
–struct–
–appear–
–appoint–

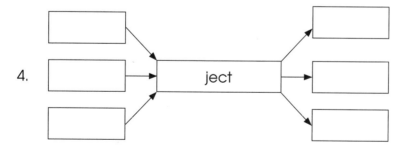

Write and Spell on Your Own

Make It Plural

Change the following words to the plural form. Write the plural of the word in the correct column.

lady	class	baby	woman	key	bush
wolf	boy	tax	banjo	ox	moose
leaf	jelly	tomato	child	loaf	knife
sheep	foot	journey	peach	rodeo	trout
goose	spaghetti	deer	half	navy	library

Add *s*	Add *es*	Change *y* to *i* and add *es*
_____	_____	_____
_____	_____	_____
_____	_____	_____
_____	_____	_____
_____	_____	_____

Change *f* to *v*	Change the spelling	Spelling does not change
_____	_____	**spaghetti**
_____	_____	_____
_____	_____	_____
_____	_____	_____
_____	_____	_____

Write and Spell on Your Own

Plural Sentences

Complete each sentence with the plural form of the italicized word.

1. I have one pink *dress,* but many blue _____**dresses**_____.

2. You can use your ticket to fly to one *city* or three different _____.

3. A black *calf* got out of the field and the other _____ followed it.

4. I have seen many inactive _____ but only one active *volcano.*

5. Uncle Peter bought one *radio* for his car and two _____ for his house.

6. The cat caught one *mouse* and is now looking for more _____.

7. We have a stone *chimney* on our cabin and two brick _____ on our house.

8. Sue has an old *piano* at home but can use one of the three grand

   _____ at school.

© 2007, 2000, 1984 by Frances Bloom and Deborah Bloom Coates

Write and Spell on Your Own

UNIT CS3 | Apostrophes

Make a Contraction

1. Cross out the letters that will be replaced by an apostrophe to write a contraction.
2. Write the contraction for the two words.
3. Write a sentence for each contraction.

we are	**we're**	**We're very busy.**
are not	_____	_____
is not	_____	_____
could have	_____	_____
there is	_____	_____
who will	_____	_____
you are	_____	_____
let us	_____	_____
you have	_____	_____
he would	_____	_____
had not	_____	_____

Form a Contraction

1. Join the following words with *is*. Write the contractions.

she	that	who	where	here
she's	_____	_____	_____	_____

2. Join the following words with *would*. Write the contractions.

you	they	we	who	he	I
you'd	_____	_____	_____	_____	_____

3. Join the following words with *will*. Write the contractions.

he	that	they	there	we	you
he'll	_____	_____	_____	_____	_____

Write and Spell on Your Own

COMPLEMENTARY SKILLS

What Is It?

1. Answer the question, "What is it?" for each sentence.
2. Find your answer from the words in the box.
3. Write the answer in a complete sentence that begins with a contraction.

1. They swim in icy waters.   **They're polar bears.**

2. It has wings.   _____

3. I live under the ground.   _____

4. They went to the moon.   _____

5. I have a broken leg.   _____

6. That is all correct.   _____

7. We cheer for our team.   _____

8. She paints beautiful pictures.   _____

9. He helps us learn to read.   _____

cast	perfect	bird
polar bears ✓	astronauts	alligators
pencil	cheerleaders	artist
worm	teacher	baby

Can *I'll* Be *Ill*?

Some contractions spell a different word if the apostrophe is left out.

1. Circle each contraction that could be a different word without the apostrophe.
2. Use a separate piece of paper to write both words in one sentence.

Example: I'll, ill   I'll be *ill* if I eat too much candy.

I'll	I'm	that's	she'll	couldn't	she'd	it's
we'll	we've	we're	when's	wasn't	we'd	

Pick Your Words

On a separate piece of paper, write seven sentences, each containing one word from each column. Use the plural possessive form of the words in Column A.

Example: The geese's feathers were wet.

Column A	Column B	Column C
cat	homes	spotted
man	feathers	fun
elf	toys	torn
child	tools	dull
goose	coats	wet
girl	books	rusty
sister-in-law	games	bright
	paws	new
	whiskers	cheery

Make It Possessive

Use the possessive form of the word in parentheses to complete each sentence. Some of the words form the plural possessive.

1. (ferry)   Both **ferries'** captains looked tired at the end of the day.

2. (actor)   The _____ makeup was wearing off.

3. (jockey)   The _____ horse did not do well in the first race.

4. (daughter)   My two _____ rooms were rather sloppy.

5. (group)   The _____ tickets were available at the box office.

6. (friend)   My three _____ pictures were in the art exhibit.

7. (thief)   The police removed both of the _____ masks.

8. (wolf)   All the _____ cubs stayed in their dens.

9. (island)   The three _____ beaches look alike.

10. (Philips)   The _____ van holds seven passengers.

11. (tree)   The _____ branches broke in the storm.

Write and Spell on Your Own

Abbreviate Your Notes

Rewrite these notes using abbreviations for the italicized words.

1. Please meet me on *Saturday* at 12:30 *in the afternoon.*

   _____

   _____

2. May I borrow five *tablespoons* of honey and a *pint* of cream?

   _____

   _____

3. Our *company* is moving to a new *building* next *Tuesday, March* 28.

   _____

   _____

4. The *vice president* of our club will meet with the *governor* this coming *November.*

   _____

   _____

5. *Doctor* Jones drove at sixty *miles per hour* on the new *highway* to deliver the *package* on time.

   _____

   _____

COMPLEMENTARY SKILLS

Abbreviated Questions

Answer the questions in complete sentences with abbreviations.

1. Who is the president of the United States?

   _____

2. What is your height and weight?

   _____

3. How many inches are in a foot?

   _____

4. Would you mail a letter at the railroad or at the post office?

   _____

5. What day comes after Tuesday?

   _____

Rewrite Using Abbreviations

Rewrite the following using abbreviations.

1. Mister Juan Perez, Treasurer

   _____

2. She lives on Cedar Street off Maple Avenue and Smith Boulevard.

   _____

3. Sixty seconds equal one minute.

   _____

4. A milligram is a metric unit of weight equal to $\frac{1}{1000}$ gram.

   _____

5. Lisa is four feet, eight inches tall.

   _____

Write and Spell on Your Own

APPENDIX A

Graded Word Lists

The graded word list assists the teacher in identifying the grade level of the words that might be added in each unit. It also provides irregular words that may be appropriate as sight words for units in Parts 2 and 3. Plurals are not included in this list except when they are formed irregularly.

The teacher can do the following to introduce these words:

- Discuss the meanings of the words.
- Point out the similarities and differences among groups of words.
- Post the words in the room for visual reinforcement.
- Post in the room advertisements, comic strips, or any other appropriate material that contains these words.
- Use selected words in the games and activities described in each unit, such as hangman, word search, crossword puzzles, and on-the-board activities.

The students can do the following:

- Use the words in sentences, phrases, or creative writing.
- Write notes to each other that include the assigned words. (Partners can check each other for spelling accuracy.)
- Make up and exchange puzzles.
- Use the words to create their own comic strips, advertisements, greeting cards, questionnaires, slogans, or signs.
- Pair off to test each other on assigned words.
- Keep a card file of words they have difficulty spelling.

Grade 2

a	come	had	log	ran	two
after	crow	happy	long	rat	
all		has	look	read	under
am	day	have		red	up
an	dear	he	made	rip	us
and	did	help	make	rob	
are	do	her	man	run	very
armchair	dog	here	me		
at	doll	him	milk	said	want
away	down	his	mother	Santa	was
	drip	home	my	saw	water
baby	drown	hop		say	we
back		house	name	school	went
ball		how	new	see	were
barnyard	eye	hug	night	she	what
be			no	slap	when
bed	find	I	not	snore	white
big	five	if		so	who
bit	for	in	of	some	wig
black	four	is	off	store	will
book	from	it	on		win
box	fun		one	take	with
boy		jet	other	that	work
	gave		ouch	the	
cab	get	know	our	them	yes
came	girl		out	then	you
can	give	last	over	there	your
car	glad	lasted		they	
cat	go	lick	pat	this	zoo
chin	going	like	play	three	
chip	good	little	pretty	to	
clap	got	live	put	today	

Grade 3

about	ago	along	another	anything	around
afternoon	air	already	answer	apple	as
again	airplane	also	ant	arithmetic	ask
age	almost	always	any	arm	asked

Appendix A: Graded Word Lists

asleep
assembly
ate
aunt
ax

bad
bag
barn
beak
bean
bear
beautiful
because
bee
been
before
begging
behind
bell
best
better
bind
bird
birthday
blue
boast
boat
both
bread
bright
bring
broke
brother
brought
brown
bud
buffalo
bug
built
busy
buy
by

cage
cake
call
called
candy
canned
cannot
cap
card
care
carry
catch
caught
chair
chicken
child
children
Christmas
church
city
class
claw
clean
cleaning
close
clothes
coat
coconut
cold
color
colored
comes
coming
cone
cool
corn
could
couldn't
country
cousin
cover
covered
cow
cowboy

crew
cried
crook
cry
cucumber
curl
cut

dad
daddy
dance
dancer
dark
daytime
December
demon
desk
dew
didn't
different
dinner
dish
does
doing
done
don't
door
downtown
dress
drink
dry

each
early
Easter
eating
egg
eight
employ
end
enough
ever
every
everything

fable
face
facing
fairy
fall
far
farm
farmer
fast
fastest
fat
father
feed
feet
fell
female
few
fifth
fight
fill
fine
fire
firm
first
fish
fishing
flag
flew
flower
fly
foil
food
foot
forget
forgot
found
Friday
friend
front
full
funny

game
garden

gets
gives
glass
gloom
glow
goes
gold
gone
good-bye
grab
grade
grandmother
grass
gray
great
green
groom
ground
grow
guess

hair
half
Halloween
hand
hard
hat
haven't
having
hay
head
hear
heard
heel
held
helped
hide
high
higher
hill
hitting
hold
hood
hope

hopped
horse
host
hot
hugged
hummed
humor
hundred
hurt
hut

I'll
I'm
ice
Indian
inside
into
isn't
it's

Jeep
jump
jumped
just

keep
kidnap
kind
kitten
knew

lady
lake
land
lantern
large
late
later
lay
leak
learn
learned
leave
leaves

398

left	met	paint	remember	skipping	takes
let	meter	pair	rest	sky	talk
letter	might	papa	ride	sled	tall
light	mine	paper	riding	sleep	teach
lighter	mined	park	right	small	teacher
liked	mining	party	ring	snow	teaches
likes	minus	pass	river	snowball	teeth
liking	miss	passed	robin	snowed	tell
lilac	Miss	patting	robot	snowing	telling
line	money	paw	rode	snowman	tells
lived	monkey	pen	roll	something	ten
lives	mopping	pencil	room	sometime	than
loan	more	people	round	song	thank
looked	morning	perch	runs	soon	Thanksgiving
looking	most	pet		sorry	that's
looks	motel	petted	saddle	spend	their
lost	mouse	piano	same	spool	these
lot	mouth	pick	sand	spring	thing
lots	move	picked	sang	star	think
love	moved	picture	Santa Claus	start	thinking
loved	much	pie	sat	started	third
loving	must	piece	Saturday	stay	thought
low		place	says	stayed	through
lunch	named	plant	second	stick	throw
	names	played	seeing	still	tie
mail	near	playing	seen	stool	till
mailbox	neck	plays	send	stop	time
makes	nest	please	sent	story	together
making	never	poor	set	stray	told
male	news	prefix	seven	street	tomorrow
malt	next	pull	shall	string	tonight
mamma	nice	puppy	sheep	study	too
many	nine		shoe	stupid	took
mapped	noon	rabbit	shook	summer	top
marble	nothing	radar	short	sun	tow
March	now	radio	should	Sunday	town
mark		raid	slck	sunning	toy
may	o'clock	rain	side	supper	train
maybe	old	raindrop	since	suppose	tray
mean	once	raining	sing	sure	tree
meat	only	razor	singing	sweet	tried
meet	or	reading	sister		truly
men	outside	ready	sit	table	try
merry	owl	real	six	tail	trying

tugged
tulip
turn

uncle
until
upon
upset
use
used

vacation
valentine
visit
vitamin
volcano

walk
walking
wanted
wants

warm
wash
watch
way
wear
weather
week
well
wet
where

which
while
why
wind
window
winner
winning
winter
wiped
wish

won't
wood
woods
word
working
would
write
writing
wrote

yard
yawn
year
yellow
yet

zebra
zipper

Grade 4

able	balloon	board	candle	company	dirty
above	band	body	can't	contest	doctor
across	bang	boot	capital	cook	doesn't
add	bank	born	careful	cooked	dollar
address	bark	bottle	carried	cookies	downstairs
afraid	baseball	bottom	carrots	corner	drank
against	basket	bought	cart	cost	draw
ahead	basketball	bow	cattle	costly	drawing
aircraft	bath	boxes	cause	cotton	dream
airline	beach	branch	cave	count	dreamed
airmail	beat	branches	center	couple	dressed
all right	became	brave	central	course	dresses
alone	become	bravely	cents	crack	drew
among	began	break	chalk	cream	dried
animal	begin	breakfast	chew	creek	drill
answered	being	bridge	chief	cross	drive
anyone	believe	broom	circus	crossed	driving
anyway	belong	brush	clay	crossing	drop
anywhere	below	build	clear	cute	dropped
April	belt	building	climate		drove
aren't	berries	bunch	cllmb	dam	duck
arrow	beside	burn	climbed	dead	dug
art	between	butter	clock	December	during
atom	bicycle	buying	closer	deck	dust
August	bigger		cloth	deep	
avenue	biggest	cabin	clothing	deer	ear
awful	bite	calf	clown	die	east
awhile	blew	camel	club	died	easy
awoke	block	camp	coal	dime	eaten
	blow	canal	coffee	dirt	eighth

either	fool	heart	king	match	opened
electric	football	hello	kiss	May	orange
elephant	forest	helping	kitchen	meal	others
eleven	fourth	hen	kite	means	ought
else	fox	hers	kitty	meeting	ours
engine	free	herself	knife	melt	own
English	fresh	hid	knock	middle	
enjoy	friendly	himself		mile	pack
enjoyed	frog	history	Labor Day	mill	package
eve	frost	hit	ladder	mind	pail
even	fruit	hole	laid	minute	painted
evening	fry	hoping	lamb	missed	pan
everybody	fur	horn	lamp	Monday	parents
everyone	furniture	hospital	language	month	part
except		hour	lard	moonlight	pasture
excuse	gas	hungry	larger	mountain	pay
	gate	hunt	largest	moving	peak
fair	gather	hunting	laugh	mud	peanut
family	geography	hurry	laughed	muddy	peas
faster	germs		learning	music	pennies
feast	getting	ice cream	least	myself	penny
February	gift	I'd	leg		person
fed	given	ill	lesson	nail	picnic
feeding	giving	important	library	nearly	pig
feel	God	inch	lie	neck	pigeon
feeling	goose	inches	life	need	pile
felt	grand	ink	lion	needle	pin
fence	grandma	insects	listen	New Year	pine
field	grandpa	instead	lit	noise	pipe
fifteen	group	iron	living	none	playground
fifteenth	grown-up	I've	load	north	playhouse
fifty	grows		lock	nose	playmate
filled	gum	jack	lonesome	November	pleased
finger	gun	January	longer	number	poem
finish		job	loose	nut	pole
firecrackers	hall	July	loud		pond
fix	handle	jumping	lovely	ocean	pony
flat	hang	June	luck	October	popcorn
flies	happen	jungle	lucky	office	porch
four	happened		lumber	often	post
flying	hasn't	kept		oh	potato
follow	hate	kill	machine	oil	potatoes
following	health	killed	mad	older	present
follows	hearing	kind	maple	open	president

prevent
prize
program
proud
public
pulled
pulling
pump
pupil
puppies
puts
putting

queen
quick
quickly
quiet
quit
quite

rabbits
race
rag
railway
rained
rainy
raise
rather
reach
reached
reader
reads
reason
receive
received
recess
reindeer
report
ribbon
rice

rich
riddle
ringing
road
rock
roof
rooms
rope
rose
ruler
running

safe
salt
sank
save
schoolhouse
sea
seat
seed
self
sell
sending
September
sets
sew
sewing
shark
ship
shoe
shoot
shot
showed
silk
silver
sincerely
sitting
size
skate
skating

skin
sleigh
slid
slide
sliding
soap
soft
soil
sold
somebody
someone
son
songs
sooner
sore
south
speak
spell
spent
spill
squirrel
stack
stairs
stand
state
station
stationery
staying
step
stepped
sting
stocking
stone
stood
stopped
stories
storm
stove
straight
strange

strong
stuck
studies
such
sudden
suddenly
sugar
suit
sung
supposed
surely
surprise
surprised
sweater
swim
swimming
swing

tables
tack
taken
taking
taught
tea
teaching
team
tear
tease
telephone
tent
theater
thick
thin
thirty
though
thousand
threw
Thursday
tiger
tin

tired
tooth
track
trap
trick
trip
trouble
truck
Tuesday
tumble
turkey
turned
twelfth
twelve
twenty
twenty-five
twice
twin

underwear
unknown
upstairs
uses

Valentine's
    Day
valley

wagon
wait
waited
walked
walks
wall
war
washed
washing
wasn't
watched
watching

wax
wears
Wednesday
west
whole
whose
wide
wild
window
windy
wing
wire
wished
wishes
wishing
witch
without
woke
wolf
woman
women
won
wonder
wonderful
wool
world
wouldn't
written
wrong

young
you're
yours
yourself

zone

Grade 5

absent	badge	bone	catalog	collar	dangerous
accent	badly	bookcase	celebrate	colt	darling
account	bake	booklet	cellar	comb	dart
ache	bakery	bore	cement	comic	dash
acre	bale	borrow	cent	concern	date
act	banking	boss	certain	consent	daughter
added	bar	bother	certainly	content	deaf
addition	bare	bowl	chain	copies	deal
adorable	barrel	brag	chance	copy	dearest
adore	base	brain	change	correct	death
adventure	basement	brass	changed	correction	decide
afterward	bathing	brick	chase	costs	decimal
alive	battle	bubble	chased	costume	dentist
although	bay	buck	chat	cough	depart
amount	bead	bucket	cheat	countries	department
ancestor	beam	buggy	check	county	depot
anger	beauty	bulb	cheese	court	desert
angry	bedroom	bump	cherries	crawl	dessert
ankle	bedtime	burglar	cherry	crayon	destroy
annoy	beech	buried	chest	crazy	difference
answering	bee	burned	chimney	cries	dim
anybody	beg	bush	chocolate	crocodile	dining
anyhow	begged	bushes	choice	crooked	discovered
anymore	beginning	button	choose	crop	disease
apart	begins	buttonhole	chose	crouch	distance
appreciate	behave		chosen	crowd	ditch
apron	bench	calves	chubby	crumb	divide
arid	Bible	camera	chum	crush	divided
army	blackboard	canary	circle	cure	division
artist	blade	cane	classes	curly	dock
ashamed	blanket	canoe	classmate	cutting	dodge
Atlantic	bleed	cape	closed		dominion
attend	bless	captain	closet	daily	dormant
attic	blood	captured	closing	dainty	double
auditorium	bloom	carefully	coach	damage	downward
author	blouse	carload	coarse	damp	dozen
auto	blowing	carol	coast	danced	drag
automobile	bog	carries	coastline	dances	dresser
average	bold	carrying	cocoon	dancing	driver
awfully	bomb	carve	coil	dandy	drug
	bond	case	coin	danger	drum

drunk	fearfully	frozen	handful	humid	knee
	fellow	fuel	handkerchief	humidity	knives
eagle	fender	furnace	harder	hung	knocked
earn	festival	fuse	hardly	hunted	known
earth	fever		hardware	hunter	
easier	fiddle	gain	harp	hurried	lace
easily	fighting	garage	haul		ladies
eastward	figure	giant	hazy	idea	lane
edge	file	girl's	headache	ideal	lap
education	film	globe	headquarters	imagine	lately
eighteen	fir	gloves	heal	Indians	laughing
empty	fire engine	glue	healthy	inertia	law
ended	fishhook	goal	heap	inn	lawn
enjoyable	fit	goat	heat	inner	laying
enter	fixed	goddess	heavy	intent	lazy
envelope	flap	golf	he'd	interest	lead
environment	flash	goods	hedge	invite	leader
erect	flashlight	gotten	helmet	invited	leaf
Eskimo	flavor	grace	herd	island	leather
especially	flight	grain	here's	itch	leaving
evermore	float	grammar	he's		led
examination	flock	grandfather	hidden	jacket	lemon
excel	flood	grandparents	highest	jail	lemonade
excellent	flow	grape	high school	jar	length
excite	followed	grapefruit	hike	jaw	less
exciting	ford	gravel	hind	jelly	let's
exercise	foreign	graze	hitch	jerk	lettuce
exhibit	forgotten	grew	hog	jingle	level
expect	fork	groan	holding	join	lift
export	form	groceries	holiday	joined	lightweight
extra	formed	grocery	homeward	joke	likely
	fort	grounds	honey	journey	limb
factory	forth	grove	honor	juice	lime
fade	forty	growing	hoof	juicy	limp
fail	forward	growl	hook	junior	lined
falling	foul	grown	horizontal	junk	lining
fallow	fourteen	gulf	horseback		links
fame	fraction	gym	hose	keen	listened
fare	frank		hotel	keeper	listening
fasten	freckles	habit	hours	keeping	lively
favor	freely	hadn't	household	kerchief	livestock
favorite	freeze	hamburger	however	key	loaf
fawn	fright	hammer	howl	kick	loafing
fearful	froze	handed	hub	kit	love

lovingly	motorboat	onion	pickling	princess	remark
lower	motorman	operetta	pilgrims	probably	remembered
lump	mottoes	orchestra	pillow	pronounce	remove
lying	mounted	order	pint	property	report
	movie	ourselves	pioneer	protect	respect
magic	museum	outdoors	pitch	protest	restore
main	musician	outfit	pitcher	puddle	return
mainland		outline	placed	pulley	rid
mainly	nature	outskirts	plain	pumpkin	rifle
mar	nearby	outstanding	plan	purely	ripe
march	neat	outward	plane	purple	rise
mark	necktie	oven	planned	purse	rising
market	needed	overcharge	plate	push	risk
marred	needs	overcoat	platform		rivers
married	neighbor	overcome	player	quart	roast
master	nephew	overflow	pleasant	quarter	rocket
mate	net	overlook	pleasure	quest	rolled
matter	newspaper	overslept	plenty	question	roller
mayor	nicely	overturn	plot	quietly	rooster
meadow	nickel	owe	plow	quilt	root
meantime	niece	owner	pocket		rot
measles	nobody	ownership	pocketbook	raccoon	rotten
measure	nor		point	racket	rough
medal	northeastern	Pacific	poke	ragged	row
medicine	northward	packing	polar	railroad	rub
melted	northwestern	page	police	rainbow	rubber
mess	note	paid	policeman	rainfall	rug
mice	notebook	painting	polite	raised	rugged
midyear	noted	palace	pool	rake	ruin
missing	notice	pants	porcupine	rally	rule
mist	noticeable	parade	postal	ramp	
mistake	nurse	parties	post office	ranch	sack
mistaken	nursery	parts	pottery	rang	sad
mittens		passing	pound	range	safety
mixed	oak	past	pour	rank	sail
mob	oasis	paste	powder	rare	saint
monster	oatmeal	patch	practice	raw	sake
monthly	oat	path	practicing	ray	sale
mood	obey	peaches	pray	reaches	salmon
moon	odd	pearl	preach	reform	salty
moss	offer	peel	prepare	refugee	sandbar
mostly	officer	penmanship	press	regards	savage
moth	oldest	perhaps	price	regular	saved
motor	one's	phone	prince	remain	saving

saying	shell	smaller	stage	tackle
scar	shelter	smart	stalk	tag
scare	shift	smell	stall	talked
scarecrow	shine	smile	stamp	talking
scarf	shining	smoke	standing	talks
scoop	ships	smooth	standpoint	tame
scooter	shirt	snake	stands	tan
score	shock	sneak	starting	tank
scoreboard	shoes	sneeze	starts	tape
scorekeeper	shooting	snowplow	stays	taxi
scout	shop	soak	steal	teammate
scoutmaster	shore	sob	steel	temper
scowl	shoulder	socks	stiff	tennis
scrapbook	shout	somewhat	stock	term
screen	shovel	somewhere	stockyard	terrible
scrub	shows	sort	stoop	test
seashore	shut	sound	strain	thanks
season	shy	soup	stranger	themselves
secretary	side	southeastern	straw	there's
seek	sidewalk	southward	strawberries	they'd
seem	sight	southwest	streak	they're
seemed	sing	southwestern	stream	thinks
seems	signed	space	streamline	thirteen
sees	sink	spaghetti	street	thread
select	sir	spare	strip	thrill
selling	sixteen	sparrow	stubborn	throat
sends	sixth	speaker	studied	throwing
sentence	sixty	speaking	stuff	thumb
separate	ski	spear	stump	tight
serve	skim	speed	stunt	tiny
setting	skinned	spinach	subject	tip
settle	skunk	split	suit	tire
seventeen	slant	spoil	sum	toast
seventh	slaves	spoke	sunny	toe
several	sleeping	spoken	sunrise	tomato
shack	sleepy	sport	sunshine	tomatoes
shade	sleeve	sportsmanship	supermarket	tone
shake	slept	spot	swamp	tools
shape	slice	spread	swan	tore
sharp	slim	spy	sway	toss
sharpen	slip	square	sweep	touch
she'd	slippers	squeak	swell	touchdown
shed	slow	squeeze		tour
sheet	slowly	stable	tablet	tourist

toward	turkeys	visiting	westward	wrap
town	turning	vote	we've	wrapped
trade	turnpike		whale	wrist
traffic		waiting	whatever	writes
trail	umbrella	wake	wheat	
trailer	undergo	walls	wheel	yard
training	understand	walnut	whenever	yarn
tramp	understanding	waste	whether	yell
travel	unhappy	waterpower	whistle	you'd
traveled	uniform	wave	whom	you'll
treasure	unit	ways	wicked	you've
treat	unless	weak	wife	
tribe	unload	weakness	wilderness	zero
tributary	unwilling	wearing	windmill	
tries	upward	we'd	wine	
trim	useful	weed	wooden	
troop	using	weigh	wore	
trout	usually	weighed	work	
true		welcome	worked	
trunk	vine	we'll	worm	
truth	violin	we're	worse	
tub	visited	western	worth	

Grade 6

© 2007, 2000, 1984 by Frances Bloom and Deborah Bloom Coates

ability	admitted	alarm	answerable	article
absence	adopted	album	anxious	ashes
accept	advance	alfalfa	apartment	aside
accident	advantage	alike	apiece	assignment
accidentally	advertisement	allow	appear	assistance
accomplish	advice	allowance	appearance	association
according	advise	allowed	apply	astronaut
achieve	aerial	altogether	appointed	attached
acquainted	afford	amazed	appointment	attack
acted	agent	ambition	appreciated	attempt
action	ages	ambulance	appreciation	attendance
active	agree	American	approached	attention
activity	agreed	anchor	area	attractive
actually	agriculture	ancient	argument	audience
addition	aid	angel	arrange	autograph
addressed	aim	angle	arranged	automatic
admire	airport	angrily	arrival	autumn
admit	aisle	announced	arrive	aviation

aviator	brake	celery	committing	cruel
avoid	breaking	cell	common	curious
awake	breast	century	community	current
	breath	certificate	compared	curtain
bacon	breathe	changes	compelled	
bait	breathing	changing	complete	daddy's
baking	bride	channel	completed	dairy
balance	broken	chapter	completely	dare
balanced	brook	character	composition	dawn
banana	bruise	charge	computer	debt
banner	bugle	charged	concert	declared
banquet	bull	cheap	condition	decorate
barely	bundle	cheer	conduct	decorated
batteries	burst	cheerful	conductor	deed
beast	bury	cheerfully	conferring	defeat
beaten	burying	choir	congress	degree
beautifully	business	chop	connect	delay
becomes	butterfly	chopped	connected	delighted
becoming		chore	conquer	deliver
beef	cabbage	chorus	consider	delivered
begun	cabinet	Christian	consideration	delivery
believed	cable	churches	constitution	demand
belongs	cafeteria	citizen	contain	depend
bend	calendar	civil	continent	describe
beneath	calm	civilization	continue	description
bent	campus	claim	continued	design
beyond	canning	clerk	contract	destroyed
bid	cannon	clever	control	developed
bill	canyon	cliff	controller	development
biography	capitol	cloud	convention	devil
birth	captive	cloudy	conversation	diamond
blame	capture	clover	copper	dictionary
blank	cardboard	collect	cottage	diet
blaze	cared	collected	council	difficult
blind	careless	collection	courage	difficulty
blink	carnival	college	cracked	digging
blizzard	carpet	colonies	cradle	dip
blooming	carriage	colony	crash	direct
blossom	cash	comfort	create	direction
boil	cast	comfortable	creature	directly
border	castle	command	creep	director
borrowed	caused	commerce	crime	disappear
bound	ceiling	commercial	criminal	disappeared
boundary	celebration	committee	crowded	disappointed

discoverer	entire	famous	fountain	graph
discussion	entirely	fancy	fountain pen	grasshopper
distant	equal	farming	fragrant	grave
district	equality	farther	frame	gravity
dive	equally	fastened	freedom	grease
divider	equipment	fate	freezing	greater
doubt	equipping	fault	freight	greatest
draft	erase	favorable	fried	greatly
drawn	erased	fear	friendlier	greet
drift	escape	feather	friendship	grind
driven	Europe	feature	frightened	growth
drumming	event	feels	funeral	guard
due	everywhere	fierce	furnish	guest
dull	evidence	figures	furnished	guide
dumb	evil	final	further	gymnasium
dusty	exactly	finally	future	
duties	examined	finding		hail
duty	example	finest	gaining	halves
dying	exchange	finished	gallon	handsome
	excited	fireplace	gang	handy
earlier	excitement	fireworks	gardener	hanging
earned	exclaim	flame	gasoline	happier
eastern	excused	fled	gathered	happily
echo	excusing	fold	gathering	happiness
edition	expected	folk	gay	harbor
editor	expelled	follows	geese	harden
effect	expense	fond	general	harm
effort	expensive	fooled	generally	harness
eighty	experience	foolish	gentle	harvest
elected	explain	forbidden	gentleman	hatch
election	explained	force	gentlemen	hated
electricity	express	forced	ghost	haunted
elevator	extremely	foreigner	gleam	heaven
elk	eyebrows	forever	golden	heavily
embarrassed		forgetting	goodness	height
embroidery	fact	forgive	govern	helpful
empire	factories	forgiven	government	hero
employed	facts	formation	governor	hiding
enemies	failed	form	gown	highway
enemy	fairly	former	grabbed	hired
energy	faith	fortunate	gradual	hobby
engineer	fallen	fortune	gradually	hollow
entered	false	fought	graduate	holy
entertainment	families	foundation	grandstand	homesick

Appendix A: Graded Word Lists

honest	jolliest	located	message	nineteen
horrible	jolly	location	metal	ninety
how's	joy	lodge	method	ninth
huge	judge	lonely	midnight	noble
human		loop	mighty	northern
husband	kicked	losing	mild	noticed
hydrogen	kid	loss	milking	noticing
hygiene	kindergarten	lowest	million	
	kindly	lung	mineral	oar
iceberg	kindness		minister	object
imagination	kisses	machine	minor	objection
immediately	kneel	machinery	minority	occurring
importance	knight	madder	mint	omitted
impossible	knit	magazine	mischief	operation
improve	knob	maid	mischievous	opinion
improvement	knot	mailed	mixture	opposite
include	knowing	majesty	model	orbit
including	knowledge	major	modern	ordered
increased	knuckles	majority	moisture	ordinary
indeed		manage	moment	ore
independent	labor	manager	motive	organ
industry	lack	manner	mount	organization
influence	landed	manners	movement	original
information	largely	manual	mule	overalls
injured	latter	manufacture	multiply	
innocent	lawyer	manufacturer	mum	package
instance	lazily	manufacturing	muscles	packed
instant	leading	marked	musical	paddle
instruments	league	marriage	mystery	pajamas
intelligence	lean	marry		pale
intelligent	lets	mask	narrow	palm
intend	letting	matches	nation	pancake
invent	liberty	material	national	paraded
invention	lies	meaning	native	paragraph
inventor	lighted	meant	natural	pardon
invitation	lightening	meanwhile	naughty	parlor
ironing	lightly	mechanic	navy	particular
itself	linen	medium	nearer	partner
	liquid	member	nearest	passage
jackknife	list	memory	necessary	passenger
janitor	literature	mend	neighborhood	passive
jealous	loaves	mention	neither	patient
jewel	local	mentioned	nervous	pattern
jollier	locally	merchant	nicer	paying

peace	prettiest	rate	scenery	shopping
peek	prevention	realize	schoolmate	shouldn't
pepper	prices	reasons	science	shower
percent	primary	rebelling	scientist	showing
perfect	principal	receipt	scissors	shown
performance	principle	receiving	scold	sickness
perfume	print	recently	scrape	sideways
period	printer	record	scratch	sigh
permission	printing	recover	scream	signal
permitting	prison	referring	seacoast	silence
personal	private	refused	seal	silent
petal	problem	region	search	silly
photograph	process	regret	secret	similar
physical	produce	regretted	secretary	simple
pickle	product	reign	section	single
pier	production	relation	secure	skiing
pilot	professor	religion	seize	skill
pirate	progress	religious	seldom	skirt
planning	project	remind	semester	sliced
plantation	promise	rent	senator	slight
plastic	promised	replied	sense	slipped
poison	propeller	reply	sensible	slippery
polish	proper	request	series	smiled
ponies	protection	required	serious	snap
popular	proved	result	servant	sneakers
population	provide	returning	served	social
port	provided	reward	service	society
portable	psychologist	rolling	settled	soldier
position	puncture	rotate	settlement	solid
possession	purchase	route	settler	somehow
possible	pure	rush	seventy	soul
poster	purity	rushed	shadow	sour
posture	purpose		shaking	southern
pouring	pushed	safely	shame	spade
power	puzzle	sailed	shaped	special
powerful		sailor	share	speech
practically	quality	salad	sharing	speeding
praise	quantities	sample	sheets	speedy
prayer	quantity	sandwiches	shelves	speller
preacher	quarrel	satisfactory	shinier	spending
preferred	queer	satisfied	shiniest	spirit
prepared		scale	shiny	splendid
presence	raincoat	scarce	shipped	spoon
pretend	rapidly	scene	shipping	stake

standard	swept	title	university	weight
stared	swift	toaster	unlock	weighty
statement	sword	tobacco	upper	weren't
static	syrup	tongue	usual	wharves
stationary	system	torn		what's
steak		total	vacant	wherever
steam	tailor	touched	valuable	whip
steep	tale	toward	value	whisper
stir	tardy	towel	vanish	who's
stole	taste	tower	various	willing
stomach	tasted	trace	varnish	wise
strangely	tax	tractor	vase	within
strength	taxes	transferred	vegetable	wives
strike	teaspoon	transportation	vein	wolves
struck	telegram	traveling	verse	wondered
struggle	telegraph	treated	vessel	wondering
student	television	treaty	view	worker
style	temperature	tricycle	village	worn
submitted	temple	trimmed	visible	worried
subtraction	temptation	trousers	visitor	worry
succeed	tend	trust	voice	worship
succeeded	tender	tunnel	volleyball	worst
success	terribly	turtle	voyage	wound
suffer	thankful	twenty-five		wrecked
suggest	thanking	twins	wade	wrestle
suggested	therefore	type	waist	wring
suitable	thieves	typewriter	walrus	wrinkle
superintendent	thirsty		wander	writer
supplies	thrifty	ugly	wandering	wrung
supply	throughout	unable	warmer	
support	thrown	understood	warrior	yelled
surface	thus	union	wedding	yield
surprising	ticket	united	weekend	youngest
surrounded	timber	unity	weigh	

APPENDIX B

Answers to Write and Spell on Your Own

Part 1: Spelling Sounds

Unit 1: /a/

Words in the Bag (p. 206) . . . . Possible words: bad, bag, bat, bam, ban, mad, mat, man, map, rad, rag, rat, ram, ran, rap, had, hag, hat, ham

Wow! (p. 207) . . . . cat, cat, wag, hat, dad, hat, cat, sat, lap, hat, cat, hat, sad, hat

Rhyme Time (p. 208) . . . . 1. rat, 2. cat, 3. mat, 4. bat

Complete a Rhyme (p. 208) . . . . cat, rat, mat; cat, rat, bat; rat, mat

A Hat Full of Words (p. 209) . . . . (in any order; some words appear twice) gap, sag, sat, zap, jam, pad, lap, yap, yam, lad, pat, dab, pal, mat, ham, rag, bag, mad, had, dad, rap, ax, ad, at, an, cat, rat, tag

/a/ Puzzle (p. 210) . . . . **Across:** 1. ham, 2. mat, 3. can, 4. bat, 5. tag
Down: 1. hat, 2. man, 3. cat, 4. bag, 6. map

Unit 2: /i/

/a/ or /i/? (p. 212) . . . . 1. can, dig, lit   4. cat, ran, dip
2. map, hip, man   5. rat, sad, van
3. jam (or Jim), pig, rib

Change a Letter (p. 213) . . . . 1. bad, ban, bat, (bam)   5. had, hag, ham, has
2. fib, fig, fit, fix   6. (rad), rag, ram, rap, rat
3. hid, him, his, hit   7. mad, map, mat, (max)
4. did, dig, din, dip   8. wig, win

Word Shapes (p. 214) . . . . wig, bag, tin, hid

Tick-Tack-Tuck (p. 214) . . . . Combinations may vary.

Categories (p. 215) . . . . **A.** 1. big, 2. in, 3. lid, 4. rip
B. hip, six, pig, lip
C. 1. pig, 2. six, 3. lip, 4. hip

/i/ Puzzle (p. 216) . . . . **Across:** 2. him, 3. in, 5. big
Down: 1. win, 2. hit, 4. fix

Unit 3: /o/

One or More Than One? (p. 218) . . . . 1. pots, 2. pig, 3. map, 4. cot, 5. logs,
6. fan, 7. bat, 8. mop, 9. lips, 10. dots

Picture Puzzle (p. 219) . . . . 1. dog, log; 2. wig, pig; 3. hat, rat
1. dog, log; 2. wig, pig; 3. The hat is on the rat.

Solve the Riddles (p. 220) . . . . 1. box, 2. mop, 3. fox, 4. pot

Tick-Tack-Tuck (p. 220) . . . . Combinations may vary.

Lunchtime (p. 221) . . . . had, a, hot, dog

/o/ Puzzle (p. 222) . . . . **Across:** 2. hop, 3. pot, 5. box, 6. mop, 7. fox, 8. top, 9. dog
Down: 1. top, 2. hot, 3. pop, 4. ox, 5. box, 6. mop,
7. fog, 8. tot

Unit 4: /u/

Different Letters—
Different Words (p. 224) . . . . Possible words:
1. bud—cud, dud, mud
2. nut—but, cut, gut, hut, rut, jut, tut
3. cub—dub, hub, pub, rub, sub, tub
4. jug—bug, dug, hug, lug, mug, pug, rug, tug, jug
5. fun—bun, gun, nun, pun, run, sun
6. hum—bum, gum, rum, sum, hum, yum

Bug in a _____ ? (p. 224) . . . . The bug is in the bag.

How Are They Alike? (p. 225) . . . . 1. bus, 2. tub, 3. bug, 4. jug, 5. sun, 6. cup, 7. nut, 8. hut

Tick-Tack-Tuck (p. 225) . . . . Combinations may vary.

What Is It? (p. 226) . . . . 1. fun, 2. hop, 3. log

Word Shapes (p. 227) . . . . 1. nut, in, hut; 2. It, is, hot, pot; 3. Put the top on the pot.

Before, After, in Between (p. 228) . . . . Read columns top to bottom.
before—c-s, g-v, j-w, o-y, r-t, l-d
after—b-c, z-g, r-w, e-o, d-h, s-m
in between—g-h, b-m, k-w, o-n, e-s, y-p

ABC Mix-Up (p. 228) . . . . 1. Pat ran to Zak.
2. A cat hid in the van.
3. A big cub digs up yams.

Unit 5: /e/

Go to the Bank (p. 230) . . . . **A.** 1. pen, 2. red, 3. hen, 4. jet, 5. leg
B. 1. wet; 2. ten; 3. pet, vet; 4. bed

Riddles (p. 231) . . . . 1. bed, 2. red, 3. web, 4. jet, 5. ten, 6. vet

Tick-Tack-Tuck (p. 231) . . . . Combinations may vary.

Hen in a Pen (p. 232) . . . . Word list: hen, pen, men, ten, vet, wet, fed, bed, beg, leg;
Story completions: hen, pen; vet; wet, fed, bed; beg, leg,
hen, pen; men, hen, ten, pen

Analogies (p. 233) . . . . 1. leg, 2. pen, 3. wet, 4. men, 5. ten, 6. yes, 7. red, 8. web

Unit 6: Short Vowel Review

Change the Vowel (p. 235) . . . . 1. pot, pat, pet, pit; 2. bag, beg, big, bog, bug;
3. hut, hat, hit, hot; 4. bed, bad, bid, bud;
5. jog, jag, jig, jug; 6. pin, pan, pen, pun

Three from One (p. 236) . . . . 1. **d**—bad, mad, sad or **t**—bat, mat, sat; 2. **t**—hot, dot, jot;
3. **n**—ten, hen, men; 4. **g**—wig, big, jig;
5. **g**—bug, hug, tug or **t**—but, hut, tut

Pick a Vowel (p. 237) . . . . 1. Ben, hid, box, tub; 2. Jim, had, big, bag, gum;
3. Ten, men, got, fox, pen; 4. Bob, did, not, his, chum

Challenge: No Symbols! (p. 237) . . . . Possible answers: 1. Jim, hid, hat, rug;
2. bug, sat, top, big, web

Make It Rhyme (p. 238) . . . . 1. hat, 2. pig, 3. hop, 4. rip, 5. bag, 6. cup

Antonym Sentences (p. 239) . . . . 1. hot, 2. yes, 3. on, 4. fat, 5. sad,
6. win, 7. up, 8. in, 9. wet, 10. sit

Scrambled Sentences (p. 239) . . . . 1. The pup on the rug got wet. 2. Bud ran to get a big mop.
3. Mom got rid of that wet rug.

How Are They Different?
How Are They Alike? (p. 240) . . . . **food:** ham, gum, bun, nut, jam, yam

animals: fox, cat, bug, dog, rat, pig

Tick-Tack-Tuck (p. 240) . . . . Combinations may vary.

Unit 7: /sh/ /ch/ /th/ /wh/

Change a Letter—
Change a Word (p. 241) . . . . 1. bath, 2. chat or that, 3. shop or chop, 4. shut, 5. math,
6. then or when, 7. chum, 8. hash, 9. then or when,
10. ship or chip or whip, 11. them, 12. path, 13. this,
14. shot, 15. gash, 16. chug or thug

Scrambled Synonyms (p. 242) . . . . 1. cash, 2. dish, 3. shop, 4. ship, 5. shut, 6. thin, 7. math,
8. path, 9. chat, 10. shed, 11. dash, 12. hush, 13. chip,
14. wish, 15. thud

One Small Wish (p. 243) . . . . 1. chip, 2. lash, 3. dish, 4. bath, 5. chin, 6. shop, 7. chug,
8. gash, 9. sash, 10. fish, 11. ship

Questions (p. 244) . . . . 1. What   4. Which   7. What (or Which)
2. When   5. What   8. Where (or Who)
3. Where   6. Which   9. Who
Students' answers will vary.

Where Is Dad? (p. 245) . . . . ship

Tick-Tack-Tuck (p. 245) . . . . Combinations may vary.

Consonant Digraph Puzzle (p. 246) . . . . . **Across:** 2. shed, 4. shut, 7. chin, 8. ship, 9. rash
Down: 1. chum, 3. dish, 5. thin, 6. chop, 8. shop

Unit 8: Beginning *l* and *r* Blends

Expand a Word: *l* Blends (p. 247) . . . . 1. blush, flush, slush; 2. clap, flap, slap;
3. bled, fled, sled; 4. clip, blip, flip, slip

Blend a Word: *l* Blends (p. 247) . . . . 1. slap, 2. slit, 3. clash, 4. plot, 5. slip, 6. bled

Blend a Word: *r* Blends (p. 248) . . . . 1. brag, 2. brat, 3. crash, 4. trip,
5. drip, 6. trap, 7. bran, 8. trot

Change a Word: *r* Blends (p. 248) . . . . . . 1. crib; 2. brim, grim, trim, prim; 3. brush, crush, thrush;
4. drug, shrug; 5. crash, brash, trash; 6. shred, bred;
7. brag, crag, drag; 8. drip, grip, trip

Simon Says (p. 249) . . . . 1. Grab, 2. Clap, 3. Grip, 4. Flash, 5. Brush, 6. Trim,
7. Flip, 8. Plan

What Can You Do? (p. 249) . . . . 1. slam; 2. grab, frog; 3. crash; 4. plan, trip

Scrambled Sentences (p. 250) . . . .
1. A bug can drag mud.
2. Clap if they win.
3. Did Fred get my sled?
4. A bird can nest on shrubs.
5. A baby can hold small toys.
6. Brad can shut the tiny trunk.

Unit 9: More Beginning Blends, Ending Blends

Blend a Word (p. 251) . . . .
1. runt, 2. bent, 3. ant, 4. bust, 5. brand, 6. scant, 7. lamp,
8. camp, 9. band, 10. clamp, 11. tramp, 12. ramp

Expand a Word (p. 252) . . . .
1. ash, mash, smash; 2. rip, trip, strip; 3. to, top, stop;
4. me, men, mend; 5. in, pin, spin; 6. an, and, sand

What Would You Do If ...? (p. 253) . . . . . .
1. spit, 2. swim, 3. mend, 4. jump, 5. splash,
6. scrub, 7. smash, 8. rest, 9. pant, 10. stop

Homonyms—Same Word,
Different Meanings (p. 254) . . . .
1. last, 2. brush, 3. land, 4. rest, 5. hand,
6. trip, 7. band, 8. club, 9. film, 10. bump

Unit 10: Dual-Blend Words

Expand a Word (p. 255) . . . .
1. in, pin, twin; 2. end, bend or lend, may vary;
3. and, sand, bland or brand;
4. am, remaining answers vary.

Words Within Words (p. 256) . . . .
1. bend, lend, end, bed, led, bled
2. run, runt, gun, rut, gut
3. sat, cat, can, scan, an, at, scat, can't
4. tap, rap, trap, ramp, am, ram, amp, tram
5. camp, lamp, cap, lap, clap, clam, cam, am, amp

One to Two (p. 257) . . . .
1. plum, lump; 2. bran, ranch; 3. cram, ramp;
4. slum, lump; 5. clam, lamp; 6. scam, camp

Not the Same (p. 258) . . . .
1. grasp, 2. plump, 3. spend,
4. prompt, 5. blend, 6. stand, 7. split

Spelling Arithmetic (p. 259) . . . .
blend

Tick-Tack-Tuck (p. 259) . . . .
Answers may vary.

Synonym Crossword (p. 260) . . . .
Across: 2. last, 5. slim, 6. plan, 7. drag,
10. trip, 11. help, 13. snip, 14. punch
Down: 1. strap, 2. lump, 3. smash, 4. flat, 5. snap,
7. drop, 8. grab, 9. mend, 12. lend

Unit 11: Compounds

True or False? (p. 261) . . . .
1. catfish, F; 2. flagman, T; 3. sunlamp, F;
4. handbag, F; 5. pigpen, T

An ABC Story (p. 262) . . . .
A. 1. pigpen, 2. sunset, 3. hatbox
B. hatbox, pigpen, sunset

Compound Puzzle (p. 263) . . . . **Alphabetical order:** bathtub, catnap, cobweb, dishrag, dustpan, gumdrop, handbag, hatbox, pigpen, sandbox, snapshot, sunset

Puzzle
Across: 2. snapshot, 3. dustpan, 6. pigpen, 8. bathtub, 10. sandbox, 11. cobweb
Down: 1. catnap, 3. dishrag, 4. sunset, 5. handbag, 7. gumdrop, 9. hatbox

Unit 12: /ar/

Pick One (p. 266) . . . . *ar* words: barn, bark, dark, sharp, smart, yard; vowels in other words may vary.

A Sandy Mystery (p. 266) . . . . starfish

How Are They Alike? (p. 267) . . . . car, hard, yarn, tart, farm
1. farm animals, 2. made of yarn, 3. tart taste, 4. hard things, 5. car makers

Opposites (p. 267) . . . . 1. hard, 2. sharp, 3. tart, 4. dark, 5. far

Analogies (p. 268) . . . . 1. hard, 2. scarf, 3. bark, 4. start, 5. barn, 6. arm, 7. jar, 8. far

Counting Syllables (p. 268) . . . . **words:** 1. one, 2. two, 3. one, 4. two, 5. one, 6. one, 7. two, 8. one, 9. three, 10. three, 11. two, 12. three

sentences: 1. five, 2. four, 3. seven, 4. four

Barn Search (p. 269) . . . . barn, car, dark, bar, park, arm, farm, bark, card, yard, starch, art, ark, far, jar, sharp, star, march, tar, mar, arch, arc, harp, spark, hard, harsh, mart, smart, marsh, par

Words Within a Word (p. 270) . . . . **farmyard:** farm, yard, mar, arm, far; ram, am, day, may, mad, fad, dam, yam, ray

yardstick: yard, star, tar, stark, dark, ark, car, cart, dart, card; stick, sick, tick, tack, sit, sat, stay, rat, day, say, stack, rack, raid, said, drastic, sty, dry, cry, try

dogcart: dart, cart, car, art, card; dog, go, at, got, rod, coat, rag, toad, cat, do, to, cot, trod, rot, drag, tag, oat, crag, goat, toga, cord, tad

partnership: part, art, sharp, star, tarnish, partner, harp, parsnip, sharper; ship, trap, pat, sip, net, pit, sat, sit, tap, tape, pair, shape, her, stir, hip, strip, trip, rip, tip, shirt, pert, pet, share, shape, hair, air, share, pair, strap, tripe

barnyard: yarn, barn, darn, bar, yard; ran, day, ray, bay, nab, ban, bran, brand, brad, drab, dray, bray, nary

farmhand: farm, harm, far, darn, arm, hard; am, and, hand, fad, mad, had, dam, ham, fan

Unit 13: –ng, –nk

Spelling Analogies (p. 272) . . . . 1. think, 2. ring, 3. king, 4. sink, 5. sung, 6. tank, 7. strung, 8. wing, 9. punk

Haiku (p. 272) . . . . 1. swing, 2. wink, 3. blank, 4. sink, 5. bunkbed

Fact or Opinion? (p. 273) . . . . 1. rings, O; ring, F   2. strings, F; string, O
3. songs, O; songs, F   4. wings, F; wings, O

Unit 14: –ed

Change a Word (p. 275) . . . . **/t/** blushed, spanked, tramped, barked, blinked, starched
/d/ armed, filmed, darned, harmed, farmed, spilled
/ed/ lasted, prompted, branded, handed, dusted, drifted

Sounds of –ed (p. 277) . . . . **A.** 1. printed, 2. rested, 3. landed
B. 1. harmed, 2. snarled, 3. darned
C. 1. smashed, 2. helped, 3. flashed

Review Puzzle (p. 280) . . . . **Across:** 3. plant, 6. dark, 8. clap, 10. snapshot, 12. blank,
13. sad, 16. mash, 18. jog, 19. bank, 20. top,
21. rung, 23. dented
Down: 1. map, 2. sharp, 4. thin, 5. last, 7. king, 8. chin,
9. pal, 10. sunset, 11. slam, 12. brushed, 14. dash,
15. darned, 17. hard, 18. junk, 22. win

Part 2: Spelling Choices

Unit 15: /ī/

Spell Long i Words (p. 283) . . . . **i–e:** bride, quite, line, pride, dine, nine, hire, crime
y: pry, sly, spy, sky, try, shy, spry, why
igh: flight, slight, fight, might, tight, blight, fright, right

Word Play (p. 284) . . . . kit—kite, bit—bite, shin—shine, twin—twine, rid—ride,
dim—dime, by—bye, hid—hide, pin—pine, quit—quite

Expand a Word (p. 285) . . . . 1. rim, grim, grime; 2. lid, slid, slide; 3. rip, trip, strip, stripe;
4. in, fin, fine; 5. it, bit, bite; 6. in, pin, spin or pine, spine

Condense a Word (p. 285) . . . . 1. pine, pin, in; 2. gripe, grip or ripe, rip;
3. kite, kit, it; 4. snipe, snip, nip

Add an e (p. 286) . . . . 1. bite, 2. kite, 3. shine, 4. twine, 5. dime, 6. slide

Add a Letter, Change a Word (p. 286) . . 1. fright, 2. wild, 3. mine, 4. tire, 5. ride, 6. pile

Make Sense out of Nonsense (p. 287) . . . 1. pines, 2. mile, 3. live, 4. time, 5. life, 6. ripe, 7. smile, 8. vine

Idioms for Every Occasion (p. 287) . . . . . . 1. strike, 2. life, 3. bite, 4. my, 5. fight

Analogies (p. 288) . . . . 1. smile, 2. lime, 3. vines, 4. fly, 5. sky, 6. blind,
7. child, 8. dime, 9. light or bright

Sentence Stretchers (p. 288) . . . . 1. grow on vines, 2. is a dime, 3. like to fly, 4. are dry

Opposites (p. 289) . . . . 1. cry, 2. dry, 3. mine, 4. night, 5. find, 6. tight,
7. right, 8. high, 9. bright or shiny, 10. wild

What If? (p. 290) . . . . 1. hide, 2. dry, 3. light, 4. dive, 5. fly

Unit 16: /ā/ /ār/

Spell Long *a* Words (p. 291) . . . .
ay: stray, hay, day, may, clay, play, stay, pay

ai: trail, pain, aim, mail, jail, drain, stain, sail

eigh: freight, sleigh, weigh, eight

ea: great, break, steak

ei: vein, veil

a-e: cake, blade, make, date, lame, shade, late, whale, game, safe

Word Play (p. 292) . . . .
1. mad—made, tap—tape, scrap—scrape, plan—plane, fad—fade, lam—lame; sentences will vary.
2. weigh—way, made—maid, mail—male, tail—tale, break—brake, pear—pair, eight—ate; sentences will vary.

Plus or Minus an *e* (p. 292) . . . .
1. rat, 2. mad, 3. plan, 4. cape, 5. pale, 6. gap, 7. fade, 8. scrape, 9. tap, 10. can

Homophones with Long *a* (p. 293) . . . . . .
1. break, 2. tail, 3. stair, 4. fare, 5. weight, 6. great, 7. sale, 8. plane, 9. pail, 10. rains

Flying Mystery (p. 293) . . . .
freight

Stretch a Word (p. 294) . . . .
1. clay, play, slay, delay, relay (sleigh)
2. fair, pair, hair, lair, chair (pare, hare)
3. bail, fail, hail, jail, mail, nail, pail, quail, rail, sail, tail, flail, Braille, frail, wail (sale, tale, hale, male, pale, whale)
4. laid, maid, paid, raid, braid, afraid, staid (made)
5. bale, dale, gale, hale, male, pale, sale, shale, stale, tale, kale, vale, whale (bail, hail, mail, pail, sail, tail, wail)
6. crate, date, fate, gate, hate, late, mate, rate, state, plate, grate, inflate (great)

Haiku (p. 295) . . . .
1. play, game, shade; 2. sail, day, fades, flames, safe; 3. gray, mane, tail, neighs, hay; 4. play, plate; 5. raindrops, snail

Homophone Puzzle (p. 296) . . . .
Across: 2. rain, 3. pane, 4. stake, 5. weight, 8. ate, 9. plane, 14. tale, 15. hale, 16. break
Down: 1. great, 4. sail, 5. way, 6. tail, 7. vein, 10. ale, 11. eight, 12. stare, 13. pale

Unit 17: /ō/

Spell Long *o* Words (p. 297) . . . .
ow: grown, show, thrown, glow, flow

o-e: quote, note, dome, vote, slope, lone, throne, stove

oe: hoe, foe, doe, floe

oa: load, loan, boast, groan, soak, coast, oath

old: told, gold

ough: though, dough

Word Play (p. 298) . . . .
1. glob—globe, rod—rode, hop—hope, mop—mope, slop—slope, not—note; sentences will vary.
2. whole—hole, dough—doe, pole—poll, road—rode, not—knot, throne—thrown, grown—groan; sentences will vary.

Appendix B: Answers to Write and Spell on Your Own

Fact or Opinion? (p. 299) . . . .
1. show, O   2. float, F   3. throw, O
4. grow, O   5. slow, O   6. cold, O
7. sold, F   8. low, O   9. old, F

Rhyming with Long *o* (p. 300) . . . .
1. roam; 2. told; 3. rode, road; 4. vote;
5. home; 6. close; 7. doe; 8. loan

Long *o* to the Rescue (p. 300) . . . .
1. hole, 2. road, 3. stove, 4. boat,
5. toe, 6. cold, 7. cone, 8. snow

Home by Jove (p. 301) . . . .
though, coast, snow, throw, throne; coat, float, boat, shone, below, boat, poach, stove, toast

Anagrams (p. 302) . . . .
Across: 5. own, 7. throw, 8. pole, 9. stone
Down: 1. flow, 2. slope, 3. robe, 4. votes, 6. note

Step up or Down (p. 303) . . . .
Some combinations may vary.
1. cold, coat or gold, goat; 2. soak, stone;
3. slope, show; 4. grow, goat or crow, coat;
5. coast, cone or toast, tone or boast, bone

Puzzle for *oa* and *ow* Words (p. 303) . . . .
Across: 3. boat, 5. thrown, 6. snow, 7. toast
Down: 1. coat, 2. blow, 3. bow, 4. throat, 6. soap

Find and Add (p. 304). . . . .
1. mope, 2. hope, 3. note, 4. hide,
5. kite, 6. ride, 7. tube, 8. made

Unit 18: /ē/ /ēr/

Spell Long *e* Words (p. 305) . . . .
ee: steer, feet, greed, meet, screen
ea: squeal, seal, meal, wheat, gleam
ie: chief, belief, shield, field
ei: seize, leisure, either
y: baby, shady, lady

Word Play (p. 305). . . . .
streetcar, leapfrog, speedway, teacup, beehive, seacoast, meanwhile

Switching Letters (p. 306). . . . .
A. 1. leaf, 2. tea, 3. lead, 4. dear, 5. seat (or teas), 6. cheat
B. 1. lean, 2. team or meat, 3. steal or least, 4. seal, 5. meal, 6. seam

Finding Homophones (p. 307). . . . .
1. See the sea. 2. Peek at the peak. 3. Heal your heel.
4. A flea bites your dog and flees. 5. Beat the beet.

How Are They Alike? (p. 307) . . . .
(Read columns top to bottom.)
1. peach, deer, bean, beet, sheep,
seal, weed, bee, monkey, wheat
Animals: sheep, monkey, deer, seal, bee
Things We Grow: peach, bean, weed, beet, wheat

What Would You Do?
Compare and Contrast (p. 308) . . . . . .
A. cheer, squeal, plead, weep, scream, shriek
B. 1. cheer, squeal; 2. plead, weep, scream, shriek

Either...Or—Neither...Nor (p. 308) . . . .
A. 1. deep, 2. east, 3. clean
B. 1. queen, 2. here, 3. neat

The Queen and the Flea (p. 309) . . . . sea, queen, free, trees, read, leaves, steep, peaks, deer, cheer, monkey, near; flea, glee, screech, hear, queen, queen, hear, speak, glee, feel, free

Rhyming Long *e* (p. 310) . . . . **Across:** 1. feel, heal; 5. weed, bleed; 6. cheer, year; 7. peek, seek; 9. meet, street; 11. need, feed; 12. each, speech; 14. heat, feet

Down: 2. need, lead; 3. seem, dream; 4. sheep, leap; 5. chief, brief; 8. keep, steep; 10. teach, peach; 13. he, bee

Unit 19: /ow/

Spell /ow/ and /ou/ Words (p. 311) . . . . . . **ou:** pouch, crouch, mound, proud, oust, spout, found

ow: chow, vow, plow, sow, brow

owl: prowl, fowl, scowl, howl, jowl

own: town, gown, down

Word Play (p. 312) . . . . **Group A:** brown, round, stout, proud, loud

Group B: couch, owl, cloud, clown, gown, town, ground, mouth, cow, scout

Change a Word (p. 312) . . . . 1. brow, 2. town, 3. gown, 4. plow, 5. crown, 6. growl

What Do I Do? (p. 313) . . . . 1. howl, 2. growl, 3. frown or pout, 4. bow, 5. frown or pout, 6. plow, 7. spout, 8. prowl

Homonyms (p. 313) . . . . 1. F, C; 2. D, G; 3. A, H, I; 4. B, E

Compound It (p. 314) . . . . downcast, downtown, downside; inbound, inside, in-law; outbound, outcast, outfit, outside, outsmart, outwit, outlaw; snowbound; southbound; sundown; side-out

Complete an /ow/ Story (p. 314) . . . . clown, our; round, mouth; flower, brown; clown; frown; sound; how, clown; clown; pout; proud; howl, sound; bowed, clown, down; clown, found, our, town

A Poetic Shape (p. 315) . . . . Clouds, sundown, round, ground, how, clouds; How, growl, sound, pout, frown, scowl, growl, without, sound, how

/ow/ Puzzle (p. 316) . . . . **Across:** 1. ouch, 5. shout, 6. our, 8. round, 10. down, 11. crowd, 12. drown

Down: 1. out, 2. cloud, 3. loud, 4. brown, 5. sour, 7. ground, 9. now, 11. cow

More Anagrams (p. 317) . . . . **A.** 1. name, 2. smile, 3. stream, 4. poles, 5. marched, 6. late, 7. meal, 8. grown, 9. note, 10. sole

B. wolf, thin, throw, chum, brush

Unit 20

Spell /aw/ Words (p. 319) . . . . **aw:** awl, gawk, dawn, prawn, squawk

au: fault, fraud, vault, haunch, maul

all: stall, tall, hall, fall

alk: stalk, walk, balk

augh: naughty, daughter, slaughter

ough: ought, fought, sought

Appendix B: Answers to Write and Spell on Your Own

Spell It *aw* or *au?* (p. 319) . . . . claw, gaunt, drawn, launch, sprawl, haunt, jaw, straw, jaunt, law, bawl, paw, thaw, flaw, paunch, yawn, taunt, crawl, draw, taut, vault, brawn, fraud, flaunt, lawn

Add a Letter and
What Do You Have? (p. 320) . . . . 1. bawl, 2. small, 3. fawn, 4. straw, 5. haunt

Think of an Antonym (p. 320) . . . . 1. tall, 2. raw, 3. caught, 4. taught, 5. bought, 6. naughty

Analogies (p. 321) . . . . 1. caught, 2. tall, 3. claw, 4. stall, 5. dawn, 6. daughter, 7. saw, 8. small, 9. bought

Anagrams (p. 321) . . . . **Words About School:** thought, chalk, hall, taught

Words About Babies: crawl, small, daughter, bawl

Unit 21: /k/

Spell /k/ Words (p. 323) . . . . **ck:** struck, whack, quack, block

ke: drake, strike, cake, yoke, hike

k: task, hulk, shark, brisk

c: crust, camp

qu: quail, quack, quench, quite

ch: school, ache, chemist, chrome

x: fix, express

Ways To Spell /k/ (p. 324) . . . . spark, joke, smack, crack, hulk, brisk, brick, deck, bike, fake, mark, cake, sulk, choke, truck, pack, spoke, yoke

Analogies (p. 324) . . . . 1. track, 2. truck, 3. neck, 4. sick, 5. bake, 6. duck

Say and Do (p. 325) . . . . **What do we say?** 1. quack, 2. bark, 3. tick-tock, 4. cluck

What do we do? 1. kick, 2. lick, 3. buck, 4. rake

Which *k* Am I? (p. 326) . . . . 1. lake, duck; 2. ask, cook, bake, cake, bank; 3. truck, poke, snake, stick; 4. quickly, trick, ask, blacksmith; 5. like, pancake, breakfast; 6. sick, back, speak; 7. pick, frisky, take, park

Homonyms (p. 327) . . . . 1. back, 2. milk, 3. bark, 4. park, 5. bark, 6. park, 7. like, 8. back, 9. milk, 10. like, 11. check, 12. block, 13. rock, 14. block, 15. rock, 16. check

What Compound Am I? (p. 328) . . . . back, luck, black, stick, sick, nick, shack; 1. potluck, 2. chopstick, 3. blacksmith, 4. handshake, 5. nickname, 6. homesick

Words Within a Word (p. 328) . . . . 1. **clambake:** cake, back, black, bake, lack, lake, beak, leak, make, bleak, calm, clam, came
2. **bareback:** back, bake, rack, rake, beak, break, creak, care, crab
3. **racetrack:** track, rack, crack, rake, take, cake, creak, care, acre, crate
4. **quicksand:** quick, quack, sick, sack, suck, duck, disk, ask, cask, dusk, sink, sank, sunk

/k/ Puzzle (p. 329) . . . . **Across:** 1. mask, 3. park, 5. sick, 7. dark, 8. trick, 9. lock, 10. fake
Down: 1. milk, 2. kick, 4. risk, 6. crack, 7. desk, 8. tank, 9. lake

Unit 22: /ch/ /j/

Spell /ch/ and /j/ Words (p. 331) . . . .
ch: coach, mulch, trench, porch
tch: latch, sketch, thatch, clutch, hatch
ge: large, twinge, barge, page, change
dge: nudge, ridge, smudge, trudge

Spell It *ch* or *tch, ge* or *dge* (p. 331) . . . . .
ch or tch: 1. inch, 2. stitch, 3. patch, 4. witch, 5. coach, 6. crutch, 7. branch, 8. catch, 9. ditch, 10. match, 11. scratch, 12. trench, 13. stretch, 14. starch, 15. bunch, 16. march
ge or dge: 1. bridge, 2. cage, 3. charge, 4. bulge, 5. change, 6. badge, 7. page, 8. fudge, 9. strange, 10. wage, 11. judge, 12. ledge

Find the Homonyms (p. 332) . . . .
1. match, 2. inch, 3. march, 4. branch, 5. coach, 6. bridge, 7. change, 8. charge

Conversations (p. 333) . . . .
ch or tch: bench, pitch, munch, inch, lunch, catch, quench, hunch
ge or dge: page, huge, cage, bridge, ledge, strange, charge, dodge

Verbs and Nouns with
/ch/ and /j/ (p. 334) . . . .
A. Verbs: 1. scratch, 2. march, 3. punch, 4. catch, 5. fetch, 6. hitchhike, 7. scratch, 8. sketch
B. Nouns: 1. crutch, 2. stage, 3. match, 4. inch, 5. cage, 6. wage, 7. judge, 8. witch

Unit 23: /or/

Spell /or/ Words (p. 335) . . . .
or: cork, scorch, thorn, torch, forlorn
our: your, four
oor: floor, door
ore: core, snore, more, wore
oar: roar, board

Using Homophones Together (p. 335) . . .
oar or ore, sore, pour, bore, four; 1. sore, soar; 2. for, four; 3. or, oar; 4. boar, bore; 5. pour, pore

What Comes Next? (p. 336) . . . .
1. roar, 2. short, 3. four, 4. north, 5. more, 6. floor, 7. fork, 8. born

Analogies (p. 336) . . . .
1. pork, 2. four, 3. store, 4. roar, 5. oar

An /or/ Puzzle (p. 337) . . . .
Across: 2. fort, 5. horn, 6. storm, 7. North, 8. roar, 10. port
Down: 1. door, 2. form, 3. thorn, 4. snore, 6. short, 7. nor, 9. more

Unit 24: /er/

Spellings for /er/ (p. 339) . . . .
er: colder, louder, browner, stern, winter
ir: girl, chirp, bird, shirt, dirt
ur: curl, church, curb
or: worm, world, work
ear: learn, heard, earth, early

Make New Words (p. 340) . . . . **Circle (*ir*):** birch, bird, birth, chirp, dirt, fir, firm, first, flirt, gird, girth, irk, shirk, shirt, stir, third, thirst, mirth

Square (*ur*): blurt, burn, burp, burst, church, churn, cur, curb, curd, curl, curt, fur, furl, hurl, hurt, lurch, purl, spur, purse, spurn, spurt, surf, turn, urn, nurse

/er/ Rhymes (p. 340) . . . . 1. burst, 2. burn, 3. church, 4. bird, 5. worst, 6. word, 7. turn

Analogies (p. 341) . . . . 1. first, 2. shirt, 3. birth, 4. third, 5. thirst, 6. girl

Just *ir* (p. 341) . . . . **Across:** 2. third, 5. birch, 6. firm, 7. girl, 8. shirt
Down: 1. stir, 3. dirt, 4. chirp, 5. bird, 6. first

Pick an /er/ Sound (p. 342) . . . . **Across:** 2. hurt, 3. burn, 4. word, 6. church, 7. work, 8. birth, 9. learn
Down: 1. turn, 3. birth, 5. thirst, 6. curl, 7. world

More Sounds

Homophone Pairs (p. 343) . . . . **A.** night, know, knew, not, need, write, ring, threw

B. 1. need, knead; 2. knew, new; 3. write, right; 4. know, no; 5. knight, night; 6. not, knot; 7. ring, wring; 8. threw, through

Secret Messages (p. 344) . . . . **A.** Meet us at the station at noon.

B. The precious coin is in his boot.

Proverbs (p. 345) . . . . 1. C, 2. D, 3. E, 4. B, 5. A

Part 3: Spelling Rules

Unit 25: Double *f, l, s, z*

Spell Words with
Double *f, l, s, z* (p. 349) . . . . **ff:** cliff, staff, scoff, stuff

ll: quell, dwell, thrill, spell

ss: chess, bass, lass, stress

zz: buzz, fuzz, jazz

Double or Not Double? (p. 350) . . . . The following are doubled: 1. swell, 3. dull, 4. mess, 5. gruff, 6. kill, 7. still, 10. buzz, 11. fuss, 12. sell, 13. less, 16. muff, 20. fizz. Double letters are *f, l, s, z;* each word has one syllable and one vowel.

Pick an Ending (p. 351) . . . . 1. bell, shell, smell; 2. still, chill, drill; 3. cuff, fluff, bluff; 4. stress, less, press

Switch and Change (p. 351) . . . . (Some answers may vary.) 1. cash, mash, mass, mess; 2. feed, feel, fell, sell; 3. bark, bask (or mark), mask, mass; 4. list, mist, miss, kiss; 5. cape, caps, laps, lass; 6. flask, flash, clash, class; 7. test, pest, past, pass; 8. trust, crust, crest, chest, chess

Spell and a Spell Cast (p. 352) . . . . miss (1); press (2); cuff (1); stuff (1); bill (2); staff (2); cross (1); well (2); spell (2); bluff (2)

Match a Double Ending (p. 353) . . . . **Across:** 2. buzz, 3. grass, 5. grill, 6. huff, 7. pass, 9. dress, 10. stiff, 11. fill

Down: 1. jazz, 2. bill, 4. stuff, 5. glass, 6. hiss, 7. press, 8. puff, 9. drill

A Scrambled Answer (p. 353) . . . . o, m, h, e, l, l, l, i; molehill

Unit 26: Doubling Rule

Complete a Phrase (p. 355) . . . . 1. chopping or chopped, 2. braided, 3. stunning, 4. ripped or ripping, 5. shipment, 6. flagged, 7. knitted or knitting, 8. spotless, 9. wishful, 10. dropped or dropping, 11. playful, 12. flopped or flopping, 13. missed or missing, 14. patted or patting, 15. harmless, 16. sanding or sanded

Use –*ing* and –*ed* (p. 356) . . . . 1. winning, 2. flapped, 3. boiled, 4. stirred, 5. plugged, 6. enjoyed, 7. ordering, 8. forgetting, 9. beginning, 10. visited

Then and Now (p. 356) . . . . 1. planned, planning; 2. visiting, visited; 3. chopped, chopping; 4. cleaned, cleaning

–*est* Can Exaggerate (p. 357) . . . . (Answers may vary.) 1. biggest, 2. saddest, 3. darkest, 4. oldest, 5. flattest, 6. sharpest, 7. hottest, 8. coldest, 9. fattest, 10. hottest, 11. neatest, 12. plumpest

Accent and Add (p. 358) . . . . 1. be 'gin, beginning; 2. con 'trol, controlling; 3. re 'sent, resented; 4. 'gar den, gardening; 5. pre 'fer, preferred; 6. 'ga ther, gathered; 7. 'of fer, offered; 8. pre 'vent, prevented; 9. com 'mit, committing; 10. re 'bel, rebelling; 11. sub 'tract, subtracting; 12. re 'veal, revealing; 13. ad 'mit, admitted; 14. for 'got, forgotten; 15. o 'mit, omitted; 16. pa 'trol, patrolled; 17. 'gal lop, galloping; 18. re 'main, remaining

Add the Second Syllable (p. 359) . . . . 1. presenting, 2. exiting, 3. enjoyed, 4. piloted, 5. employed, 6. inventing, 7. equipping, 8. opening, 9. forbidding, 10. forgetting

A Scrambled Day (p. 359) . . . . 1. tripped, 2. spilled, 3. strapped, 4. dropped, 5. bragged, 6. gripped, 7. melted, 8. stopped

Diamante (p. 360) . . . . throwing, running, jumping, passing, shooting, winning; planning, digging, planting, growing, weeding, picking

Unit 27: –*le Rule*

Complete a Word (p. 361) . . . . (Some answers may vary.) 1. gentle, buckle, rifle; 2. jungle, juggle, cradle; 3. tremble, battle, stable; 4. uncle, pebble or peddle, ladle; 5. bundle or bungle, cripple, able; 6. ankle or angle, riddle or riffle, maple; 7. jumble, drizzle or dribble; title; 8. sparkle, kettle, fable; 9. ramble, muddle or muffle or muzzle, cable; 10. humble, dabble or dapple, trifle; 11. marble, bottle or boggle, stifle

Keep the Ending (p. 362) . . . . (Answers will vary.) 1. pimple, dimple, ample, crumple; 2. fizzle, sizzle, dazzle, muzzle; 3. bottle, cattle, settle, scuttle; 4. juggle, wiggle, haggle, toggle; 5. shuffle, raffle, scuffle, baffle; 6. table, cable, fable, stable; 7. paddle, middle, muddle, fiddle

Challenge! (p. 362) . . . . (Answers may vary.) 1. babble, table; 2. paddle, ladle; 3. waffle, rifle; 4. juggle, eagle; 5. topple, maple; 6. crackle, uncle

Can You Remember? (p. 363) . . . . 1. nimble, candle; 2. diddle, diddle, fiddle; 3. simple; 4. twinkle, twinkle, little; 5. jingle, jingle, jingle; 6. little; 7. cradle; 8. buckle

Cinquain (p. 364) . . . . 1. noble, gentle, nibble, apples 2. candle, twinkle, sparkle, dazzle

Find a Word to Stretch (p. 365) . . . . **Across:** 2. bugle, 3. rattle, 5. steeple, 6. handle, 7. settle
Down: 1. jiggle, 2. battle, 4. needle, 5. startle, 7. saddle

Unit 28: –y

Pick an Ending (p. 367) . . . . (Answers may vary.) 1. choppy, 2. shady or shaky, 3. thirty, 4. petty or peppy, 5. silly, 6. smoky, 7. ugly, 8. body or bobby or bonny or bossy, 9. buddy or bully or bunny or bury, 10. empty, 11. lazy or lady, 12. curly or curry or curvy, 13. study or stubby, 14. handy, 15. nasty

How's the Weather? (p. 367) . . . . 1. foggy, 2. sunny, 3. chilly, 4. cloudy, 5. muggy, 6. icy, 7. wintry, 8. snowy, 9. stormy, 10. hazy

y Makes a New Word (p. 368) . . . . 1. belly, 2. baggy, 3. tiny, 4. army, 5. penny, 6. carry, 7. shiny, 8. skinny, 9. slimy, 10. forty, 11. party, 12. kitty, 13. buggy, 14. grimy, 15. lady

Opposites (p. 369) . . . . 1. *large* to *tiny*; 2. *quiet* to *chatty*; 3. *big* to *skimpy*; 4. *clean* to *dusty*; 5. *gloomy* to *sunny*

Make 1 + 1 = 1 (p. 370) . . . . **Across:** 2. cherry, 4. thrifty, 7. shaggy, 9. skinny, 11. snappy, 12. muddy
Down: 1. stingy, 2. crispy, 3. rusty, 5. forty, 6. plenty, 7. sloppy, 8. grumpy, 10. buddy

Unit 29: More Endings

Add and Subtract (p. 371) . . . . taping, tapping; riding, ridding; scraping, scrapping; planing, planning; filing, filling; pining, pinning; hoping, hopping; tiling, tilling

Drop the *e* or Let It Be (p. 371) . . . . **Before a vowel drop the *e*:** exploded, completion, dazzling, creation, striding, forgiving
Before a consonant keep the *e*: merely, likely, useful, amusement, settlement, careful
If a word ends in –*le*, drop –*le* and add –*ly*: crumbly, ably, nobly

e—Use It or Drop It (p. 372) . . . . 1. skated, 2. voting, 3. taste, 4. diving, 5. waste, 6. smiling, 7. snore, 8. trades, 9. scaring, 10. arrangement, 11. saving, 12. useful

New Endings (p. 373) . . . . 1. (circle) saved, raked, exploded, timed, glared, lined, liked, dined, tuned, wiped, faded, lunged, stared
2. save, rake, explode, time, glare, line, like, dine, tune, wipe, fade, lunge, stare

Challenge: Add Endings (p. 374) . . . . 1. changing, changed, changeable; 2. outraged, outrageous; 3. canoeing, canoed; 4. mileage; 5. ridiculing, ridiculed, ridiculous; 6. tracing, traced, traceable; 7. using, used, usable, usage; 8. storing, stored, storable, storage; 9. hoeing, hoed; 10. dyeing, dyed, dyeable; 11. acreage; 12. wasting, wasted, wastage; 13. continuing, continued, continuous; 14. courageous; 15. adventuring, adventured, adventurous

Unit 30: *y* to *i*, *i* Before *e*

y Math (p. 375) . . . . **Circle:** deny, angry, fancy, frisky, musty, pity, happy, apply

Underline: enjoy, buy

1. denying, 2. angrily, 3. fanciful, 4. friskier, 5. enjoyed, 6. mustiest, 7. pitying, 8. happier, 9. buying, 10. applied, 11. boyish

To *i* or Not To *i* (p. 376) . . . . 1. relied, 2. betraying, 3. applied, 4. beautiful, 5. healthier, 6. prettiest, 7. merrily, 8. busiest, 9. employed, 10. annoying

A Crossword Challenge Review (p. 377) . **Across:** 1. chubby, 3. paddle, 4. cradle, 7. bottle, 8. loving, 10. repelled, 11. tidy, 15. flier, 16. candle, 17. scaring, 18. clapping, 19. yield
Down: 1. cuddle, 2. buckle, 5. drizzle, 6. eight, 7. brief, 9. applied, 12. dusty, 13. hill, 14. caged, 16. chief

Part 4: Complementary Skills

Unit CS1: Prefixes and Suffixes

Expand with Affixes (p. 381) . . . . (Encourage students also to add affixes other than those listed.)

week: midweek, weekly, biweekly, midweekly

like: unlike, mislike, dislike(d), liked, likely, liking, likeable

agree: disagree(d), agreed, agreeing, agreeable, agreement

kind: unkind, kinder, kindly

use: unused, reuse(d), misuse(d), disuse(d), user, used, useful, using, useable, misusing, reusing

twist: untwist, retwist, twister, twisted, twisting, twistable, untwisted, untwisting, retwisted, retwisting

load: unload(ed), reload(ed), misload(ed), loader, loaded, loading, unloading, reloading, misloading, loadable

match: unmatched, rematch, mismatch(ed), matched, matching

lock: unlock(ed), relock(ed), locker, locked, locking, lockable

Appendix B: Answers to Write and Spell on Your Own

manage: unmanageable, mismanage(d), manager, managed, managing, mismanaging, manageable, management, mismanagement

place: replace(d), misplace(d), displace(d), placing, replacing, misplacing, displacing, placeable, unplaceable, misplaceable, placement

service: reservice(d), disservice, serviced, servicing, reservicing, serviceable

Make a New Word (p. 382) . . . . 1. fastest, 2. misfortune, 3. enjoyable, 4. studying, 5. noticeable, 6. mileage, 7. misspelled, 8. artist

Two from One (p. 383) . . . . 1. unwilling, unpack; 2. reelected, recount; 3. submarine, subway; 4. misfortune, misquoted; 5. autograph, autobiography; 6. disapprove, disbanding

Prefix Phrases (p. 383) . . . . 1. rewrite, 2. unnumbered, 3. misjudge, 4. prepay, 5. intrastate, 6. postwar, 7. semicircle, 8. uneaten, 9. misbehave, 10. befriend; (Phrases will vary.)

A New Part of Speech (p. 384) . . . . 1. migration, 2. useless, 3. playful, 4. reproduction, 5. livable, 6. loneliness, 7. alphabetize, 8. friendly, 9. falsify

Linkage (p. 385) . . . . (Answers may vary.) 1. disappointed, disappointing; 2. unlocked, interlocking; 3. destruction, construction; 4. interjected, dejected, injection

Unit CS2: Plurals

Make It Plural (p. 387) . . . . **Add s:** boys, journeys, banjos, keys, rodeos

Add es: classes, taxes, tomatoes, peaches, bushes

y to i: ladies, jellies, babies, navies, libraries

f to v: wolves, leaves, halves, loaves, knives

Change the spelling: geese, feet, women, children, oxen

Spelling does not change: sheep, spaghetti, deer, moose, trout

Plural Sentences (p. 388) . . . . 1. dresses, 2. cities, 3. calves, 4. volcanoes, 5. radios, 6. mice, 7. chimneys, 8. pianos

Unit CS3: Apostrophes

Make a Contraction (p. 389) . . . . 1. we're, 2. aren't, 3. isn't, 4. could've, 5. there's, 6. who'll, 7. you're, 8. let's, 9. you've, 10. he'd, 11. hadn't

Form a Contraction (p. 389) . . . . 1. she's, that's, who's, where's, here's; 2. you'd, they'd, we'd, who'd, he'd, I'd; 3. he'll, that'll, they'll, there'll, we'll, you'll

What Is It? (p. 390) . . . . (Answers may vary.) 1. They're polar bears. 2. It's a bird. 3. I'm a worm. 4. They're astronauts. 5. I've a cast. 6. That's perfect. 7. We're cheerleaders. 8. She's an artist. 9. He's a teacher.

Can *I'll* Be *Ill*? (p. 390) . . . . **Words to use:** ill, well, were, shell, shed, wed, its

Pick Your Words (p. 391) . . . . **Plural possessive forms:** cats', men's, elves', children's, geese's, girls', sisters-in-law's

430

Make It Possessive (p. 391) . . . . 1. ferries', 2. actor's, 3. jockey's, 4. daughters', 5. group's, 6. friends', 7. thieves', 8. wolves', 9. islands', 10. Philipses', 11. tree's (or trees')

Unit CS4: Abbreviations and Acronyms

Abbreviate Your Notes (p. 393) . . . . 1. Sat., 12:30 P.M.; 2. tbs. or T, pt.; 3. co., bldg., Tues., March; 4. VP, gov., Nov.; 5. Dr., 60 mph, hwy., pkg.

Abbreviated Questions (p. 393) . . . . 1. pres., U.S.; 2. _____ ft., _____ in., _____ lbs.; 3. 12 in.; 4. P.O.; 5. Wed.

Rewrite Using Abbreviations (p. 394) . . . . 1. Mr. Juan Perez, Treas.
2. She lives on Cedar St. off Maple Ave. and Smith Blvd.
3. 60 sec. equal 1 min.
4. A mg is a metric unit of wt. equal to $\frac{1}{1000}$ g.
5. Lisa is 4 ft., 8 in. tall.